MAXIMUMPC *Guide to*

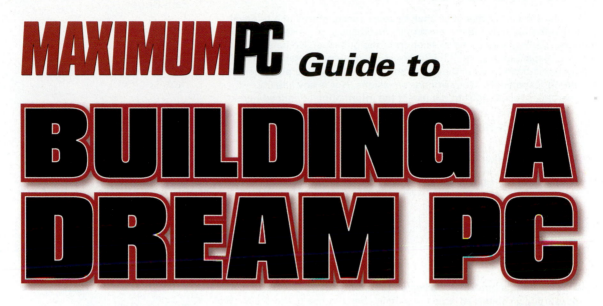

BUILDING A DREAM PC

By WILL SMITH

que®

800 East 96th Street,
Indianapolis, Indiana 46240

Maximum PC Guide to Building a Dream PC

International Standard Book Number: 0-7897-3193-2

Library of Congress Catalog Card Number: 2004107055

Printed in the United States of America

First Printing: September 2004

07   06   05   04   4   3   2

Trademarks

Warning and Disclaimer

Bulk Sales

Que Publishing offers excellent discounts on this book when ordered in quantity for bulk purchases or special sales. For more information, please contact

U.S. Corporate and Government Sales

1-800-382-3419

corpsales@pearsontechgroup.com

For sales outside the U.S., please contact

International Sales

international@pearsoned.com

Que Publishing

Publisher
Paul Boger

Associate Publisher
Greg Wiegand

Executive Editor
Rick Kughen

Development Editor
Todd Brakke

Managing Editor
Charlotte Clapp

Project Editor
Tonya Simpson

Production Editor
Seth Kerney

Indexer
Larry Sweazy

Technical Editor
Maximum PC

Publishing Coordinator
Sharry Lee Gregory

Interior Designer
Anne Jones

Maximum PC

Publisher
Chris Coelho

Editor-in-Chief
George Jones

Editors
Gordon Mah Ung
Will Smith
Logan Decker
Josh Norem

Cover Designer
Natalie Jeday

Future Network USA

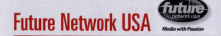

Editorial Director
Jon Phillips

MAXIMUM PC

Contents at a Glance

Table of Contents

Foreword: Why We Dream About Killer PCs

There are numerous reasons why it just plain *doesn't make sense* to build a one-off, personalized, exotic supercar in your driveway. Yes, the development, engineering, and fabrication costs would be prohibitively expensive. *True dat.* And, yes, from first pencil sketch to final wrench twist, the whole process would probably take between 1,325,000 to 1,500,000 man-hours. By the time you finished the job, the rest of world would be zipping around in hydrogen-powered aero-pods while you were still looking for a pump that dispenses dino juice.

But when it really gets down to decision-making time, the strongest argument against constructing your own Ferrari-killer keys into the issue of safety. To wit: If you were to build the supercar of your dreams—that price-is-no-object, four-wheeled rocket sled—you'd inevitably stuff it with so much horsepower, you'd probably run the vehicle into a tree on your first trip to redline.

Such is man's gluttony for power. Our lust for balls-out performance can often be self-defeating. And this is why building a dream car makes very little sense, whereas building a *dream PC* makes all the sense in the world.

After all, even the world's most witless computing newbie can still reap major benefits from owning the world's fastest PC. And anyone can play *Doom 3* without risk of injury, even at its highest resolution and effects settings. All it takes is a dream machine that's up to the task.

The book you're now reading is a practical extension of all the annual "Dream Machine" projects that *Maximum PC* ever created. In every September issue of the magazine, our editors present their interpretation of the finest hand-built PC possible, all in the hope that readers will glean useful information from our configuration decisions, and be inspired to build a dream machine of their own.

Truth be told, we're also driven by personal demons. We, too, want to build bad-ass PCs. We, too, want to explore the engineering limits of modern PC technology. And we, too, want to lord bragging rights over all the penny-ante small fries who would dare call themselves hardcore PC geeks. So, yeah, it gets personal.

I've been involved with *Maximum PC*'s Dream Machine creations since the beginning, even back when the magazine was called *boot*. The ancient history majors among us will recall that Dream Machine 1996 wasn't an actual physical creation. No, for *boot's* very first dream machine, the editors merely spec'd out a machine on paper; a blood-and-guts computer never sprang from our collective, uh… loins.

It would take another year for us to build our first *real* Dream Machine. I can still remember the tense planning meeting we held in the Northside Conference room (a dank, tomb-like space that has ironically become my office). Most of the drama surrounded our CPU choice. Hardware editor Andrew Sanchez had literally just gotten back from a visit at Intel HQ, where the Intellians revealed that a 300MHz Pentium II was imminent. The speed-bumped proc seemed like a natural fit for Dream Machine 1997, but Andrew was riddled with worry that our September issue publishing date would conflict with Intel's non-disclosure agreement (NDA).

The scene got ugly as all the editors (including myself) ganged up on Andrew, and pressured him into fudging the specifics of our publishing date when it came time for him to request the part from Intel. We wanted that CPU for Dream Machine 1997, damn it, and we were ready to do *anything* to get it in the Lab. As for Andrew, well, he went Andrew on us. He seethed in near-silence, and only spoke to repeat the following mantra: "The CPU is under NDA, and I don't want to break the trust of my press contact."

His argument, of course, was sound. NDAs absolutely suck, but if you're not prepared to honor them, then you shouldn't sign them in the first place. So we ultimately decided to play ball with Intel. The plan was for Andrew to *nicely* ask his contact to let us fudge the NDA by a few days.

In the end, a 300MHz P-II *did* make an appearance in Dream Machine 1997. Sort of. To Intel, the NDA would become a non-issue, but the company didn't have 300MHz part to give us by our construction deadline. So we ended up overclocking a 266MHz processor, and called our CPU decision resolved.

All subsequent Dream Machine projects would be affected by some type of precarious planning decision, but only because Dream Machine-caliber ambition leads to trouble. Indeed, every year we do our best to top the previous year's Dream Machine, and this usually means waiting for a last-minute component that's fresh out of quality-assurance testing. In effect, we become victims of our own high level of press access. Luckily (or unfortunately, depending on how you view the world), you folks at home need not suffer such travail. Your Dream Machine component options are limited to whatever's currently selling, so you'll never have to wrestle with even half of *Maximum PC's* configuration nightmares.

That said, building the perfect dream PC from scratch is never a walk in the park, and if you're even the least bit unsure of which parts to buy, or how to assemble your rig, then you should find the instruction in this book to be invaluable. *Maximum PC* tech editor Will Smith has not only imbued this book with his own knowledge of PC building, he's also included the strategies, tips, and opinions of all his Lab compadres. In fact, this *Maximum PC Guide to Building a Dream PC* includes far more building information than we've ever published in a regular issue of the magazine (or even our *Build the Perfect PC* newsstand special), and should serve as the definitive bible for how-to, do-it-yourself PC construction.

So go hog-wild. Build the craziest damn dream PC you can possibly imagine. The only thing you can possibly damage (or maybe even kill) are a few benchmarking records. Do it. *Do it.* Build that dream machine, and define the "maximum" in *Maximum PC*. Nothing could better validate our yearly efforts as editors.

Jon Phillips, editorial director, *Maximum PC*

About the Author

Will Smith is the Technical Editor of *Maximum PC* magazine, the ultimate magazine for PC enthusiasts on the planet. In addition to covering bleeding-edge technology for the magazine, he's also edited the mag's How-To section since its inception, edited two *Maximum PC* How-To special issues, written innumerable white papers, and once—during a week-long benchmarking orgy—tested so many videocards that he wore out a test PC's AGP slot.

He has built hundreds of computers for friends, family, co-workers, and himself since 1995, and would never, ever tell anyone "Dude, just get a Dell!"

This is his first book.

Contact info:

Email: will@maximumpc.com

Work homepage: www.maximumpc.com

Personal Homepage: willski.com

Dedication

To Gina—so you can finally build your own computer!

Acknowledgments

This book would not have been possible without the support of the entire staff of *Maximum PC* magazine—past and present. In addition to answering my incessant questions on topics ranging from the viability of Socket 939-based processors to the best way to take a picture of a Serial ATA cable, they also helped shoulder a larger load when I was buried in work on this book. Thanks for your help Boni, E-Will, George, Gordon, Josh, Katherine, Logan, Mark, Natalie, Samantha, Steve, and Tae! (Please note that the preceding list was in alphabetical order.)

I'd also like to thank my editors, Jon Phillips at Future Network USA and Todd Brakke and Rick Kughen at Que Publishing. Their questions and thoughtful critiques helped me write a book that is accessible to just about anyone who can pick up a screwdriver. Thanks, guys.

A big thank you goes to all the writers who have contributed to *Maximum PC* in recent years. I rarely found a topic that hadn't already been covered in more detail than I needed for this book in a back-issue of the magazine.

Thanks to all my friends who forgave me for disappearing and not returning phone calls for the first half of the year. There are too many of you to list, so I'll just buy a round the next time I see you guys.

Extra special thanks to my mom Leah, my dad Verlin, my sister Lynlee, and the rest of my family for their understanding during the months that my invariable answer to the question "Hey, what are you doing?" was "Working on the book."

Finally, and most importantly, I have to thank my partner and confidant, Gina. I would not have been able to write this book without her constant love and support. Not only did she keep me fed, watered, and Diet Coke'd during all-night writing rampages, she helped me start when I wanted to procrastinate and kept me going when I thought I was out of steam. She's an exceptional woman, and I'm amazed and thrilled every single day that she chose to live her life with me.

We Want to Hear from You!

As the reader of this book, *you* are our most important critic and commentator. We value your opinion and want to know what we're doing right, what we could do better, what areas you'd like to see us publish in, and any other words of wisdom you're willing to pass our way.

As an associate publisher for Que Publishing, I welcome your comments. You can email or write me directly to let me know what you did or didn't like about this book—as well as what we can do to make our books better.

Please note that I cannot help you with technical problems related to the topic of this book. We do have a User Services group, however, where I will forward specific technical questions related to the book.

When you write, please be sure to include this book's title and author as well as your name, email address, and phone number. I will carefully review your comments and share them with the author and editors who worked on the book.

Email: feedback@quepublishing.com

Mail: Greg Wiegand
Associate Publisher
Que Publishing
800 East 96th Street
Indianapolis, IN 46240 USA

For more information about this book or another Que title, visit our Web site at www.quepublishing.com. Type the ISBN (0789731932) or the title of a book in the Search field to find the page you're looking for.

Introduction

Never has it been easier to build your own computer. Since I built my first computer in 1995, I've built hundreds of computers for friends, family, co-workers, and work. When I built my first computer—a 200MHz beast with a whopping 32MB of RAM, an 8GB hard drive, an ancient SoundBlaster soundcard, and one videocard dedicated to 2D and another videocard specifically for 3D games—it took me the better part of three months to pick out the perfect components. My search to find the best bang for my meager college-student buck forced me to read every review on the Web and in all the computer magazines of the day. I read every website and every magazine I could find to learn everything I could possibly need to know about building my PC.

By reading dozens of websites and magazine articles, I learned all about setting CPU speeds with jumpers, the motherboard features I had to have, and the right way to configure my IDE drives. I was able to glean enough info to build my first PC without outside help from a half-dozen sources. Luckily for you, building your own PC is no longer such an esoteric art—everything you need to know to build your first computer is contained within the pages of this book. I've collected the computer-building expertise of all the staff members at *Maximum PC* in this volume. Everything you will need to know, from how to pick the right components to the secrets of proper hard drive configuration, is in the *Maximum PC Guide to Building a Dream PC*.

Is This Book For You?

This book is for anyone who has ever looked at a store-built PC and thought that she could do better. You don't need to know what RDRAM is to build a computer. You don't need to know the difference between a Radeon and a GeForce, or even what the big deal about 64-bit computing is. If you know how to work a Phillips-head screwdriver, and can read this book, you're ready to begin.

Even if you've already built a computer, this book contains oodles of valuable buying advice for all the important components of your computer. Our buying guides will show you how to choose the perfect videocard, the most important things to know when buying memory, the three most important considerations when you purchase a hard drive, and everything you need to know to pick out the perfect case for your new rig. If the buyer's guides aren't enough, I've also included dozens of the best PC-building tips and tricks—straight from the *Maximum PC* testing lab.

Chapter-by-Chapter Breakdown

This book is broken into two main sections. The first half is a series of detailed buyer's guides, which gives detailed tips to help you choose the perfect components for your dream PC. The second half gives step-by-step instructions that tell you exactly you how to build your new computer after you've collected your parts. Before you begin purchasing components, you should read each chapter in the buyer's guide, as some components naturally influence other components. For example, you can't plug an AMD CPU into a motherboard designed for Intel processors, and most small formfactor rigs don't have the space to accommodate a two-slot videocard. Here's what you can look forward to:

Chapter 1 is a survey-level course in how computers work. I give you 30-second descriptions of what the main components do and how they work, and show you what each component actually looks like.

The latter half of Chapter 1 also outlines six different sample rigs that you could build. They range from the ultimate gaming rig to a very basic budget PC to a kick-ass computer suitable for personal video recorder duty in your living room. If you use one of these rigs as a template, you won't be disappointed.

Chapter 2 is the first buyer's guide chapter. In it, I tell you the secret to buying a kick-ass case for your new rig and describe the possible perils you'll face when purchasing a power supply. I also cover the pros and cons of the increasingly popular small formfactor cases.

Chapter 3 tackles your computer's brain—the CPU. I talk about the real differences between Intel and AMD CPUs, the right places to scrimp on performance to save big bucks, and what you need to know to pick the perfect CPU for your machine. After all, all CPUs aren't created equal. Because a modern CPU requires a powerful cooling apparatus, I tell you what to look for when purchasing a top-class aftermarket CPU cooler.

Once you know which CPU you're going to buy, you can go motherboard shopping, which is exactly what I'll help you do in Chapter 4. Whether it's describing the perfect motherboard layout, dishing the dirt on the new BTX motherboards, or just listing the features that every modern motherboard should support, this is one of the most inclusive motherboard buying guides *Maximum PC* has ever run.

In Chapter 5, I'll tell you everything you need to know about your computer's memory. I explain why some RAM is faster than others, and why you *must* buy your memory in matched pairs. Picking poor performing memory can severely affect your system's performance. Luckily, I can show you how to avoid such a sad fate.

Chapter 6 introduces the long-term storage for your computer—the hard drive. I'll explain what you need to look out for when choosing a hard drive. Bigger isn't necessarily better; when you're talking about hard drives, speed rules size for almost every use.

Next up is optical storage—really just a fancy name for CD and DVD drives. Chapter 7 sheds some light on the many different flavors of optical drive available

today. Do you need a state-of-the-art DVD burner? (Probably.) What makes one CD burner better than another? (More than you might think.) What do you need to look for if you want to rip music from your CDs (not all drives work the same)?

There are literally thousands of websites and magazine articles devoted to picking the best videocard for your computer. I condensed all of the important information that you need to know to buy a videocard that perfectly suits your needs to help you make a well-informed decision. Whether you're a hardcore gamer, a 3D modeler, or a TV addict, there's a videocard designed for your needs. Find your videocard in Chapter 8.

Chapter 9 opens up the aural beat. The soundcard is part of the one-two punch that creates kick-ass audio from your PC. Whether you want a pro-level audio card for professional music mixing or a 7.1 gaming card to give you an edge over your enemy, I have loads of buying tips that will help you choose the perfect soundcard.

The best computer is completely useless without a good monitor. Chapter 10 tells you everything you need to know about purchasing the perfect CRT or flat-panel for your dream rig. Heck, I even show you how to pick just the right display, whether you're a gamer, a 3D artist, or just a web browser.

The other half of your PC's audio system are the speakers or headphones. In Chapter 11, I'll show you all the options available in PC audio output, from super-budget priced headphones to multimedia speaker rigs that are powerful enough to loosen your bowels. I'll tell you everything you need to know to buy brilliant-sounding speakers.

If you're anything like me, floppy disks disgust you. They hold a pathetic 1.44MB of data, they're fragile, and they're slow. But you need portable storage for your PC. In Chapter 12, I'll tell you about all the different portable storage options, from tiny external hard drives to keychain USB drives that you can slip into your pocket.

Chapter 13 concludes the buyer's guide chapters by telling you how to safely shop online. If you follow our ten tips, you can rest assured that you'll receive your components without getting ripped off.

Now that you've purchased all your hardware, it's time to assemble your rig. Before you start, you should sit down and read Chapter 14 in its entirety. I used loads of large, full-color photographs to show you exactly how you'll install every component in your new computer. From the proper way to seat a video-card in the AGP slot to the amount of pressure you'll need to apply to lock your memory into place, I show you everything you need to know to build your computer right the first time.

In Chapter 15, I'll show you how to use the power of RAID—it stands for Redundant Array of Inexpensive Disks—to improve the performance and reliability of your hard drives. By pairing identical drives, you can increase their performance, lessen your chances of data loss, or just increase the amount of storage space you have available.

Chapter 16 is a compilation of all the best low-level tweaks that we've run in *Maximum PC* magazine. I'll show you how to shorten your boot time, squeeze a little more performance out of your new rig, and increase its reliability by making some quick and easy adjustments to your PC's BIOS.

Once you've tweaked your BIOS to the max, I'll show you how to get the most performance from Windows XP. The collection of Windows XP tweaks in Chapter 17 is the result of the decades of experience the editors of *Maximum PC* have with Windows. Learn how to strip nonessential features from Windows for a big performance boost and protect your new machine from the dangerous viruses and worms that run rampant across the Internet.

In Chapter 18 I'll tell you how to take your smoothly running XP machine and make a set of custom recovery CDs or DVDs that you can use in the event of a disaster to restore your PC to its "like-new" condition. It's easy to make recovery disks—it only takes a few minutes, and can save you hours if your PC does get infected with a malicious virus or even just annoying spyware.

When you're building your first PC, things are bound to go wrong. This is to be expected, and you shouldn't get upset. Instead, turn to Chapter 19, where

Maximum PC's computer repair guru, the Doctor, covers every possible thing that can go wrong with a newly PC. Whether you're fixing a problem or just trying to avoid one, you should heed the Doc's advice.

Closing Thoughts

That's really all there is to it. Building your own computer is great fun, a fantastic way to learn more about computers, and it can be intensely rewarding. After almost 10 years of building my own rigs, I can't imagine ever using a computer that I didn't assemble myself. By building your own computer, you know everything about your machine. You'll know exactly what hardware is in your rig. You'll know exactly what software is running on your machine.

Most of all, you'll have the satisfaction of knowing that your machine is unique. You choose the parts to perfectly suit your needs. You installed exactly the software you need, no more and no less. By building your own rig, you make your PC an extension of yourself, and that's pretty damn cool.

Now it's time to get out there, pick up your screwdriver, and build your PC!

—Will Smith
San Francisco, CA
July 4, 2004

Chapter One

Planning the PC That's Right for You

Or... One Man's Dream Machine Is Another's Hellspawn Hardware Nightmare

Behold the majesty! Dream Machine 2003—hand-built by editor-commandos in the *Maximum PC* Lab—is a lightning-fast gaming rig, equipped with the fastest hardware money could buy in September 2003.

Building your own PC is definitely more challenging than order-ing a pre-built machine from Dell or purchasing a HP box from Circuit City—but, hoo-wee, it's a satisfying way to spend a Saturday afternoon! Indeed, if you eschew buying a pre-fab system and instead go the do-it-yourself route, you'll end up with a lean, mean computing machine that includes the exact features that you need the most. You'll also gain a much deeper understanding of how PCs actually work if you build your machine at home.

Yeah, yeah, we know: We had you at "building." But before you begin tin-kering in earnest, it's vital that you formulate a project plan—or your Dream Machine might turn into a silicon-soaked night-mare. Thus the purpose of this chapter. So get out your mechanical pencil, because in a short time you'll need to begin scribbling to-do notes and shopping lists in the margins of this book.

Hey, This Ain't Rocket Science

Here's the big secret that your geeky friends don't want you to know: Building a PC doesn't require oracu-lar wisdom, the secrets of the engi-neering elite, or even any fancy tools. You don't need to know how to read binary code, and you don't have to understand how a piece of sili-con is fabbed into a CPU. All you really need are a few components, a good plan, a few hours, a Philips head screwdriver, and a little tech know-how, *Maximum PC*-style.

So, first things first. Before you begin sharpening up your screw-drivers for the kill, you need to fig-ure out what you want to use your PC for. Different dream machines demand different components. While a gaming rig demands the fastest

3D accelerator possible, a media center PC for your living room might simply do better with the quietest 3D accelerator. Not sure what kind of PC you want to build? Don't fear. In this chapter, we'll introduce you to the basic parts that all PCs require, and outline the configurations of six dif-ferent Dream Machines, from the ultimate gaming machine to the ultimate 3D rendering box. We also show you the precise component "load out" that we used to build our own Dream Machine 2003, the PC featured on the preceding page.

After you've decided what kind of PC you want to build, it's time to formu-late a budget. By faithfully follow-ing a budget during each phase of your building project, you won't fall victim to any rude surprises when you tally the final bill. To this end, this chap-ter also clues you in to *Maximum PC's* best budget-stretching tips and tricks, which can help you get the most of your PC-building buck.

Motherboards Aren't Supposed to Get Hot

Finally, if you don't know a motherboard from an ironing board, don't worry. The lion's share of this book tells you everything you'll ever need to know about picking spe-cific parts for your personalized Dream Machine. We'll go component-by-component, showing you exactly how different parts work, how to tell the good ones from the bad ones, and how to purchase parts without getting ripped off. After you've collected all the components for your perfect PC, we'll then walk you through a complete step-by-step PC con-struction guide, revealing every-thing you'll need to know for assembly, configuration, tweaking, and maintenance.

OK, enough with prelims. It's time for the big show...

Parts at a Glance

Let's take a quick peek at the components that are universal to all PCs

The Silverstone SST-TJ03 combines form and functionality. Its burnished silver exterior hides a chassis that's light enough for easy transport, but sturdy enough to withstand frequent travel.

The Case

Getting the right case for your Dream Machine is imperative. Your enclosure will house just about every component your machine requires in order to function, so you need to make sure that the one you choose is large enough to suit your needs, and sturdy enough to withstand the physical torture typical hardcore PC enthusiasts inflict.

Your case's physical dimensions and interior structure should be prepared to hold your motherboard of choice. The case should have enough open bays for all your optical and hard drives, as well as enough mounting points for all the fans you'll ever want to install. You might also be on the lookout for cases that come with pre-installed amenities, such as front-mounted USB and FireWire ports, and integrated temperature monitors. Your case's basic construction material—maybe aluminum, maybe plastic, maybe even cardboard if you're living on the edge— also requires some consideration, as we'll be discussing later on.

Your case could cost as little as $45 or as much as $1,500. Most standard tower cases cost about $100, but specialized cases (such as shoebox-sized "small formfactor" boxes and massive workstation cases) can cost more.

The Power Supply Unit

In simple terms, a Power Supply Unit (PSU) converts the alternating current from your wall into the direct current required by PC components. Yeah, sounds simple enough, but nothing will bring an otherwise functional PC to its knees faster than an inadequate, under-powered PSU. When choosing your PSU, you'll want to ensure that it can output more power than your components will require, so make sure that your unit is up to the task. There are literally hundreds of power supply units on the market, ranging from bare-bones PSUs that do nothing but supply juice to components, to deluxe PSUs that include fancy lights and super-silent fans.

The PC Power & Cooling Silencer 400 provides enough power for even the thirstiest of PCs, yet it's quiet enough to run in almost any hush-hush environment.

Motherboard

Either directly or indirectly, all of your PC components will plug into your motherboard (or "mobo"), which fulfills the role of "data traffic cop," making sure all your various components work together, and exchange data as quickly as possible.

Because each motherboard only works with a handful of CPUs, it's important that you consider your mobo and CPU purchases as a single buying decision. These two parts must be compatible. Your mobo also determines the type of memory you'll be using, and even defines the type and number of storage drives that you'll be able to run. Many modern motherboards also include "onboard" features that can save you time and money. For example, if you buy a motherboard with onboard networking and audio chips, you won't have to buy and install add-in Ethernet cards and soundcards. Whatever mobo you decide on, you'll want to make sure that it includes support for a few new data-transfer standards: USB 2.0, Gigabit Ethernet, and Serial ATA.

The Albatron K8X800 ProII supports the latest AMD processors, and includes must-have integrated features, such as Serial ATA RAID and dual-channel DDR memory support.

CPU

Without a CPU, your Dream Machine is nothing more than a box filled with some processed sand, copper, aluminum, and trace amounts of gold, tin, and silver. However, with a CPU—a modern CPU—your Dream Machine is more powerful than every computer running on Planet Earth, circa 1970.

CPU stands for "central processing unit." This little chip pretty much performs all of a PC's math calculations, save those executed by dedicated 3D accelerators. CPUs are differentiated by the number of calculations they can perform every second, the amount of cache memory they have onboard, and the speed at which they interact with a system's motherboard. Most of the other parts in your PC either store data or shuffle data, but your CPU actually processes data. For hobbyist PC builders, there are two families of CPU to choose from: AMD and Intel. Each processor family has different strengths and weaknesses, and there are dozens of CPUs within each family.

The Athlon 64 FX processor is arguably the fastest CPU you can buy today for 3D gaming.

Memory

Random access memory, also known as RAM, serves as a short-term storage receptacle for whatever data your CPU is chewing on. Each program you open requisitions a section of RAM and stores data in this section, moving chunks in and out as necessary. RAM is "volatile" memory. This means that when the power to your RAM is shut off, the information that was stored inside is irretrievably lost.

RAM typically comes packaged on small circuit boards (known as *sticks* or *modules*) that include several identical memory chips that work together. Make sure that you buy memory that's compatible with your motherboard and CPU. Most mobos support just one type of memory running at only a few different speeds. If you purchase memory that's slower or faster than what your motherboard and CPU support, your system may not run properly. It's also vital that your Dream Machine have enough total memory. Luckily, memory is very cheap, so everyone can afford *Maximum PC*'s minimum recommended amount of 512MB.

These 512MB sticks of Corsair PC3200 DDR SDRAM work with both AMD- and Intel-based systems.

With platters that spin at 10,000rpm, the 72GB Western Digital Raptor is the fastest Serial ATA hard drive on the planet.

Hard Drives

Whereas your RAM serves as a short-term storage receptacle, your hard drive functions as long-term storage. Unlike volatile system memory, a hard drive physically writes data to a magnetic disk, and this data remains intact, even if your PC is powered off. Saving data to your hard drive takes an order of magnitude longer than saving the same data to RAM, but hard drive space is also an order of magnitude cheaper than RAM space. Hard drives that hold up to 300GB of data are available for less than $300!

Capacity isn't all that matters when picking out a hard drive. You also need to look at the drive's rotation speed, as well as the size of its onboard memory cache. The faster your hard drive's rotation speed, the more data it can transfer every second. Having a large hard drive cache, meanwhile, can greatly reduce the time it takes for your drive to access files.

Optical Drives

We call them optical drives, but they're really just storage drives used for reading and writing CDs and DVDs. Data transfer rates for various drives are typically described by an "x-rating," such as 40×. Please note, however, that a 40× drive may not write discs twice as quickly as a 20× drive. More about this in the chapter dedicated to optical drives.

Picking the perfect optical drive lets you write (that is, "record" or "burn") a DVD in seconds. Picking the wrong drive gives you nothing but compatibility headaches. The problem is rooted in the fact that most optical drives that burn DVDs support only one of two different standards, either DVD-R/RW or DVD+R/RW. Luckily, however, both DVD standards offer write-once and rewritable formats, and both standards create discs that run in most set-top DVD players. There are also several DVD "combo" burners that support both recordable DVD formats.

The Sony DRU-530A can burn both DVD-R and DVD+R media, making it one of the most flexible optical drives you can buy.

Videocard

Once upon a time, your computer's videocard did nothing more than output text to a low-resolution monitor. Those days are long past. Modern videocards include graphics processing units (GPUs) that execute intense math calculations, and are every bit as complex as modern CPUs. GPUs perform all the number-crunching needed to draw complex 3D scenes and special effects at speeds fast enough to please 3D gamers and content developers. This requires a helluva lot of number-crunching prowess, and gobs of onboard video memory. Yes, today's videocards still send basic two-dimensional images to your desktop monitor, but they also do a whole lot more.

Picking the proper videocard is important for everyone, but absolutely vital to 3D gamers. Pick the right card, and you'll be able to play the latest games at their highest possible detail settings. Pick the wrong card, and you'll doom yourself to, well, a life of watching *American Idol*.

The GeForce FX 5950 is one of the best videocards you can buy for games. Because its core and memory are clocked so high, it requires a mongo-large heatsink/fan.

Soundcard

Modern soundcards do much more than process idiotic "boing" sounds or "You've got mail" greetings. Indeed, a good soundcard can turn a normal PC into the centerpiece of a home theater sound system. So don't skimp. And don't automatically assume that you'll need to purchase an add-in card like the one pictured here. Many motherboard manufacturers now integrate audio-processing chips directly onboard.

Whether integrated or on a separate PCI card, a soundcard lets your PC record or play back sound in many different formats—from the Dolby Digital 5.1 format encoded on DVD movies to the AAC format used by iTunes. Really good soundcards even relieve your CPU of audio-processing chores, and this can lead to faster frame rates in 3D games. Some soundcards also include "breakout boxes"—interface panels that mount on the front of your computer, and include connectors for USB, FireWire, headphones, and so on.

The Sound Blaster Audigy ZX supports full 7.1 channel, 24-bit audio output.

Monitors

Do we really need to explain your monitor's purpose? It's the one and only visual interface to what your PC is actually doing. Duh. But just because its purpose is simple, you shouldn't assume your purchasing decision will be as well. Like all other components, the perfect monitor depends on your intended uses. While a large-screen projector is perfect for a living room PC that plays DVD movies, it's completely inappropriate for day-to-day office work. Similarly, while an LCD flat-panel would be perfect for a small computer located in the kitchen, it just won't do for serious gaming.

When choosing your monitor, you'll be faced with a bewildering array of technologies. Even traditional CRT-based monitors range from under $100 to more than $1,500. HDTVs and DLP projectors? They cost a whole lot more.

The Samsung 180T's 18-inch display runs a native resolution of 1280×1024 pixels.

Speakers

Computer speakers take the unamplified output from your soundcard, amplify it, and then play it back (as loud and as majestically as possible, if they're running in the *Maximum PC* Lab). Most multimedia sound rigs include several smaller speakers—satellites—that produce high and middle frequencies. Low frequencies are handled by a larger speaker—a subwoofer—that can be placed wherever it is convenient.

The Klipsch ProMedia 5.1 Ultra isn't the loudest 5.1 speaker system we've tested, but it provides some of the best audio fidelity we've ever heard.

A good set of PC speakers will thunder during 3D gaming deathmatches and whisper during string sonatas, but not all speakers are appropriate for every use. While a great set of gaming and movie-viewing speakers will have great frequency response and a powerful subwoofer, a high-quality "studio monitor" speaker for PC audio editing will have a perfectly flat response, and reproduce sound exactly as it was recorded.

Mouse and Keyboard (Input Devices)

A good mouse and keyboard are absolutely vital for healthy and comfortable computing, so don't simply purchase the cheapest input device you can find. After all, whenever you're working on your PC, it's inevitable that you're manipulating either device about 90 percent of the time (and if you're not touching your mouse and keyboard that often, it's not called "working on your PC," it's called "sitting"). The upshot is that it's worth spending a few extra bucks on input devices that suit your own hands and habits.

Also be aware that cheap optical mouse devices have low-resolution sensors that are less precise than their more expensive brethren. Whether you're editing digital images or fighting for your life in an online deathmatch, you need the most precision you can get.

The Logitech Elite Keyboard and the Microsoft Intellimouse Explorer 4.0 are de rigueur for serious gamers.

Cooling

Your computer includes several components that generate astounding amounts of heat—your CPU and videocard will typically be the worst offenders. These parts must remain cool, or they'll overheat and your PC will malfunction. So running your computer without sufficient cooling devices is a big no-no. Most people cool their PCs with fans and heatsinks. By attaching large heatsinks to hot components and then using fans to blow cool air over the heatsinks, hot CPUs and videocards can be adequately cooled. Unfortunately, some fans make a lot of noise. People who want quieter computers frequently eschew fans for unconventional cooling methods—for example, water-cooling and phase-change cooling systems.

This Zalman fan/heatsink combo isn't just functional, it's also a work of industrial art.

Cables

Picking the right cables for your system is every bit as important as picking the right components. If your cables aren't capable of transferring data as fast as the rest of your components, they'll retard overall performance.

Your PC cables may serve a utilitarian function, but they need not be boring to look at.

Operating System

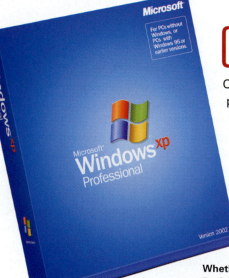

Once your hardware is assembled and working properly, you'll need a proper operating system in order to actually use your computer. Right now, the best OS for desktop use is Windows XP. Its rock-solid stability, blazing-fast performance, and up-to-date hardware support give it the edge.

Whether you choose the bare-bones Home version or the feature-loaded Professional edition, the only OS for power users is Windows XP.

Dream PCs: Six Case Studies of Perfection

There's no perfect PC for everyone, so it's time to decide what type suits you best

N ow that you've got a general idea of what makes a computer tick, it's time to decide what you want to put into your Dream Machine. To help you along that path, on the following pages we've configured six different Dream Machine possibilities, each dedicated to a particular task.

Sure, all of the six PCs share commonalities. They all run some type of CPU. They all hook up to some type of monitor. And—yes, Timmy—they all would probably teach you some valuable life lessons over time. But make no mistake, very few modern PCs can "do it all." That's because the very definition of what constitutes a personal computer has exploded beyond scopes once imaginable. In the beginning, PCs were used for basic word processing functions. Then they became tools for graphic design and other types of content creation (movie-making, sound-mixing, that sort of thing). Then they became video gaming machines. And now they can replace your home stereo, DVD player, and TiVo recorder.

In this chapter, we'll introduce you to all the decision-making you'll need to consider before you begin ordering parts. On the following pages you might discover some tech terms that elude you, so please make sure to read Chapters 2 through 12 for glossary definitions as well as deeper explanations of component categories.

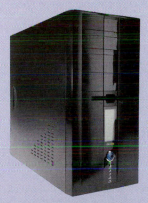

The Dream
Baseline PC

The Dream
Entertainment
Center PC

The Dream
Gaming PC

The Dream
Budget PC

The Dream Content
Creation PC

The Dream
Mini PC

The Dream Baseline PC
From strong foundations come strong houses

You don't play games, and you do serious image, video, or sound editing. All you need is a plain vanilla PC to read email, browse the web, type out an occasional personal letter, and file taxes online every April. You don't need all the special hardware required to render 3D models, edit studio-quality audio, or play back DVD movies across 42 diagonal inches.

You just need a fast, no-frills, honest PC.

But just because you don't plan to use your computer for any kind of specialized tasks, it doesn't mean you don't deserve a Dream Machine. *Maximum PC* believes that even a "normal machine" can have a dreamy parts configuration, one that does everyday tasks with aplomb, but doesn't cost a lot of money.

First, you'll need to pick out a case and power supply. A standard PC doesn't demand a fancy case, but it does need a case large enough to hold all your hardware. It also requires a power supply capable of powering all your components. For your baseline PC, we recommend you choose a nice-looking—but not flashy—mid-tower ATX case that includes a built-in 350-watt power supply. If you're not going to play games, there's no reason to shell out big bucks for the fastest CPU/motherboard combo possible. So, given today's offerings, for example, you'd do well to pick up a 3.2GHz Pentium 4 processor and an Intel D875PBZ mobo, which cost just a few hundred dollars total. The current highest-performing gaming CPU is the Athlon 64 FX-53, but it costs the better part of $500, and is complete overkill for anyone who isn't really into games. In fact, even a 3.4GHz Pentium 4 would be considered excessive for a baseline PC. That's why the 3.2GHz P4 is currently a great value from a price/performance perspective. It costs a few hundred bucks less than the highest-performing CPU, but actually delivers 75 percent of that CPU's performance.

As for the D875PBZ motherboard, it's a fully-featured, mid-price board. It includes built-in networking and FireWire support, which saves you from having to buy add-in PCI cards that offer the same functionality. See the benefit here? When configuring a baseline system, you should pick a mobo with as many integrated features as possible. Only integrated sound and video support should be disregarded (and even integrated sound is up for debate—while all integrated video is considered unacceptable among *Maximum PC* editors, some mobos actually have very acceptable sound support care of nVidia nForce-class chipsets).

We should also note that the D875PBZ motherboard can take advantage of high-speed PC3200 DDR memory. Does a baseline system need the fastest-possible memory? Not necessarily. But it always pays to have a motherboard that's primed to support faster memory types. Who knows? Some day you might find a bag full of higher-speed memory sitting on park bench. It could happen!

Now it's time to pick a baseline videocard. If you truly intend to avoid all 3D games and applications, you can cheap out on the videocard—there's just no reason at all to shell out $500 for a top-of-the-line gaming card. In fact, if you're not going to be playing games, just about any videocard you can buy will fill your needs perfectly, so buy the cheapest you can find.

That said, a mid-range card (think $200) will give you a great balance of 2D image quality in regular applications, and decent performance in today's games. One competent mid-ranger to consider is the ATI Radeon 9600 XT, which costs a little more than $100 and can drive two monitors to boot. The 9600 XT's GPU is powerful enough to run most games; it just doesn't offer the frame rate capabilities of more expensive cards.

Next up: Your baseline soundcard. Whether it's for listening to MP3s or making free phone calls across the Internet, you'll need some type of audio support in your PC. For your baseline purposes, you might consider Creative Lab's SoundBlaster Audigy 2 LS. Creative Labs pretty much owns the soundcard market (which means the company's hardware suffers relatively few software conflicts), and the LS is a good mid-range offering that can play and record DVD-Audio quality files in perfect 24-bit precision.

Of course, the best soundcard in the world is worthless if you don't have speakers capable of playing the sweet, sweet melodies that your PC produces. This is where Logitech's Z-2200 systems come in. Instead of shelling out big bucks for a fancy surround-sound speaker system with seven speakers, you can go with the Z-2200, which is the best two-channel system we've ever tested. These 200-watt monsters are so loud, they literally rattled the walls in our testing labs.

When it comes to baseline storage, we suggest you go with a single hard drive and a single optical drive. When picking the hard drive, look at three main things: its storage capacity, its rotational speed, and its cache size. We would never consider building a system with less than 180GB of storage, and we would never recommend any drive with a rotational speed slower than 7200rpm. Sure, there are great bargains on huge drives that spin at a mere 5400rpm, but they're not fit for human consumption (boot-up times, application loading times, and large file loading times all suffer at 5400rpm). Cache size is less important, but, if possible, you should still go for a drive with 8MB of onboard cache. Onboard cache memory speeds up data transfers, so the more, the better. In fact, we now consider 2MB of onboard cache to be the hard drive minimum.

The Radeon 9600 XT is a great general-purpose videocard. It's fast in day-to-day desktop use, and provides decent speed for games to boot.

The Logitech Z-2200 2.1 speaker rig is not only THX-certified, it's also damn loud.

For your optical drive, you'll want a "combo burner" that can burn CDs as well as both DVD formats (DVD+RW and DVD-RW). If you intend to burn a bunch of DVDs, your optical drive's DVD burning speed should be rated at 8×. At this performance rating, most DVD burners burn a full disk in about eight minutes. CD-writing speed is also important, so make sure your combo burner is rated with a CD-R burn speed of at least 24×. Otherwise, you'll find yourself waiting for your disks to burn, while other PC enthusiasts frolic outside, enjoying their idle time.

For day-to-day computing that eschews gaming, a flat-panel LCD display is perfect for most baseliners. LCDs take up very little desk space, are easy to lift, and cost less and less every day. Look for a 17-inch display with a native resolution of 1280×1024.

Finally, because your baseline PC won't be used for 3D gaming firefights that require absolutely perfect mouse tracking, you can afford to use a wireless keyboard and mouse combo. When you're purchasing any wireless input device, make sure it uses a radio to communicate with your PC. There's nothing more annoying than an infrared mouse that must retain a "line of sight" with its base station. After all, you go with wireless peripherals because you want to minimize annoyances, not increase them, right?

Baseline PC Cheat Sheet

- By choosing a mid-range CPU, you can keep your PC's performance high, but its price tag reasonably low. Top-of-the-line CPUs always command a budget-bashing price premium.
- Ensuring you have enough memory is the key to great PC performance, especially for day-to-day Windows tasks. Make sure you have at least 512MB.
- A great set of 2.1 speakers will let you play your music loud, without having to bother with wiring an unwieldy 5.1 speaker rig that you may never even use.
- For a normal PC, you won't need any fancy cooling rigs, but rather just a couple of fans and a quiet heatsink/fan combo for your CPU.

Baseline PC Shopping List

Here are some specific product recommendations for a killer baseline building project

Generic Mid-Tower Case

There's no reason to spend a load of dough on a fancy aluminum case when it's just going to sit quietly under your desk. All your case needs is the ability to hold all your components, enough mounting points for one or two interior fans, and a 350W power supply. We recommend the Antec Lanboy—it's made of aluminum and boasts the requisite 350W power supply. (www.antec-inc.com)

3.2GHz Pentium 4 CPU

With 3.2GHz of pure processing power under its heat spreader, the 3.2GHz P4 has more than enough juice for common consumer software apps. This particular P4 also boasts HyperThreading technology, which lets the CPU execute two application tasks at once—perfect for multitasking. As for the fan-heatsink combo that comes with this P4, it's all the direct cooling this processor needs. (www.intel.com)

Plextor 708A DVD Combo Burner

If you want to burn it, the Plextor 708A can handle the job, and quickly to boot. It can back up your data, burn DVD movies, create audio CDs—anything. Such is the beauty of a single optical drive that supports all known optical media. (www.plextor.com)

Western Digital 1800JB Hard Drive

With 180GB of storage, a 7200rpm platter speed, and a whopping 8MB of cache, the 1800JB offers a winning blend of affordable performance and a near-bottomless pit of capacity. RAID arrays and 10,000rpm are plenty faster, sure, but the 1800JB is perfect for baseline computing. (www.westerndigital.com)

The Dream Gaming PC
For gamers, all that matters is raw 3D processing speed

Let's face it: In the hyper-competitive world of online gaming, having a faster machine than an opponent is a huge advantage. Frame rate equals life. That said, however, speed is nothing without style. When you hit the LAN party circuit, you shouldn't just dazzle your competition with your mad deathmatch skills; you should also wow them with a tricked-out case. We're partial to aluminum cases for modding. The aluminum body is easy to completely disassemble, which makes it easier for you to cut holes, paint, or otherwise modify body panels.

When outfitting a system with high-end gaming hardware, it's vital that your power supply provide enough go-fast juice. You shouldn't settle for a PSU with a rating less than 400W. Spending a few extra bucks on a premium PSU essentially precludes unpredictable crashes and restarts during zero hour.

There's really only one choice for your dream gaming CPU: The Athlon 64 FX is fast enough, it's good enough, and doggone it, gamers just like it. In specific terms, you might consider pairing an FX-53 with an Asus SK8V, simply the fastest Athlon 64 mobo available. When you buy this mobo, also pick up a couple of gigabytes of PC3200 SDRAM to ensure all your games have plenty of room to stretch their proverbial legs.

When you're buying a videocard for your dream gaming rig, you need to read the latest issue of *Maximum PC* to determine the current frame rate champion—and then settle for nothing less. Never buy a videocard that has fewer than eight pipelines, lacks the latest programmable shader support (DirectX 9.x), or comes with less than 256MB of RAM. Because a videocard is so crucial to gaming performance, you need the mack-daddy performance king, not only for today's games, but also for tomorrow's.

If you want the best sound for your games and don't want to sacrifice frame rate, go for a Creative Labs Audigy card. The Audigy 2 ZS series of soundcards delivers perfect 24-bit multi-channel gaming harmony when paired with a great set of 5.1 (or higher) speakers. Bass rules in the gaming speaker category; you should feel every bullet impact and explosion. To reproduce that kind of rocking bass, your speakers should include a large, powerful subwoofer.

The perfect gaming rig will ideally have two monitors, a stay-at-home CRT and a travel-sized flat panel. Your CRT should be large—21-inches is ideal—come in at a reasonable price, and have pixel-perfect color reproduction. Aperture grille CRTs tend to have more brilliant colors than shadow-mask CRTs, so go "AG" and don't look back. That said, not even a *Maximum PC* editor would consider hauling a 21-inch behemoth to a LAN party, so to go on the road, we recommend you use a 17-inch LCD flat-panel LCD. Look for a fast pixel response time, DVI support, and a native resolution suitable for gaming (1280×1024 or lower).

In an online deathmatch, shaving a second or two off the time it takes to load the next map can give you extra time to beat an enemy to a weapon. For this reason, don't settle for less than a 10,000rpm Serial ATA drive. Look for hard drives with an average seek time under 5ms, if you want to stay on top of your game. Optical drives aren't all that important to gamers, but you should consider purchasing either a combo drive with full DVD support or a standalone

At the heart of any gaming rig lies a powerful videocard. The Radeon 9800 XT is the fastest videocard you can currently buy.

There's nothing quite like a Raptor to shorten your map loading times in games. With a 10,000 rpm spindle speed, it's the fastest desktop hard drive on the planet.

DVD-ROM drive and a CD burner. If and when games are only available in the DVD format, you won't want to be left out in the cold.

When it comes to 3D gaming, your mouse and keyboard are your sword and shield. So to protect yourself, you need the fastest mouse available, and the most responsive keyboard on the market. Don't consider an optical mouse with a resolution lower than 800dpi, or one with fewer than three buttons. Keyboards are more difficult to recommend. The only way you can tell if you're going to like a keyboard is to try it. Go to a local retailer, and pay close attention to key noise, key action, and the placement of individual keys.

Gaming PC Cheat Sheet

- Speed is the number one goal with a gaming rig, so get the fastest CPU, videocard, hard drive, and memory you can buy. You don't want to die at the hands of a less-skilled gamer because your machine couldn't keep up.

- If you want a few easy style points, get a case window and add some cold-cathode lights to illuminate your rig.

- Choose your weapons wisely. Your mouse and keyboard are the way you interact with your game. You don't want an inferior or uncomfortable weapon.

- You can never have too much memory. With 2GB of RAM, your gaming rig won't run short when it comes to storing large, high-resolution textures.

Gaming PC Shopping List

Here are some specific product recommendations for an awesome gaming PC

ATI Radeon X800 XT Platinum Edition

The heart of any gaming rig is its videocard. Without a top-class videocard, an otherwise perfect gaming rig might as well be a Macintosh. The X800 XT Platinum Edition includes a whopping 256MB of onboard memory, and features full acceleration for all DirectX 9 programmable shader functions. (www.ati.com)

AMD Athlon 64 FX-53

The Athlon 64 FX-53 supports HyperTransport, a technology that supercharges the data bus between the CPU and the rest of the system (and, yes, HyperTransport can speed up 3D frame rates). The CPU's core architecture—rich with floating-point number-crunching prowess—is also perfectly suited to the very calculations that games need to execute. (www.amd.com)

Western Digital WD740G Raptor Hard Drives

A pair of RAIDed Raptors will help you load new maps and levels faster than your competition, giving you yet another edge over a poorly equipped competitor. Because their disk platters spin at 10,000rpm, the Raptors have lower seek times and faster transfer rates than any other consumer hard drives on the planet. In a RAID array, they're almost too fast to measure. (www.westerndigital.com)

Microsoft Intellimouse Explorer 4.0

A fast 800dpi sensor will give you pixel-perfect accuracy whenever you take aim at an opponent. The Intellimouse's four-button design and revolutionary tilting mouse wheel put any command you wish at your fingertips. (www.microsoft.com/hardware)

Logitech Z-680

An 8-inch front-firing subwoofer and tweeter-less satellites are the secret to this 5.1 speaker rig. The subwoofer cranks thunderous bass, while the satellites produce crisp mid- and high-frequency sounds thanks to the aluminum phase-cap in each satellite. (www.logitech.com)

Dream Content Creation Machine
Performance and reliability are your primary concerns for a content creation rig

This is the big one, Elizabeth! Content creation PCs—machines used for drawing and rendering 3D models, and editing high-end movie, audio, and image files—demand very specialized hardware, and need to offer a higher level of data protection than vanilla PCs. Indeed, the ultimate content creation box could costs tens of thousands of dollars, and for this very reason, few content creation PCs end up being appropriate for all the jobs listed previously. So let's first tackle some universals common to all content-creation machines, and then get into specific hardware choices for specific tasks.

First, you'll need to be running dual CPUs. Most games aren't written to take advantage of more than one processor, but almost every serious content-creation app will take full advantage of a dual-processor system. Choosing dual-processors means you'll be buying hyper-expensive Intel Xeon or AMD Opteron CPUs, but that's life—when you're developing content for hire, time is money. You'll also need to spend a few extra bucks in order to buy a motherboard from a company with dual-processor expertise. At *Maximum PC*, we generally go with Tyan boards for all the dual-proc test systems we build. Your total system memory amount is also important. We recommend a minimum of 1GB of RAM, but 2GB or more is preferred. The more physical memory you have, the less often your system will have to use the much slower hard drive to store temporary files.

When configuring your hard drive subsystem, think redundancy first, performance second. At bare minimum, you'll want two identical drives that hold your operating system, applications, and data, and they should be mirrored using RAID1. This config ensures that if one drive fails, its mirror will still be ready to serve up exactly the same data. If you want to go even more extreme, you can go with four drives—two 10,000rpm Serial ATA drives mirrored in RAID1 for your OS and apps, and two 7200rpms drives mirrored in RAID1 for your actual document files. Also, anyone who wants to edit uncompressed, high-definition video needs the fastest drives available for data as well. This means 15,000rpm SCSI drives in a RAID5 array. If you're not going to be editing high-def video, you can settle for slower, larger data drives. Finally, if you use applications that put page files on your hard drive (think Photoshop), no matter how much RAM you have, you can improve performance by dedicating a single, fast hard drive to both your application swap files and your Windows swap file.

For your optical drive, you should return once again to a DVD-combo drive. You'll be backing up large amounts of data, so speed is essential. The rest of the parts for a dream content creation rig are pretty straightforward, but you'll need to spec out parts per your needs. For example, video editors need a way to get video into and out of the system. Thus, if you want to build a content creation rig for video editing, you'll need a video-capture device that will work with all the formats that you want to use.

3D modelers, meanwhile, will need a workstation-class videocard—one with drivers certified for their modeling application of choice. And, of course, anyone who works with images of any type would do well to have a high-end aperture grille CRT. Sony even makes a 24-inch CRT, especially for people who work in CAD programs.

The Tyan Thunder K8W gives you everything you need in a dual-CPU board. It supports two Opteron processors and includes an AGP port, unlike many dual proc boards intended for servers.

The Sony F520 consistently produces the most accurate image quality we've ever seen in a CRT monitor.

Into audio-editing? If so, you'll need a high resolution, pro-level soundcard and a great set of "reference speakers" (also known as studio monitors). That's right: Any speaker set that imparts its own personality to what you hear is strictly verboten!

Photoshop freaks need no equipment more specialized than a good monitor, but having a good tablet can make editing photos much easier. Instead of trying to mimic brushstrokes with an unwieldy mouse, a tablet lets you use a pen-shaped stylus to make your mark on your PSD.

Content Creation PC Cheat Sheet

- Tune your Content Creation PC shopping list to fit your preferred applications. For example, don't spend a bunch of money on a high-end soundcard if you're just going to be creating 3D models.
- Multimedia speakers are great for a gaming rig, but they just don't cut it for audio editing. Get a set of "flat" reference speakers, so you'll hear sounds exactly as they were recorded.
- Data redundancy is key with content-creation machines. You don't want to risk a moment's downtime, so you'll need, at minimum, RAID1 mirroring for all your drives.
- Make certain you buy a case with plenty of room for expansion. External drives simply don't perform well enough for most content creation apps, so you'll need lots of internal drives, and lots of drive bays to hold them.

Content Creation PC Shopping list

Here are some specific product recommendations for the ultimate content-creation box

Tyan Thunder K8W

The great price and awesome 64-bit performance of the AMD Opteron CPU makes it a no-brainer for most content-creation systems. And for the latest Opteron processors, there is simply no better motherboard than this Tyan beauty. Its four memory banks give each processor its own dedicated pool of memory, eliminating traditional bottlenecks in dual-CPU configurations.

nVidia Quadro FX 3000

The latest Quadro card from nVidia combines the power of DirectX 9 programmable shaders and the most reliable, quality-tested graphics drivers in the business. The card's 256-bit memory interface gives you top-class performance, whether you're tweaking a model in *3ds max* or editing a new deathmatch map in *UnrealEd*.

Hitachi UltraStar 10K300

With 300GB of storage, the UltraStar 10K300 is the biggest 10,000rpm drive money can buy. Unlike puny Serial ATA drives, the UltraStar actually comes in real capacities, and it's only 1-inch high, so you can put four of these bad boys in pretty much any case.

Sony F520

A good monitor is absolutely vital to many content creation apps. The 21-inch F520 delivers pixel-perfect accuracy in every app you use. What's that you say? You're only doing audio editing? We have a 15-inch VGA monitor in the corner for you, weevil eyes.

Wacom Intuos2 Tablet

This large-format, high-performance graphics tablet gives you plenty of room to sketch, draw, or mark up in any graphics application, without having to futz around with a wimpy mouse or trackball.

Dream Entertainment Center PC

Speed, capacity, and silence a perfect entertainment PC make

The perfect Entertainment Center PC fulfills a variety of roles. It serves as a digital audio jukebox, a DVD home theater player, a gaming console, and a TiVo-like digital video recorder. It should be small and quiet enough to fit into your living room, but have enough storage capacity to hold several hundred hours of recorded TV shows and at least 15,000 digitally encoded songs. It should also be able to burn DVDs and CDs for archiving, and it should do all of this virtually silently.

Not just any bare-bones case will work for an Entertainment Center PC. Not only does your case need to be small, it needs to be quiet, and have plenty of room for expansion. Ideally, a small formfactor case will include room for a couple of hard drives, an AGP card, and a couple of PCI cards. And as you'll quickly discover when you begin shopping for a small formfactor case, most come of these babies come with wee motherboards already installed.

Because space is limited in a small formfactor system, we recommend motherboards with quality onboard components. Not only does this mean the machine should have onboard FireWire and networking support, it should also have a good onboard sound solution—which means your motherboard choices will be limited to nForce 2 chipset-based boards. So, assuming that you're buying a barebones system with a pre-installed nForce2 mobo, you need to decide what speed Athlon XP you're going to run. Don't immediately think "faster is better." Faster CPUs can actually be bad for entertainment center PCs, because lower-performance CPUs can be cooled with slower—and thus quieter—fans.

The nForce2 chipset includes an integrated Dolby Digital decoder. So, unlike pretty much every soundcard available, an nForce2-based mobo can convert any sounds your PC can produce into the Dolby Digital 5.1 format on the fly (even DirectSound3D positional sounds from games can be converted). Because Dolby Digital 5.1 is the format used by most home theater receivers, this means the nForce 2 has a huge advantage in the living room. Most normal PC soundcards only output 5.1 sound in an analog format, and it's awkward to integrate them into a home theater sound system.

Your dream Entertainment Center PC will need both a videocard and a TV tuner, and there's nothing that handles both of those jobs better than the ATI All-in-Wonder cards. Because space in a home theater rig is at a premium, the one-slot All-in-Wonder is vital. The current All-in-Wonder cards can't decode HDTV signals, but we expect to see a two-slot HDTV-enabled All-in-Wonder by the end of 2004. All of the All-in-Wonder cards include software that will help you make your entertainment PC better. We especially dig ATI's personal video recorder software and the DVD player.

Because digital audio and video files take up so much space, storage subsystems are key to an Entertainment Center PC. In today's market, we recommend you consider two 300GB Maxtor DiamondMax drives for your storage needs. With 600GB of total storage, your PC will easily handle 25,000 songs with 350GB to spare for DVR usage and movie storage.

You'll also want a fast DVD combo burner, one capable of burning DVD+R/RW, DVD-R/RW, and CD-R/RW so you can archive movies and TV shows, as well as burn audio CDs. Look for a drive that can burn a full CD in less than four minutes and a full DVD in a little under ten.

There are literally hundreds of options for an Entertainment Center sound system. While you could simply "settle" for a high-end multimedia speaker rig like the Klipsch ProMedia 5.1 Ultras, you might do better to invest in a little more oomph. Yep, we're talking true home theater speakers, the kind that cost thousands of dollars. But, hey, you're worth it.

The Shuttle SN45G XPC barebones case is smaller than a tower, but it holds more hardware than a standard small formfactor box.

Nothing says home theater quite like a giant plasma display. The Pioneer PDP-5040HD is 50 inches of beautiful PC monitor.

Finally, when it comes to dream displays, your options are so numerous, it's downright scary. Although there are compelling reasons to choose large CRT-based monitors, DLP-powered front projectors, and even rear-projection LCD and CRT HDTVs, we ourselves dig large-screen plasma displays. You'll ultimately need to balance size and expense when you pick out a display.

Dream Entertainment Center PC Cheat Sheet

- Audio reproduction is key. Pair your system with either a top-class 5.1 multimedia speaker rig, or go all the way with a home theater amplifier and a set of real home theater speakers.

- Large hard drives are the secret sauce in any Entertainment PC. So get the largest drives you can—but just make sure they're quiet.

- Make absolutely certain that your wireless gear communicates with your computer using radio, not infrared. Infrared comms require line-of-sight with the receiver unit, but radio does not.

- A fitting display is crucial. You don't necessarily need to shell out five grand for a plasma display, but you don't want to watch DVD movies on a 15-inch CRT, either.

Entertainment PC Shopping list

Here are some specific product recommendations for your dreamy entertainment center

Pioneer PDP-5040HD

This massive 50-inch plasma display may just be the ultimate PC display. Its native resolution is 1280×768, which is perfect for watching movies and TV, and even playing an occasional game. (www.pioneerelectronics.com)

Klipsch Reference Series Home Theater Speakers

These are the best home theater speakers we've tested. By going with "speaker separates," you can customize your speaker config for the specific room you intend to use. At *Maximum PC* HQ, we chose two powerful front-channel speakers, a crystal-clear center channel, a pair of rear satellites, and a downward-firing 12-inch subwoofer to deliver the sound from our Entertainment Center PC. (www.klipsch.com)

All-in-Wonder 9600 XT HDTV

The latest entry in the All-in-Wonder series adds two more tuners to an already kick-ass videocard. Its included remote has a rudimentary mouse control, and one-click support for many common entertainment PC functions. With support for over-the-air HDTV reception and the only really usable HDTV DVR solution we've seen, there's literally no reason to use any card but this. (www.ati.com)

Shuttle SN45G XPC

The original small formfactor, but still the best. The Shuttle SN45G sports an nForce2 motherboard, room for a pair of hard drives, an AGP slot, and a PCI slot. Besides, you can't beat the clean styling and kick-ass access to important components, like USB and FireWire ports, on the front panel. (www.shuttle.com)

Mouse & Keyboard

The perfect mouse and keyboard are less vital than a great remote to a home entertainment PC. We recommend the Gyration Ultra Pro mouse and keyboard. The Gyration's gyroscopic sensor requires no surface for pixel-accurate movement, and the keyboard is great for living room use. (www.gyration.com)

The Dream Budget PC
You don't always need a massive budget in order to build a kick-ass PC

Building a Dream Budget PC is more about finding balance than raw speed. Indeed, to check in with a machine that costs less than $1,500, you'll need to sacrifice some amenities and top-shelf performance, but you won't necessarily need to sacrifice personal satisfaction.

Start your Budget PC with a great bargain case. Look for a generic mid-tower job with enough room to grow a little and a decent power supply—think 300W minimum. You'll need at least three 3.5-inch bays, two 5.25-inch bays, and room for a standard five-slot ATX motherboard.

When purchasing a CPU, you'll need to strike a good balance between price and performance. Generally, for a budget box, you won't want to spend more than $200 for your processor, but don't let the low price scare you! You should be able to find a light-ning-quick processor at that price. When you pick out your CPU, look for a companion mother-board that includes important components onboard. It's ultimately cheaper to spend an extra $40 on a full-fea-tured motherboard than to buy a network card, Serial ATA card, and FireWire card later.

Picking a budget videocard used to be as simple as buying any nVidia-based GeForce4 Ti 4200-based board. But, unfortunately, it's not that easy anymore. So when purchasing a videocard, look at the $200 price point; the best values are generally found there. Also, consider buying an "OEM" or "white-box" version of a faster board. You won't get a bunch of bundled games, but you probably wouldn't play those games anyway.

The Chenbro Gaming Bomb is a great-looking case, and with an included power supply, it's a great bargain at under $50.

Even if your motherboard includes onboard sound, you should consider adding a decent add-in sound card. In addition to pulling the sound processing load off of your CPU, a standalone card should also give you better-sounding audio. You can also find some great deals by buying an OEM soundcard without all the bundled-in software that you'll never use.

With your main components covered, it's time to think about storage. Since your budget will preclude a pair of RAIDed Raptors, you should consider pairing a small-but-fast drive with a larger-capacity slow drive. Install your operating system on the small, fast drive, and your apps and documents on the large, slow drive. A small 10,000rpm drive should run you about $100, and larger-but-slower 7200rpm drives will cost even less. As for optical drives, a DVD combo burner is an amenity that no one should sacrifice. Luckily, you can find great burner bargains by buying previous-generation technology. Thus, if 16× burners are hot, consider buying a 4× or 8× burner. We'd much rather have the added flexibility of a drive that supports both DVD for-mats than the extra burning speed afforded by a single-format drive.

There's no reason to blow a load of money on a flat-panel monitor for a budget box, especially when you can get a great big CRT for less money. Indeed, you can pick up a great 19-inch CRT for about $150. Make sure you get a display with a flat tube, though, or you'll curse your penny-pinching ways every time you sit down at the computer.

The GeForce FX 5900 XT is a fully featured 3D gaming card, but costs much less than the competition.

There's no reason to spend a bunch of cash on a keyboard, as long as you buy one that's comfortable. You should be able to pick up a decent 104-key keyboard for about $15, check your local office supply stores for the best deals. Even if you're on a budget, a high precision mouse is still vital. Don't settle for anything less than an 800dpi optical sensor, or you'll have problems with fine-detail work, even in Windows.

Dream Budget PC Cheat Sheet

- It almost goes without saying, but when you're building a budget PC, you need to stick very closely to your budget. It's easy to spend a few more dollars here and there, and end up $1,000 over your goal.

- For a budget box, target components that are one or even two generations old. If new 400GB hard drives just arrived, consider buying a slightly smaller 300GB drive instead.

- Remember that you don't have to buy your entire machine at once. Sometimes it's easier to upgrade your old machine in waves rather than shelling out for a whole new box.

- Although it's tempting, don't scrimp on memory or hard disk storage space. 512MB of system memory and 80GB of hard disk space are the bare minimums you should consider. You'll definitely regret it if your applications bog down or you're constantly running out of disk space.

Dream Budget PC Shopping List

Here are some specific product recommendations for the perfect budget PC

Chenbro Gaming Bomb

It's cheap, well-equipped, and easy on the eyes. Unlike other inexpensive cases, the Gaming Bomb comes with a 300W power supply and a bunch of other cool features. We especially like the pre-cut case window and the selection of different colored front bezels. No detail is too small; the Bomb's intake fans even have air filters. (www.chenbro.com)

GeForce FX 5900 XT

Despite its bargain price, the 5900 XT includes a fully featured GeForce FX chip, complete with eight pipelines and a full complement of programmable shader processors. The only difference between this board and its more expensive brethren is that it only has 128MB of RAM and its clock speeds are slightly slower. (www.nvidia.com)

Logitech MX500

With the same 800dpi optical sensor as the wireless MX700, the Logitech MX500 provides pixel-perfect accuracy on any surface. Left-handers rejoice: The MX500's ambidextrous design denies no one from enjoying everything this mouse has to offer. (www.logitech.com)

Windows XP Home Edition

Although the truly budget-conscious will install one of the free versions of Linux, we just can't recommend that home users burden themselves with maintaining a Linux system. Windows XP Home costs about $100, but it's more than worth it in the time you'll save. After all, would you rather be tweaking your OS, or using your system? (www.microsoft.com/windowsxp)

The Dream Mini PC
When you're talking about small formfactor boxes, size does matter

There are so many uses for a Dream Mini PC that it's hard to list them all. When paired with a svelte LCD flat panel, a Mini PC can fit unobtrusively into rooms that normally don't accommodate PCs, such as the kitchen or family room. Small formfactor machines are also well suited for travel. We love loading up a stacked Shuttle XPC to tote to LAN parties.

For your mini-PC case, you'll want to focus on connector options and drive bay options. Your case needs to include all the connection types that you'll ever want, because you won't be able to make a bunch of upgrades at a later date. Moreover, the motherboard that comes pre-installed in your mini case should essentially include support for "onboard everything." This means onboard audio, networking, FireWire, Serial ATA, and USB 2.0.

Obviously, your case choice will limit the options you have in the motherboard department. So, if nothing else, make sure that your mobo has at least one PCI slot and one AGP slot. You should also make sure that your board uses the latest chipset for your CPU platform. You don't want to buy an already-outdated chipset that will unnecessarily deny you CPU upgrades down the line.

Your videocard decision depends mostly on your intended uses. If you want to play games, you'll want to buy the fastest single-slot 3D accelerator you can find. On the other hand, if you only want to use your PC for checking email and web browsing, you're safe settling for the integrated, onboard graphics that your mobo most surely offers.

Because most small formfactor cases include only a pair of internal 3.5-inch hard drive bays, it's very important to equip your machine with a drive that's large enough and fast enough for your needs. Buy the largest 7200rpm drive you can find that includes 8MB of cache. That way, you'll have more than enough room for dozens of games and thousands of songs, as well as damn skippy performance across the board. Even the best 7200rpm drives can't compare to a 10,000rpm barn burner, but that's just one of the sacrifices you have to make when building a dream mini PC.

On the optical drive front, we demand the flexibility of a DVD combo burner, and, like always, faster is better than slower. If your combo burner can't burn a full DVD in eight minutes, consider buying one that doesn't suck. As it's your only optical drive, you should also pay close attention to CD-burning and ripping speeds. Don't settle for any drive that's rated slower than a 24× for CD burning and 40× for audio CD ripping.

There's no better monitor to pair with the small PC than a small flat-panel LCD. Look for a mid-priced 18-inch flat panel—expect to spend around $400. We wouldn't consider running apps that demand pixel-perfect accuracy on a $400 flat panel, but it should be entirely acceptable for web browsing and playing the occasional game.

As for speakers, there's just no reason to shell out big bucks for a multi-channel 5.1 rig if your PC is going to sit in the kitchen. For this reason alone, simple stereo speakers make the most sense. However, if you intend to take your small formfactor on the road, you'll want an audio output solution that's a little more portable. Any headphones you buy should have near-perfect audio fidelity, be comfortable enough to wear for long sessions, and have a nice long cord. For desk use, a set of big, closed ear phones create a rich, full listening environment, and actually sound better than many PC speakers.

The Shuttle SB75G2 is the latest Shuttle XPC small formfactor case from the originators of the species.

The latest version of the Hitachi Deskstar, the 7K250, is a lightning-quick 250GB Serial ATA drive.

Your mouse and keyboard decisions will come down to personal choice. We're quite fond of the Microsoft Natural MultiMedia keyboard for extended use. It even includes built-in play controls for music and video files. For basic mousing, you need look no further than the Logitech MX300. This little ambidextrous mouse shares the same 800dpi optical sensor with the other mouse devices in the MX series.

Dream Mini PC Cheat Sheet

- A mini PC's biggest enemy is heat. Make sure that the airflow through your tiny case is enough to keep hot components like your videocard, CPU, and hard drives cool.

- Sometimes high-end, power-hungry videocards wreak havoc on delicate small formfactor power supplies. Consider upgrading your case's default power supply if you are going to use a fast videocard.

- Not all parts will actually fit in all small formfactor cases. Check your case manufacturer's online forums and documentation before you purchase parts, and make sure your videocard actually fits in the machine.

Mini PC Shopping List

Here are some specific product recommendations for the perfect mini-PC

Hitachi Deskstar

This super-sized 400GB drive is a benchmark monster, and faster than all other 7200rpm hard drives we've tested. Fluid-dynamic bearings keep the Deskstar whisper-quiet, even when it's running full bore. It's a little more expensive than most other massive drives, but it's performance and extra space more than make up for the added cost. (www.hgst.com)

Shuttle SB75G2 XPC

Shuttle invented the small formfactor case paradigm with its original XPC. Newer versions only improve on the original concept, packing faster and better hardware into smaller cases. The SB75G2 uses an Intel i875 chipset and supports both 533MHz and 800MHz Pentium 4 CPUs. It also includes onboard LAN, Serial ATA, and FireWire, so you won't have to sacrifice the only PCI slot to an interface board. (www.shuttle.com)

Sennheiser HD-580 Headphones

Most LAN parties ban real speakers, so you'll be glad you brought your high-end headphones all the way from home. The Sennheisers are pricey, but they last forever. End users can easily replace every damageable part, from the headphone cables to the ear cup pads. (www.sennheiser.com)

Plextor PX-708A Dual-Format DVD Burner

The sexy Plexy can write to every relevant optical format on the planet, which is crucial because it fills the only 5.25-inch drive bay in the Shuttle chassis. It's not just a fast DVD burner either, we measured speeds close to 40× using the 708A for CD audio extraction. (www.plextor.com)

Flat-Out Awesome

Every September, our magazine staff unveils its annual dream machine project. What you see here is how last year's dream machine (code-named "DM2003") would look if it suddenly exploded, and all of its parts landed in some type of logical placement, flat on the floor of the *Maximum PC* Lab. Let this presentation serve as a visual inventory—you can see at a glance all the different parts you'll need to accumulate for an archetypical dream machine project.

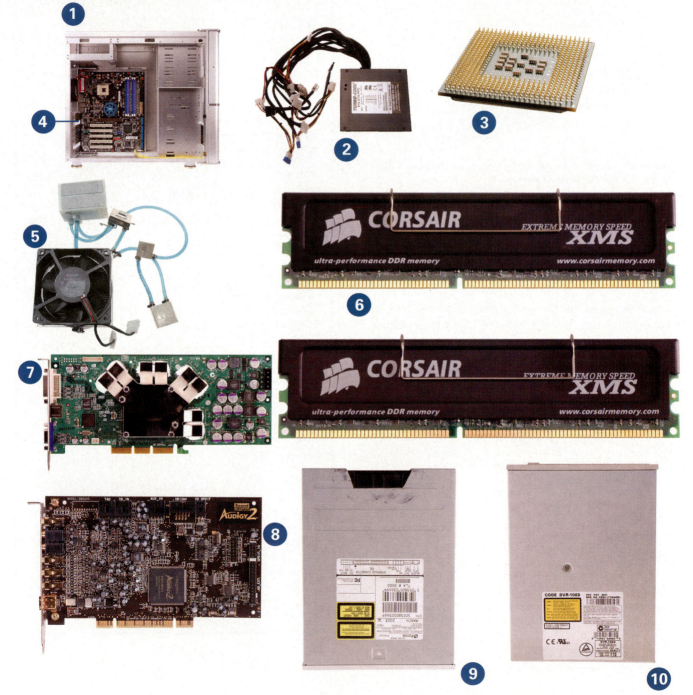

The Damage

(1) Case: CoolerMaster TAC-T01

(2) Power Supply: PC Power and Cooling Turbo Cool 510 Deluxe

(3) CPU: 3.2GHz Pentium 4

(4) Motherboard: ABIT IC7-G

(5) Cooling: Voodoo F1 Liquid Cooling

(6) Memory: Two 512MB sticks of Corsair Micro XMS4000

(7) Videocard: nVidia GeForce FX 5900 Ultra

(8) Soundcard: Sound Blaster Audigy 2 Gamer

(9) CD-RW: Plextor Premium 52×32×52

(10) DVD Burner: Pioneer DVR-A06

(11) Media Reader: Atech Pro-9 Multiple Flash Card reader

(12) 10,000rpm Hard Drives: Two 36GB WD Raptors

(13) 7200rpm Hard Drives: Two 250GB WD Special Edition Caviars

(14) CRT Monitor: Sony F520

LCD Monitor: Sharp LL-T2020B

(15) Speakers: Logitech Z-680 5.1s

(16) Keyboard: Key Tronic LifeTime

(17) Mouse: Logitech MX700

(18) Cables: Black Hole Cables BlackFlash Special Edition Network cable; BlackFlash Onyx power cable; and miscellaneous ATA/SATA cables

(19) OS: Windows XP Pro

Final Considerations

Before you purchase any parts, please consider the following buying strategies.

Buying Yesterday's Fastest Gear to Save Money Today

Not all of us can afford to buy the latest, greatest $500 videocard every time we want to build a new computer. Luckily, there's a secret that most people don't know about: After a new product is announced, the street price of the old hardware that's being replaced usually plummets. If you pay attention to product announcements, you can take advantage of hardware retailers that need to clear out old stock before new stock arrives. And for parts where speed is less important than price (for example, optical drives), you can safely purchase products that are two or three generations old.

Bottom Line: If the Radeon 9800 XT is the fastest videocard on the market, you can usually save a bundle by buying this card's immediate predecessors. The just-replaced videocard is frequently only a few frames per second slower than the new videocard, anyhow.

Buying the Fastest Today to Stay Ahead of the Curve

If you're not comfortable frequently upgrading your box to stay on top of things, you can stretch the length of time between upgrade cycles by buying top-end hardware as soon as it's available. (Just make sure you don't do this for every generation of product—that would be overkill.)

Bottom Line: If you can keep yourself from upgrading to the latest-greatest hardware every generation, being an early adopter can be a smart purchasing scheme.

Keeping a Watchful Eye on Inevitable Releases

Keeping track of technologies on the horizon is vital if you're going to keep from getting ripped off. For example, if motherboards that include a brand new data bus standard are just a few weeks away from being ready, don't be a dumkoff by buying a soon-to-be-obsolete mobo today. Read *Maximum PC*'s tech previews to stay on top!

Bottom Line: Know when to expect new videocards, CPUs, and chipsets so you won't get an unpleasant surprise after a big purchase.

Choosing Between Online and Walk-in Retailers

It's very satisfying to walk into a store, spend some money, and walk out with all the parts you need to build your Dream Machine. But unless instant gratification is worth a 15 percent penalty to you, it's worth the extra time to do your shopping online instead. By using online shopping sites like Pricewatch.com, you can avoid paying state sales taxes, and save a bundle of cash by buying non-retail parts.

Bottom Line: You can save a bunch of money by buying PC parts online. You must beware of retailers that skimp on the warranty, charge exorbitant shipping rates, or just plain rip off their customers. If it sounds too good to be true, it probably is.

Final Thoughts

Building your own PC is an adventure. As you read this book, you'll gain a better understanding of how your computer works, but you still need to take small steps to get from newbie status to veteran PC builder. First, decide what you want to use your PC for. Next, come up with a budget for your project. Then select the hardware you want to use in by reading reviews in *Maximum PC* and online. Read this book, then set aside a day to assemble your new computer. Most of all, have fun!

Chapter Two

Cases and Power Supplies

Building your Dream Machine begins with two very basic components

A heavily modified CoolerMaster WaveMaster enclosure served as the case for our Dream Machine 2003 project. We must confess that we outsourced the etching for the polycarb window. It was Voodoo PC's custom-designed water-cooling rig that was the true assembly challenge.

Before you can even think about assembling your PC, you need to pick out a case and power supply that will perfectly suit your needs. These aren't simple tasks. For most systems, the case is the only indication a casual observer has to differentiate your dream—which you poured thousands of dollars and dozens of hours into—from a craptastic $300 eMachine. You want a case that is functional and looks nice. A perfect power supply is less flashy, but there are dire consequences for anyone foolhardy enough to use an underpowered power supply in their performance PC.

The case you choose for your new PC affects every other decision you will make when building a computer. After all, there's no need to buy a giant, full-size tower case if you're simply going to stuff it with a small battery of components. Conversely, you simply can't fit the multiple hard drives, and larger-than-normal sound and videocards you need for a top-class content creation box into a small formfactor case. There are literally hundreds of different cases available today, so you should be able to find the perfect case that fits your needs, budget, and own personal sense of style.

A good power supply is kind of like a good wallet. You have to have one and you use it every single day, but you never think about its actual "functionality" unless something goes wrong. And, even though your friends probably won't notice that you're carrying around a $400 Italian cowhide beauty, they'll definitely notice if you routinely pull out a cheapo nylon and Velcro wallet. Because power supplies aren't particularly sexy, no one notices them, but *you'll* definitely notice all the signs of a bad power supply: crashes and system instability. Power supply problems are also notoriously difficult to troubleshoot because they appear to be basic Windows problems or the fault of other components (such as system RAM).

In short, a sub-par power supply will leave your system crying for Mommy.

In terms of function, all your power supply has to do is convert the alternating current that enters your home into direct current for your PC's components,

right? Wrong. It does need to provide your PC with juice, but it also needs to be quiet enough to keep you sane, as well as even out the inevitable electrical sags and spikes that occur.

So what makes a good case great? And how much power is enough for your power supply? It really all depends on what type of PC you plan to build. Let's start with the case.

Takin' It Case-by-Case

The vast majority of PC cases you can buy today are based on either the ATX spec or a variation of the ATX spec. Formfactor specs like ATX define everything about your PC's physical configuration, from the placement of motherboard mounting points, to the direction air flows through the case, to the basic layout of compatible motherboards. Indeed, the type of case you purchase will determine the type of motherboard you'll be able to use in your PC, and it's for this very reason that both cases and motherboards share common spec names.

The PC Power and Cooling Turbo-Cool 510 Deluxe provided the Dream Machine 2003 with 510W of sustained power. With that much power, we had plenty of headroom for loads of optical drives, hard drives, and the fastest processor on the planet.

So, your motherboard—or *mobo*—needs to fit inside your case. That's easy to understand, but the different variations of the ATX spec can confuse matters. ATX cases and mobos come in more sizes than miniskirts. In order from smallest to largest, there are flex-ATX, mini-ATX, micro-ATX, and just plain ATX cases and motherboards. You can always fit a smaller ATX spec into a case that's rated for a larger size of ATX mobo, but a larger board just won't fit into a smaller case. So, make sure your case is big enough for your mobo.

There's another new motherboard spec on the horizon called BTX. The new BTX spec helps solve the cooling and space issues that plague some current ATX cases. In fact, if you want to build a new machine and you're reading this after October 2004, you should definitely investigate BTX cases and motherboards before you make a purchase.

So What Makes the Perfect Case?

The perfect case does exactly what you need it to do. For example, someone building a workstation will want a huge case with lots of expandability for future hard drives, as well as plenty of fan mounts to keep the system icy cool. On the other hand, an entertainment PC for the living room should be based on a small case running a small number of fans for maximum quiet. Of course, in exchange for the small size and limited cooling opportunities, you sacrifice the capability to add a lot of hardware to your machine. Your typical gaming rig uses a basic mid-tower case, but there's no fundamental reason why you can't use a portable, small formfactor case for a high-performing gaming rig.

Before you can choose the perfect case, you really need to know exactly what you want to use your Dream Machine for. There's no perfect case for every computer, and before buying one, it's difficult to tell which features will actually be useful once your machine is up and running, and which features will just annoy you every time you boot up.

Many mid-towers include features designed for the PC enthusiast. This one has a temperature monitor and a pre-cut case window. Unless you want to carve a custom design on your case, it's much easier to buy a case with a pre-cut window.

That said, in many instances, it's easy to recognize poor case design and shoddy workmanship. Be on the lookout for interior pieces with sharp metallic edges that need to be sanded down. Touch one the wrong way during a component installation, and you'll shred your hands. And then there are the dreaded cramped cases—enclosures with such poor interior design, you'll find it difficult to remove hard drives, optical drives, and PCI cards. Other cases offer intrinsically bad cooling. For example, airflow may be constricted by drive placement. And another case might even be inordinately loud.

However, it's not always so easy to recognize poor case design.

Ask the Case and Power Supply Doctor

Q: Can I scavenge the power supply from my old PC?

A: As a general rule, yes. However, some large PC vendors (such as Dell and HP) use custom-designed, proprietary PSUs that only work with their own custom-designed, proprietary cases and mobos. So don't automatically assume that you can use a power supply from one of these manufacturers with a stock motherboard or vice versa.

The Good, Bad, and Ugly of Case Design

A removable motherboard tray makes upgrading your CPU or memory a snap. Just slide the tray from the case, do what you need to, and slide it back in.

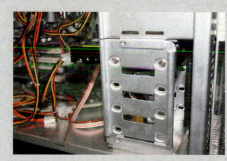

A removable hard drive cage is a great idea, but if you have to remove both side panels from the case to remove the cage, what's the point? Drive cages should make it easier to work with your drives, not more difficult!

This CoolerMaster case has an annoying metal plate that blocks access to the PCI and AGP mounting screws. Sure, they cut a hole in the plate to give you easier access, but there's no reason for the plate to be there in the first place.

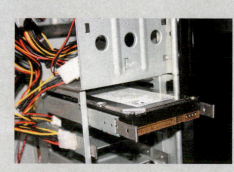

This is the way access to hard drives should be! In the Antec Sonata, each hard drive is lovingly mounted to a bracket, which then slides perfectly into the case. Access to your hard drives is easy because the business end of the drive actually faces the case door. Nice work!

One *Maximum PC* editor once bought a mid-tower box with a "safety switch" that was supposed to prevent you from accidentally turning the machine off—you had to both push *and* twist the switch to power down. Unfortunately, it was an ATX case, so to force a shutdown, you had to twist the spring-loaded button and keep it twisted and held down for five finger-crippling seconds. The editor initially thought that the "safety switch" would be a cool feature, but it turned out to be completely useless and a literal pain to use!

The lesson here is that getting hands-on time with a case is absolutely vital, especially as it could serve you through two or more upgrade cycles. If our editor had had the opportunity to test the power switch gimmick before he bought the case, he never would have purchased it. Doh!

which is an ideal combination. Steel and plastic cases are inexpensive, sturdy, and they conduct electricity to prevent static buildup.

When you're purchasing a case, make sure that the area around the motherboard is easily accessible. Do the cages around the optical and hard drive bays cover the area the motherboard will occupy? Will a hard drive cage prevent you from installing long PCI or AGP cards? Are metal edges inside the case folded over to blunt jagged, finger-slicing edges? Are there plenty of fan mounts on the front, back, and top of the case? Are there enough internal and external drive bays for all the gear you want to install in your PC? These are all questions that a *Maximum PC* editor asks himself before recommending a case to a friend.

Getting Materialistic

A great case needs more than a perfect design—it must also must be made from the right materials. Today's cases are made from everything from plastic and steel, to crystal-clear Lexan, to aluminum. We've even heard of manufacturers building custom gold-plated PCs for special customers. Because aluminum is so light and strong, it's the perfect metal material for PC cases—but aluminum is also much more expensive than other materials. A good aluminum case can run upwards of $250. Lexan and other Plexiglas-type materials seem like they'd be perfect for computer cases, but we can't recommend them for anything but wacky theme cases that absolutely demand that "glass house" look. Because plastic doesn't conduct electricity, it's possible for a Lexan case to act like a primitive capacitor and store a powerful static shock that could damage your components. Most computer cases are made of steel and plastic,

The Chenbro Gaming Bomb has everything a budget builder would need. If you're building a PC on a budget, you should be able to find a case that includes a decent power supply, but still costs less than $50.

Kick-Ass Construction Tip

Look for a case with a removable motherboard tray. It's much easier to install a mobo, CPU, and heatsink when the entire assembly is outside the cramped confines of a small mid-tower case.

So What's the Right Case for You?

The mid-tower case is the mid-size sedan of the case world—practical, sensible, accommodating, ubiquitous. There are generic mid-towers available for rock-bottom prices; costly, dead-sexy mid-towers crafted from exotic materials; and plenty of "bling-bling, lowered Honda" analogues (in other words, cheap cases outfitted with fancy lighting systems and heavy modifications).

We usually build gaming rigs and basic workstations into mid-tower cases. It's hard to beat the room for expansion and the great airflow they provide. The only real problem is that mid-towers are becoming relatively large in the larger scheme of case design, and can be quite noisy out of the box. But no matter how noisy a mid-tower is, remember that it's much easier to quiet a loud PC than it is to add more drive bays and PCI slots to a too-small case!

When you're shopping for an ATX mid-tower case, make sure that it has plenty of expansion bays for both 3.5-inch hard drives and 5.25-inch optical drives. We expect a minimum of three external 5.25-inch bays, two external 3.5-inch bays, and three more internal 3.5-inch bays. External bays have slot covers, which can be removed to make a piece of hardware accessible from the outside of the case. Optical drives require external drive bays—otherwise you wouldn't be able to insert any disks! Internal 5.25-inch bays are less important because almost everything that uses a 5.25-inch bay is external only, but you can install a 3.5-inch hard drive in a larger bay with an adapter if you ever feel the storage crunch. We also love to see removable motherboard trays inside of mid-tower cases; these make mobo and CPU upgrades painless. Instead of installing your motherboard inside the cramped confines of your case, you can simply slide the mobo tray out of the machine, install the motherboard, memory, CPU, and sometimes even the CPU heatsink, and then slide the tray back into the case. A removable drive cage or well-implemented drive rails are a plus, too. Drive rails are small metal or plastic rails that mount to

Making Sure Your PSU Delivers Enough Juice

To determine your Dream Machine's minimum power supply requirements, add the number of watts used for each component in your system and then multiply your result by 1.8.

Component	Typical Requirement
AGP Videocard	30–50W
Average PCI Card	5–10W
Floppy Drive	5W
Optical Drives	10–20W
5,400rpm Hard Drive	5–10W
7,200rpm Hard Drive	5–15W
10,000rpm Hard Drive	5–20W
Case/CPU Fans	3W (ea.)
Cold Cathode Lights	3W (ea.)
Motherboard (w/o CPU or RAM)	20–30W
RAM	20W per 256MB
Pentium 4 Processor	70W
AMD Athlon XP, 64, or FX Processor	60–90W

Source: PC Power and Cooling

the side of your optical drives, where they serve as guides that let you quickly slide the drives in and out of the case. Mounting your optical drives on rails makes removing or upgrading them painless, but can decrease the life of your drives if the rails don't fit very snugly in their slots.

On the other end of the spectrum are small form-factor cases, such as the Shuttle XPC. These shoebox-sized cases trade expansion opportunities for their small size, and almost always include a pre-installed, custom-fitted motherboard. We love to use small form-factor boxes to build home entertainment PCs destined for the living room, for portable PCs to bring to

The Silverstone SST-LCO1 is our recommended desktop case. The horizontal desktop case is perfect for a living room PC because of its horizontal shape and matte black finish, which let it blend in with a home theater component rack.

LAN parties, and for inconspicuous PCs to hide in a tiny home office. Small formfactor machines should include plenty of key features on the pre-installed motherboard: an audio chip, a graphics chip, support for USB 2.0, Ethernet, and FireWire. By offering all this support out of the box, they save you the trouble of buying any add-in cards, except maybe a true 3D videocard. The mobos in these small formfactor cases should boast an AGP slot and at least one PCI slot. A pair of 5.25-inch and 3.5-inch external bays, and at least one 3.5-inch internal drive bay, are mandatory as well.

As for full-tower cases, they're tempting to most power users. After all, who wouldn't want an enclosure with 12 drive bays and room for more than a dozen fans? Well, while they might sound good during the back and forth of your own internal monologue, you should resist oversized cases unless you actually *need* tons of space. Full-tower cases tend to run very loudly and can be difficult to work in. For example, when using a full-tower case, the 18-inch length limit of old-style parallel ATA cables can come into play. In a full-tower case, the distance from the bottom of your mobo (where IDE connectors frequently reside) to your upper-most 5.25-inch slot is often longer than 18 inches. So even if you buy a huge case, you might not be able to take advantage of every drive bay. In reality, only workstations and servers really demand the kind of space that a full-size case provides. So if you're not building one of those two types of machines, save a few bucks and get a mid-tower instead.

Small formfactor cases are the current oddball darlings for anyone who wants to avoid the sensible mid-tower route, but there are indeed other alternatives for Dream Machine-building rebels. For example, desktop

"pizza box" cases offer another option for the home builder. In a desktop case, the motherboard is mounted on the floor of the enclosure. Desktop cases have fallen out of favor in the last few years because they're more cramped and have fewer drive bays than tower cases. However, these pizza box-formfactor cases *are* still available, and they're perfect for use in high-end entertainment computers. In fact, there are several desktop cases that are designed to blend in with other components in a stereo rack. If you choose to build your PC in a desktop case, pay close attention to airflow. You'll need to pay close attention to your IDE and power cables to ensure that they don't block the flow of cool air into the case, or warm air out of the case.

One last word of warning about your case choice: We frequently hear from readers who tried to save a few bucks by purchasing the cheapest case they could find, only to find themselves upgrading a few short months later. Remember that your case isn't just the foundation for every other piece of hardware that you install in your PC, it's also one of the few components that you can keep through several upgrades. In fact, some *Maximum PC* editors have been known to use a favorite case for three, four, or even five years. Although most other hardware specs change every six months, case formfactors rarely change more frequently than every five years. *So don't skimp.* Buy a case that can accommodate a healthy battery of parts, and make sure it's durable enough to withstand years of banging around and abuse. (Some of our guys like to perform the "Can I sit on it?" test, figuring that if it can support 200-odd pounds of *Maximum PC* editorship, it can last a few total-product upgrade cycles.)

There are literally hundreds of different PC cases available today. They come in all sizes, shapes, and materials. So whether you choose a super-premium aluminum case or a supersized steel full-tower, there's a case out there that perfectly fits your needs.

Getting to Know Your Power Connectors

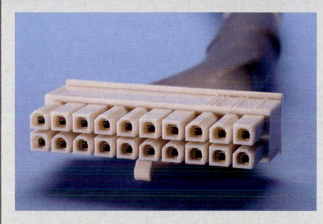

This large connector delivers electricity in three flavors to your motherboard—12V, 5V, and 3.3V. It also carries the signal for the soft power-on/off feature of ATX motherboards to the power supply.

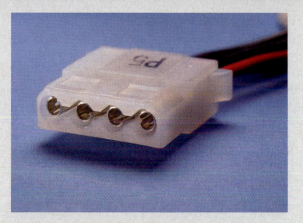

These 4-pin connectors are used to deliver 5V and 12V lines to most internal peripherals, including hard drives, optical drives, and videocards that need more power than the AGP slot provides.

Newer Serial ATA drives use a new type of power connector. This new 15-pin connector enables hot-swapping of Serial ATA drives in certain circumstances.

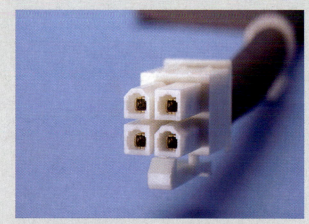

To ensure that modern processors receive enough power, Intel added this 4-pin power connector to the ATX spec. It delivers a pair of 12V leads, more than enough for even the fastest processors.

Power Up

Whether you plan to use a power supply that comes pre-installed in a case, or opt for an add-in power supply that's packaged separately, you need to ensure that your PSU (power supply unit), case, and motherboard all support the same spec. So, if your mobo and case are based on the ATX spec, make sure you purchase an ATX power supply, or you'll be without juice when you really need it.

In addition to converting the alternating current (AC) that comes from your wall outlets into the direct current (DC) required by your PC components, your PSU helps pull hot air out of the case interior. That's because ATX power supplies come with built-in fans. We'll get into cooling issues later in this book, but for now, let's focus on electrical issues.

Power-hungry parts—hard drives, optical drives, your videocard, and your CPU—especially require a constant flow of clean DC power to work properly. If your power supply can't keep up with your hardware's requirements, your system will be unstable, suffering frequent crashes at the worst possible moments. The amount of power a power supply can output is measured in watts (often abbreviated to a simple W). So, what you need to do is make sure that the combined maximum power load of all your components is significantly *lower* than your power supply's maximum rating. Will your components need up to 250W in worst-case scenarios? Fine. Then go out and buy a 450W, high-quality, no-excuses PSU. You'll be glad you invested in the headroom.

Think of your power supply as a pitcher full of water and your components as cups. The amount of water in the pitcher is equal to the power output of your power supply. Meanwhile, each component you connect to the PC—whether it's a hard drive, optical drive, PCI card, AGP card, CPU, stick of RAM, or USB device—is a small cup. So, if your "power pitcher" runs out of water before filling all your "component cups," your machine will just plain crash. Scary, right? Then plan ahead. Don't skimp. Get a high-capacity pitcher than can handle your current load of cups, as well as any extra cups you might add in the future. And we need not remind you that the CPU or video-card you buy today might require much less power than the parts you might upgrade to tomorrow.

Have You Cleaned Your Power Lately?

Running out of power isn't all you that have to worry about. Your components also demand *clean* power from the PSU. So, if the amount of power coming from the power supply fluctuates too much, your machine will crash. A high-quality power supply can actually "even out" the small spikes and sags that plague most residential electrical service, so it's important to get a PSU that's built for stability.

Kick-Ass Construction Tip

A good rule of thumb for power supplies is that the heavier they are, the better they are. Converting electricity from AC to DC generates heat, which a power supply dissipates with weighty heatsinks and fans. So, when presented with two seemingly identical power supplies, buy the heavier one. Yeah, this all sounds like voodoo science, but trust us: It's grounded in fact.

The PC Power and Cooling Turbo-Cool 510 is the premiere power supply money can buy. It delivers clean, consistent power to even the thirstiest components.

Beware of the craptacular power supplies that ship with most cases. Although there are always exceptions, most cases ship with low-quality PSUs that don't actually meet their advertised power rating when running above normal room temperature. That's right: As the temperature inside the power supply rises, the actual power output of the supply goes down. And when power output goes down, you run a greater risk of system crashes. Also, today's hot-running CPUs and videocards frequently heat the air *entering* the power supply to more than 100°F, and the resulting decrease in power output starves these power-hungry components. Without plenty of clean power, your PC will crash. This is a bad thing.

Now, all that said, we've found that the power supplies that come with small formfactor cases are usually decent. Why? Because these small formfactor cases are engineered within an inch of their lives, and their manufacturers put a lot of focus on electrical and cooling issues. Also, these small cases offer scant upgrading opportunities, so the manufacturer can easily predict the maximum number of new components an upgrader might add, and then reliably calculate the maximum draw on the PSU. If you end up getting a small formfactor case for your Dream Machine, make sure it has a top-rate power supply, because the PSUs for these wee dealies are very difficult to upgrade.

What to Buy on the Aftermarket

Now, if you can't trust the wattage rating of a preinstalled PSU loaded into a cheapo case, what options do you have? We recommend sucking down the extra cost and purchasing a high-end supply. After all, if you're going to spend two or three thousand dollars on PC components, you don't want to fry them because your bargain-basement PSU surged when it should have sagged. We think that PC Power and Cooling (www.pcpowerandcooling.com) makes the best power supplies available today, but they aren't cheap. We've used PC Power and Cooling supplies for every single annual Dream Machine project ever built for one simple reason: Their power supplies are *hardcore*.

Case and PSU Spec Speak

Formfactor
The formfactor is the maximum size of motherboard the case will accommodate. If your case's box claims support for a full-size ATX motherboard, you should be able to fit every ATX motherboard on the planet into it, from the tiny flex-ATX up to a massive dual-processor full-ATX mobo. Also keep your eyes peeled for new BTX cases and power supplies later this year.

5.25-inch bays
These external drive bays are lined up on the front of your case. You'll mount your optical drives as well as any internally mounted breakout boxes or full-size fan bus devices here.

3.5-inch bays
The 3.5-inch bays can be either internal or external. You'll use the internal 3.5-inch bays exclusively for hard drives, but the externals can be used for all sorts of different things, from front-mounted USB ports to fan bus controllers that will let you manually adjust how much air moves through your case.

Peak Power Output
The peak power output is the maximum amount of power that a power supply can provide your PC for a short period of time. This is the number that most companies use to differentiate power supplies.

Sustained Power Output
The maximum amount of power that your power supply can provide the PC indefinitely at load. This number is usually more important than the actual peak load. Most power-related crashes occur when a system draws more power than the power supply can provide over a longer period of time.

In fact, we've run puny 250W supplies from PC Power and Cooling that have eaten cheapo 400W PSUs for dinner. That's right: The 400W jobs have let us down, whereas the PC P and C supplies—saddled with a 150W disadvantage—have given us blissfully uneventful stability.

PC P and C's Silencer series PSUs are perfect for most machines. Silencers come in 310W and 410W ratings, and use slow-moving, large fans to keep components cool without making too much noise. Now, if your system boasts a full magazine of power-hungry components, consider upgrading to the Turbo-Cool 510. It is, without a doubt, the best power supply money can buy. It produces 650W peak and 510W continuous, which is more than enough juice for even the beefiest workstation.

Fanless power supplies that stay cool with just a massive heatsink (instead of a fan) are relative newcomers to the power supply world. In fact, they're so new, we haven't actually gotten one into the *Maximum PC* Lab yet. Their principle is simple: Instead of using a noisy fan to pull air through the PSU and out the back of your case, these "passively cooled" PSUs uses a series of heat pipes (metal rods that transfer heat from one place to another) to transfer heat to a large heatsink that sticks out of the back of your case. Passively-cooled power supplies aren't for neophytes, and there's one very important thing to consider before purchasing one: Because you won't have a PSU fan venting the hot air that builds up in your case interior, you'll need to vent the hot air your CPU produces

some other way. In real-world terms, this mean you'll either have to mount a fan behind the CPU, or go with a more exotic cooling method—such as water-cooling. We trust that if you add a passively-cooled power supply to a system with a basic water-cooling rig, you'll be just fine (and you'll also have a fanless, almost perfectly quiet PC!).

Like a good case, you should be able to use your power supply for more than one upgrade. Money spent on a high-quality PSU will save you from having to constantly replace frizzle-fried parts.

What Is BTX and Why Is It So Damn Cool?

The ATX case premiered in July 1995 when the Pentium II was the fastest processor around and a 300MHz machine was stupid-fast. Back then, CPU heatsinks didn't have fans, and videocards didn't even have heatsinks!

Fast forward nine years, and some of the decisions that made sense when ATX was new make much less sense today. For example, in an ATX case, fresh cool air is sucked into the front, over hot hard drives, over the videocard and memory, and finally over the CPU. So, instead of fresh, cool air flowing over the CPU, the poor processor gets pre-warmed air. That's just not good.

However, there's a new formfactor on the horizon, and it aims to make good on ATX's failings. BTX—which stands for Balanced Technology Extended—updates both case layout and motherboard design for modern mid-tower systems. The biggest change is that cool air is given a straight shot from an intake on the front of the case, over the CPU, and then out the back. To accommodate this change, motherboard layout is redefined (the CPU assumes a different position on the mobo), and key PC components—such as hard drives and expansion slots—are rearranged.

As we shipped this book to press, we still hadn't tested (or even seen) our first BTX case or mobo, but we expect to see the first of them in late 2004 and early 2005. The new spec is a definite improvement over the aging ATX standard, and is something we're looking forward to at *Maximum PC*.

Dream Machine 2004 Contenders

Every year, Maximum PC editors assemble the best computer components on the planet, and build the biggest, baddest, best machine in the world! Money is no object! Without any further ado, here are the leading candidates for the 2004 Dream Machine's case and power supply:

Silverstone SST-TJ03

The Silverstone SST-TJ03 has everything it takes to contain the raw power of a Dream Machine. It's built from aircraft-grade aluminum and comes in both silver (pictured here) and black. We especially like the fact that it includes six external 5.25-inch bays and another six internal 3.5-inch bays.

PC Power and Cooling Turbo-Cool 510

Every Dream Machine Maximum PC has ever built has included a PC Power and Cooling power supply. We don't expect any changes this year, either. Look for a PC Power and Cooling Turbo-Cool 510 Deluxe in the 2004 Dream Machine.

Chapter Three

CPUs

Perhaps the most crucial part in any computer, the CPU serves as your rig's brain

We used a Pentium 4 3.2GHz in the 2003 Dream Machine. At the time, it was undeniably the fastest CPU on the planet, and we overclocked it to make it even faster!

One of the most important questions you're going to face when spec'ing a new dream PC is, "Which CPU do I buy?" This question immediately raises a second question—"Intel or AMD?"—which in turn raises a whole host of questions on which motherboard to buy and what kind of RAM to use. And then there's the issue of raw speed: "How much clock speed does one really need?"

Before we delve into the particular products that each CPU company has to offer, let's take a quick look at the first thing on everyone's mind when choosing a processor: the mighty megahertz question.

Megahertz: Does It Really Matter?

Watching the stunning increase in Intel clock speeds over the years, many of us have been conditioned to think that megahertz is the most important determinant of CPU performance. A 2.4GHz CPU is faster than a 2.2GHz CPU. It's simple math, right?

No, not always. Clock speed can often be a misleading indicator of a processor's actual real-world horsepower. The two leading CPU families—the Intel Pentium 4 clan and the Athlon XP/FX brood—use distinctly different number-crunching strategies that affect overall performance in very real-world ways. Although clock speed is always an important metric of brute strength (especially when comparing two CPUs that share the same architectural DNA), other CPU design factors come into play.

To give you an idea of how different CPU designs can lead to wildly varying performance results, consider the original Pentium 4 (P4). Launched at a speed of 1.5GHz, many people reasonably assumed the P4 would be much faster than the Pentium III, which at the time was hitting a top frequency speed of 1.1GHz. Unfortunately, however, because of core architecture differences between the two chips, the P4 was actually *slower* in many applications available at that time—this, despite its 400MHz clock speed advantage!

So why the performance drop? One reason is that when the P4 was first released, most applications weren't yet optimized to take advantage of the CPU's special instruction set, code-named SSE2. In due time, software developers would re-code their apps for SSE2, and when they did—boom!—the P4 suddenly showed much better performance. It was a simple matter of waiting for the software to "catch up" to a hardware architecture change. Nonetheless, until those apps were re-coded, they weren't taking full advantage of the P4's particular architecture.

The other culprit that made the P4 look dog-slow when it was released was its lengthy, 20-stage

The original Athlon 64 CPU just used a single channel memory interface, but that didn't really affect performance that badly.

instruction pipeline. Long pipelines help facilitate high clock frequencies, but for many jobs that a CPU might have to execute, they can also lead to performance inefficiencies (and thus bad benchmark results). *Maximum PC* columnist and chip guru Tom Halfhill explains:

A CPU pipeline is like a factory assembly line; it divides work into a sequence of stages. In a CPU, "work" is executing a program instruction. Several instructions can move through the pipeline at the same time, with each instruction in a different stage of completion. During each clock cycle, the CPU can retire the results of one instruction at the end of the pipeline while fetching a new instruction into the front of the pipeline.

Longer pipelines allow a chip to run faster because each stage has less-complicated circuitry. The time it takes for the slowest stage to do its work is the limiting factor for the whole pipeline, so dividing a slow, complicated stage into two or more simpler stages relieves the bottleneck. Super-long pipelines have drawbacks, however. Branch instructions require the CPU to flush partially completed instructions out of the pipeline and replace them with new ones. It's like a factory foreman suddenly ordering an assembly line to make pick-up trucks instead of sedans—the partially completed sedans must be discarded. To avoid this problem, modern CPUs try to predict the outcome of branches. But if the branch prediction stinks, the length of the super-long length of the pipeline can actually hurt performance.

And therein lay the P4's pipelining problem. Many tests—such as those based on office apps—are rife with conditional branches. These tests bogged down in the P4's super-pipelined architecture. The Intel PIII and AMD Athlon XP processors, meanwhile, processed these tests quite handily, despite their clock speed disadvantage. The whole situation was a textbook example of why clock speed isn't the be-all, end-all of performance.

The classic 32-bit Athlon XP CPU was the budget workhorse for several years, but it's fallen by the wayside with the introduction of newer 64-bit Athlons.

But it's now been more than three years since the P4 was introduced. The CPU's branch-prediction logic has improved, and the very clock-speed increases made possible by the P4's lengthy pipeline have more than compensated for the CPU's intrinsic inefficiencies. Now buzzing along at more than double its introductory clock speed, the Pentium 4 is the recognized performance leader. In short, the long pipeline is paying off.

This doesn't mean, however, that an Athlon XP running at 2.2GHz is always going to be a lower performer than a Pentium 4 running at 2.5GHz. Because the Athlon XP's architecture is particularly well-suited to floating-point calculations, the CPU performs very well in floating-point-heavy apps such as 3D games. This means that for many types of a software, an Athlon XP can complete more work in a single clock cycle than could a Pentium 4. The new 64-bit Athlon FX CPUs continue the AMD tradition of doing more per clock cycle than the Pentium 4, so you really can't judge a modern processor by its clock speed.

So that's our spiel on CPU theory! It should give you a good foundation of knowledge as we move on to discussions of specific Intel and AMD CPUs.

Kick-Ass Construction Tip

The socket designed to hold your CPU is also known as a Zero Insertion Force socket. That means that it should take absolutely no physical pressure to mount the CPU in its socket, if it's aligned properly. If you find yourself pushing down on your CPU during mobo mounting, you're likely doing great damage to it. So don't!

Intel, the Processor Giant

Intel is the largest semiconductor manufacturer on the planet, and as such, it's had a hand in developing a majority of the technologies powering modern PCs. The company has been the major force behind PCI, AGP, PC100, AC97, USB, and PCI Express. That said, Intel's biggest claim to fame has been the Pentium processor and its heirs. The Pentium 4 is currently the company's flagship CPU. Although you can still buy Pentium IIIs, they've long been banished from desktop systems in retail channels. Indeed, if you want to save money on your dream machine, don't get stingy by buying a PIII. There are far better places to shave off a few dollars and cents. Here's a quick look at your *Maximum PC*-endorsed, Intel-based CPU options.

The Celeron CPU is a basic Pentium 4 core, but the performance is severely limited by its tiny 128KB L2 cache.

- **Pentium 4:** There are currently several different versions of Intel's flagchip on the market. First, there's the P4A, a.k.a. the original "Northwood" Pentium 4 with 512KB of cache. It runs on a 400MHz memory bus and uses a 0.13-micron core. Second, we have the P4B. It's also a Northwood, but runs on a 533MHz bus. Third and fourth, there's the P4C, which uses an 800MHz bus, and the Prescott P4E, which uses both 533MHz and 800MHz buses.

  The P4 architecture has a lot of frequency headroom left in it; we expect it to reach 5GHz and beyond! The P4 is also unique in its support for Hyper-Threading, which essentially splits a single physical CPU into two virtual CPUs. So while one application is running floating-point operations, another can use other CPU resources that aren't being tapped. It's a boon to people who run multiple applications simultaneously. Hyper-Threading is available on most P4 processors running at 2.8GHz and faster.

  The standard Pentium 4 Northwood is a great general-purpose CPU. It's very fast for all apps, and can really crank out the floating-point calculations that are crucial for gaming, digital audio, and digital video. That said, once the Prescott-based CPUs exceed 3.6GHz, we expect them to replace the Northwood-based CPUs as Intel's "everyman" processors. However, if you have "more specialized" processor requirements, there are several other Intel CPUs worth considering. Read on...

- **Pentium 4: Extreme Edition:** In late 2003, Intel unleashed the high-end, limited-run Pentium 4: Extreme Edition processor. For an ultra-premium $1,000 price tag, the Extreme Edition pairs a 3.2GHz Pentium 4 Northwood core with a humongous full-speed 2MB L2 cache. It all adds up to beaucoup gaming performance. In reality, the Extreme Edition has more in common with the even more expensive Xeon processor (see the following bullet). In fact, the only Xeon feature the Extreme Edition lacks is multi-processor support. So, if you want to run dual procs in an Intel rig, you've gotta go Xeon.

Kick-Ass Construction Tip

Always use some sort of heat-conductive agent between your CPU and heatsink. Without it, air trapped in the gaps of your imperceptibly irregular heatsink surface will hamper your cooler's ability to dissipate processor heat. Thermal paste or a thermal pad will fill those gaps, and allow the heatsink to draw away heat from the CPU more efficiently.

- **Xeon:** Rest assured, you will pay dearly for dual-processor privileges. Although based on the vanilla P4, the Xeon adds a host of features designed for high-end servers that make these procs enormously expensive. Indeed, an extra 1.5MB of L2 cache does not come cheap. Unless you're building a content-creation rig, you really don't need to be running two processors in tandem, so if you want the performance benefits of a 2MB L2 cache, get a P4 Extreme Edition.

- **Celeron:** Intel's current Celeron version is a Pentium 4-based processor that boasts just 128KB of L2 cache and is confined to a 400MHz bus. The current Cellies even operate in most motherboards designed for 400MHz-bus and 533MHz-bus P4s. The Celeron offers more than enough torque for granny to browse the Net, but gamers and other power users would be better served by purchasing a slower Pentium 4 than a faster Celeron.

AMD, the Feisty Upstart

In the five years since the introduction of AMD's Athlon line of processors, the Athlon has consistently given the Pentium III and Pentium 4 a run for their money. The ultimate humiliation came when AMD beat Intel to the 1GHz mark. Now, after years of eating dust, AMD has tasted the sweet nectar of victory and has no intention of giving up. The company's Athlon 64/FX CPU is currently its flagship consumer CPU,

which was the PC world's first desktop CPU to include support for 64-bit apps and operating systems. As you read this book, older 32-bit Athlon XP processors might still be available, but they are definitely dinosaurs. Here's a look at AMD's current consumer-level offerings.

- **Athlon FX:** The latest 64-bit processors from AMD—dubbed Athlon FX—give smokin' fast performance in today's games and demanding content-creation apps. The FX series absolutely blows away the standard Pentium 4 in most memory-bandwidth dependent tests (read: almost all benchmarks). The Athlon FX core runs at a much lower clock speed than the P4, but the chip benefits greatly from an integrated 128-bit memory controller.

  Yes, the Athlon FX is quite a performer, but it doesn't offer very inviting upgrading options. You see, instead of making its memory controller part of the motherboard chipset (the traditional approach Intel still uses), AMD integrated the memory controller Athlon FX into the CPU itself. This integration enables the memory controller to provide a lightning-fast connection between the CPU and system memory, but it also limits the CPU to using a single type of memory. To wit: When we went to press, the memory

This Alpha cooler's unique design allows you to mount whatever fan you want to the cooler. If you plan on overclocking, you can connect a small, high-speed fan. If you're more concerned with minimizing noise, you can use a larger, low-speed fan.

Chipset Compatibility Chart

Each CPU is only compatible with certain specific chipsets. Here's the list of all Pentium 4, Athlon FX, and Athlon XP chipsets available now, and the system bus speeds they support:

Chipset	Processor Type	Fastest Memory Supported
Intel 875P	Pentium 4, Celeron	DDR400 Dual-Channel
Intel 865G	Pentium 4, Celeron	DDR400 Dual-Channel
Intel 865PE	Pentium 4, Celeron	DDR400 Dual-Channel
Intel 865P	Pentium 4, Celeron	DDR333 Dual-Channel
Intel 850E	Pentium 4, Celeron	PC1066 RAMBUS Dual-Channel
Via PT880	Pentium 4, Celeron	DDR400 Dual-Channel
Via PT800	Pentium 4, Celeron	DDR400 Single-Channel
Via K8T880 Pro	Athlon 64, Athlon FX	(Determined by CPU)
Via K8T800 Pro	Athlon 64, Athlon FX	(Determined by CPU)
Via KT880	Athlon XP	DDR400 Single-Channel
Via KT600	Athlon XP	DDR400 Single-Channel
nVidia	Athlon 64, Athlon FX	(Determined by CPU) nForce3 250
nVidia	Athlon 64, Athlon FX	(Determined by CPU) nForce3 150
nVidia nForce2	Athlon XP	DDR400 Dual-Channel

controllers integrated into the Athlon FX-51 and FX-53 CPUs only supported DDR400 memory. So, when faster DDR-II memory comes out later this year, FX-51 and FX-53 owners will need to buy *new* CPUs if they want to upgrade to faster motherboards and faster memory.

That's quite a gotcha, and you've been warned. Nonetheless, the Athlon FX series of processors performs nearly as fast as the Pentium 4 Extreme Edition, and at a fraction of the cost. We recommend the Athlon FX for any PC builder looking for top-class performance at a reasonable price. Just be prepared to give your Athlon FX machine away to your nephew by the time *Doom* 4 or 5 rolls around.

- **Athlon 64:** AMD's first consumer-level, 64-bit CPU for Windows-based PCs is the Athlon 64. (Yes, it's true that Apple was the first company to rush a 64-bit PC proc out with the G5 series, but we're not talking about building Macs, Billy.) Based on the same "Hammer" core as the Opteron processor, the Athlon 64 has one key feature that differentiates it from its FX brother: It's handcuffed by a single-channel memory controller. That's right: The plain-vanilla Athlon 64 only supports a 64-bit memory controller, whereas the FX series has a *dual-channel* 128-bit controller that can move twice as much data with the same speed memory. The Athlon 64's performance suffers because of this memory bandwidth deficiency, making it a poor choice for demanding power users.

- **Athlon XP:** The Athlon XP remains a budget PC builder's favorite. Its 32-bit core still performs extremely well, even with demanding applications and games. The fastest version in the Athlon XP lineage clocks in at 2.2GHz, uses a 0.13-micron process, packs in 512KB of L2 cache, and runs on a 400MHz bus. It was designed to be a screamer in floating-point software (games and digital media apps) and actually outperforms the Pentium 4 when both chips are running at the same clock frequency. And herein lies the problem: The Athlon XP simply can't reach the high clock frequencies achieved by the P4. Still, the Athlon XP's floating-point performance makes it ideally suited for older mathematic and scientific applications that have not been optimized for the Pentium 4.

Before you buy an Athlon XP, you need to know about AMD's goofy performance-rating scheme. Instead of just tagging their XPs with a clock-speed rating, the CPUs are assigned a rather arbitrary name based on relative Pentium 4 performance. Thus, a 2.167GHz Athlon XP running on a 333MHz bus is marketed as an "Athlon XP 3000+." What does the 3000+ mean? AMD swears on a stack of *Maximum PCs* that it's not a tip-off that the CPU runs as fast a 3GHz P4, but we don't buy it. It's just a little too convenient that the performance numbers perfectly line up with Intel's clock speeds.

For regular-old consumers, the numbering scheme actually makes sense, as the average Joe and Jane don't have the time (or technical savvy) to understand that a 2.2GHz CPU can run as fast as a 2.8GHz CPU in many applications. For hobbyists, however, the performance rating scheme presents a confusing mess. For example,

Oddly enough, the Zalman CNPS6500 Series of coolers is very effective at quietly cooling both Athlon and Pentium 4 processors. If you choose to use a nonstandard shaped cooler, make sure it will fit in your PC.

AMD has two 3000+ CPUs—the original one clocked at 2.167GHz and running on a 333MHz bus, and a newer version clocked at 2.1GHz on a 400MHz bus. AMD's variables (clock speed, bus speed, and cache size) are many, and lead to confusion. For example, it's usually better to sacrifice a few megahertz for a larger L2 cache and a 400MHz bus speed, but there's no way to know exactly what you're getting by looking at a silly performance rating.

That said, as long as you do a little extra research when buying an Athlon XP, you'll be OK. In fact, most stores and websites are very clear about labeling the attributes of specific Athlon XPs so you don't get mixed up.

- **Athlon MP:** Take an Athlon XP, test it for compatibility in a dual-processor configuration, confirm that it passes, and then label it "Athlon MP." That's pretty much the Athlon MP story. It's just an XP chip that's multi-processor-ready. The Athlon MP was supposed to be AMD's big push into the server-scale arena, but it has been hindered by a lack of chipset support. The 760MPX is still the only chipset ordained for Athlon MP support, but it runs a puny 266MHz memory bus and wimpy DDR266 memory. In fact, poor chipset support and the kick-ass performance of newer AMD Opteron chips have doomed the Athlon MP to the scrap heap. So don't buy one of these stinkers, no matter what!

Ask the CPU Doctor

Q: My machine randomly reboots after several hours of playing games or watching movies—what could it be?

A: A likely culprit when you have spontaneous reboots is an overheated CPU. If you suspect that your CPU is running too hot, you can usually monitor the CPU temperature using a special utility that comes with your motherboard. If your CPU is running much above 40° Celsius, you should consider replacing your CPU cooler to get more air moving over the core.

- **Opteron:** AMD's 64-bit server and workstation processor is called Opteron. Like the Athlon FX and Athlon 64 processors, the Opteron breaks from tradition by embedding a dual-channel memory controller directly into the CPU die. Its large, integrated L2 cache helps the Opteron shine in high-intensity server apps, but its lower clock speed really hurts performance in consumer apps, such as games and video-encoding software. Because the Opteron isn't intended for desktop use, we recommend it only for people looking to build high-powered servers and workstations.

The Good, Bad, and the Ugly of CPU Cooler Design

Words of Wisdom: You're only as cool as your CPU cooler!

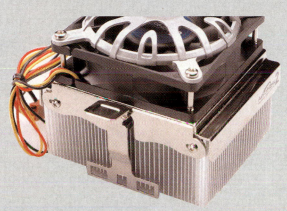

The copper core on this Thermaltake cooler helps the heatsink pull heat away from the CPU and into the rest of the system. Some coolers are made entirely of copper, but we prefer that the copper core in a heatsink be made of another material. Because copper is very soft, it's easy to damage all-copper heatsinks.

The type of spring clip on this Athlon XP cooler requires a frightening amount of force to latch onto the CPU socket. If you're building an Athlon XP, be especially careful when you attach the heatsink to the CPU socket, as it's very easy to crush the unprotected CPU core and render your CPU unworkable.

This Alpha cooler looks swanky, but it's very difficult to mount on your CPU socket. Instead of a standard mounting bracket, you have to physically screw it into a bracket that attaches to your mobo. This is definitely a heatsink to avoid if you plan on frequently upgrading your CPU.

By using a large, slow fan on this Thermaltake Athlon 64 cooler, this heatsink can keep hot CPUs cool, without making a whole lot of noise. Look for a CPU heatsink with a large slow-moving fan instead of a smaller fast fan.

Anatomy of the Prescott Pentium 4

To get a sense of how tiny the 90nm process is compared with the current 130nm process, note that Prescott has more than twice the number of transistors than the current Northwood Pentium 4, yet is 33mm² smaller. To imagine the size we're talking about, consider this: A nanometer is only 3 to 5 atoms wide, and the period at the end of this sentence is 250,000 nanometers across.

Prescott still retains the 12KB trace cache of the original Pentium 4 but increases the L1 data cache to 16KB from 8KB. Unlike older CPU designs, like the Pentium III, the P4 series can store up to 12KB of simple instructions that have been decoded from x86 instructions into what Intel calls micro-ops. Since the instructions are stored in a decoded state and ready to be executed, the CPU experiences an increase in performance.

Caches are a necessary evil of today's computers. The world would be a better place if CPUs didn't have to use big fat caches to make up for slow-ass system RAM. Prescott's cache is double that of the Northwood 1MB. Like all CPUs, cache memory is made from expensive SRAM. In the Prescott core, the 1MB of L2 accounts for roughly 48 million of the 125 million transistors.

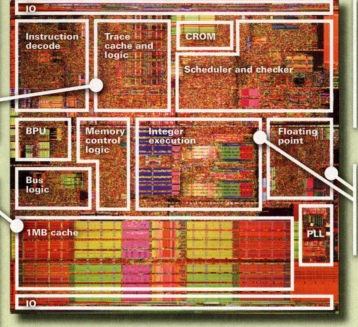

Other enhancements in Prescott:
• An improved branch predictor speeds up productivity applications.
• Twelve additional store buffers over the Northwood's 24 help keep data moving through the ultra-long pipeline.
• Two more write combining buffers (for a total of eight) help reduce bus traffic.

There are no additional floating-point units in the heart of the Prescott, but Intel has added an additional integer multiplication unit that no longer shares resources with the floating point multiplication unit, which will result in reduced processing latency.

Prescott's improved process
• Prescott features a seven-layer vertical process vs. Northwood's six layers, which helps reduce the transistor density on the core and reduce the wire delay, or latency of signals moving through the core. Think of a layer as a floor in a building; more vertical layers saves horizontal space.

• Prescott CPUs will also use carbon doped oxide to increase the wire transfers in the transistors as well as nickel silicide to improve speed through lower resistance.
• Intel will use strained silicon in the Prescott core so electrons can flow faster.

• **Duron:** The Duron is AMD's version of Intel's Celeron. A budget chip built from a derivative of the Athlon XP, the Duron has only 64KB of L2 cache and is limited to a 200MHz system bus. In the early days of the Athlon XP, the Duron could outperform a low-end Celeron, but today it's solidly outclassed by Intel's current-generation Celeron. AMD shelved the Duron earlier this year, and has pushed the Athlon XP into the low-end market to compete with the Celeron. The price on an old, dust-gathering Duron processor might be right, but the performance sure isn't.

What'll It Be, Bub? Intel or AMD?

Intel or AMD? It can be a tough choice. But it's not all about cache sizes, transistor counts, and which one has the better commercials. The perfect CPU for you will greatly depend on what you intend to do with it.

If you're interested in playing games, the Pentium 4 Extreme Edition is the leader for now, but the Athlon FX-53 is nipping right at its heels. And once you factor in that Athlon FX chips cost significantly less than the hard-to-find Extreme Editions, you have compelling arguments for each platform. Don't discount the standard Pentium 4, either. It delivers strong performance and value, and shouldn't be overlooked.

If gaming isn't your top priority, there are other factors that should influence your choice. If you intend to handle a lot of media-intense chores such as MP3 encoding and DV editing, or if you're interested in 3D rendering apps (such as Lightwave 3D or 3ds max, which have been specifically coded for Intel instructions), then the P4 is the way to go.

We don't recommend investing your hard-earned cash in Pentium III, Duron, Celeron, or Athlon MP chips, as these are all dead-ends, upgrading-wise. Xeons and Opterons are too expensive when purchased in pairs for the vast majority of consumers, and there's a good argument that says first-time PC builders should not be playing around with dual-processor projects.

Keeping Your CPU Cool

At this point, you should have a pretty good idea of which CPU type to purchase, so it's time to give some attention to CPU cooling. Every modern processor needs a good amount of cooling to dissipate the heat generated by today's power-hungry transistors. The vast array of CPU cooling devices you can buy today even intimidates *Maximum PC* editors, but we'll let you in on a little secret: Most people—even enthusiast PC builders—can safely stick with the stock cooler that comes bundled in retail CPU packaging. Both Intel and AMD spend millions of dollars developing custom-tailored fan/heatsink combos that are quieter and more effective than many aftermarket coolers.

CPU Spec Speak

Cache Size
Your CPU's cache—also called L2 cache—is high-speed RAM, built directly onto the CPU core. As a general rule, the more cache your processor has, the faster it will run hardcore applications and games. Don't settle for a CPU with less than 512KB of L2 cache.

Bus Speed
The speed at which the CPU communicates with system memory, typically measured in megahertz. Because the CPU multiplier in most processors is locked, increasing bus speed is the only way most people can overclock their systems.

CPU Multiplier
An integer that determines a CPU's core clock speed. Modern CPUs will only run when the motherboard is set at a factory-specified clock multiplier. The system simply won't boot if the clock multiplier is set to a unauthorized value in the BIOS. You can calculate your CPU's multiplier by dividing the CPU's rated core speed by the bus speed. For example, early 400MHz processors ran a 100MHz system bus on a 4× multiplier.

Memory Controller
A specialized section of the motherboard's chipset (or in the case of the Athlon 64 family, the CPU itself) designed to direct memory traffic and support specific memory types. Usually the memory controller is located in the motherboard's northbridge chip, allowing motherboard manufacturers to pop new northbridge chips on their boards whenever a new memory standard hits the market.

Core Speed
The speed of the CPU, usually measured in either megahertz or gigahertz.

Floating-Point Number
A number bearing decimal points, such as 9.89. CPUs have more difficulty crunching floating-point numbers than integer numbers (whole numbers). Floating-point calculations offer a higher level of precision, and are integral to 3D games.

Branch Prediction
The capability of a CPU to predict conditional branches. The sophistication of this feature varies greatly, from static prediction (always guessing a branch will fork in the same direction) to dynamic prediction (basing a prediction on previous behavior). When you click an OK button in an interface menu, you are effectively fulfilling a branching prophecy! (It's a gross simplification, Timmy, but we're trying to keep things easy.)

This Innovatek water-cooling rig will keep your PC cool, and it's virtually silent to boot.

Now, there are indeed reasons to upgrade from stock cooling. Running your CPU at a higher-than-rated clock speed—also known as *overclocking*—generates more heat than most stock fans are designed to dissipate. So overclockers definitely need more powerful coolers. Also, if you're building a PC for your living room, you might want to consider a quieter solution. By combining larger, slower-moving fans and larger-than-normal heatsinks, some aftermarket coolers designed for low noise output can pull heat away from a CPU every bit as effectively as Intel and AMD coolers.

Another good way to minimize noise is to consider installing a *fanbus*. Not to be confused with the short bus, you can use a fanbus to control the speed at which your fans turn. Fanbuses usually fit into a spare 5.25-inch drive bay, and are then connected to all the fans in your system. Once you've connected all your fans, you can use the controls built into the fanbus to adjust fan speeds as necessary. When you're working in Word, you can crank the speed down, but when you're fragging online, you can ratchet up the fan speed to keep your components cool.

Fancier fanbuses even include temperature sensors that you can place near the area that a controlled fan keeps cool. When the temperature rises, the fanbus turns the fan speed up automatically. When everything is cool again, the fanbus slows the fan back down to its quiet mode.If you're truly fanatical about noise reduction and/or overclocking, consider water-cooling kits. Most water-cooling rigs use nearly silent aquarium pumps to move a constant stream of chilly water through a cooling block that attaches directly to your hot CPU. Just be warned that water-cooling is not for everyone. In addition to the danger of a system-destroying leak, water-cooled systems require much more maintenance than air-cooled PCs. You have to maintain water levels and keep a constant eye peeled for leaks.

Does your case sport a window? If it does, you should definitely consider upgrading your CPU heatsink to one that brings a little more bling! After all, what's the point of having a fancy case window if you just have plain vanilla parts inside? There are lots of Pentium 4, Athlon XP, and Athlon FX heatsinks that light up, just plain look cool, or both.

Regardless of your reasons, when purchasing a third-party CPU heatsink, make sure it's rated for your CPU. That means it can dissipate as much heat as that CPU will generate at stock clock speeds, and includes the special mounting brackets required to attach to your CPU's socket.

Dream Machine 2004 Contender

Here's a close-up look at the odds-on favorite CPU and CPU cooler for next year's Dream Machine

AMD Athlon FX-53

What's the secret sauce in the Athlon FX? The on-chip memory controller gives the CPU ready access to your system RAM, letting it squeeze every ounce of performance from your high-speed memory. The FX CPU—and the other Athlon 64-based processors, for that matter—are also extremely good at floating-point math. Games and CPU-heavy multimedia apps, such as video and audio encoders and decoders, are notorious users of floating-point math.

The extremely efficient use of memory bandwidth and lightning-fast floating-point performance make the Athlon FX-53 a strong contender for Dream Machine 2004. In fact, the Athlon FX-53 is the fastest CPU we've tested for games, and damn near anything else for that matter. The FX-53 even smokes the more expensive Pentium 4 Extreme Edition in all but a few benchmarks.

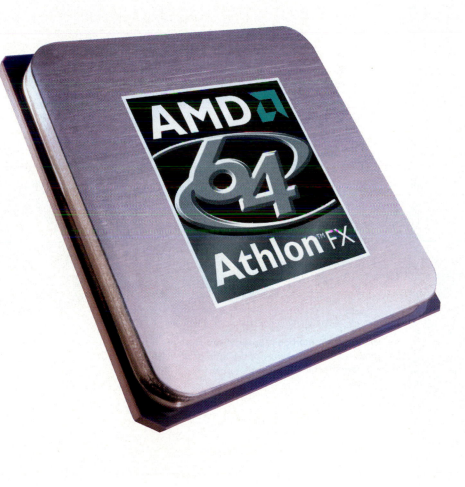

Chapter Four

Motherboards

It's the main clearing station for all your PC's data—so you better pick the right one

The Abit IC-7G motherboard brought top-class performance and all the features of the Intel 875P chipset to the Dream Machine 2003.

We'll assume that if you're ready to begin mulling your mobo decision, you've already decided which CPU you want to use for your Dream Machine. So sit back and relax—you're about to enjoy a relative walk in the park, PC configuration-wise. Picking the perfect motherboard is really just a matter of deciding which core-logic chipset you want to use, and then finding a board with the perfect set of integrated, onboard features.

Well, sort of. You'll also need to make sure that your prospective board fits inside your case. And, of course, you'll want a board that's received *Maximum PC's* blessing for no-nonsense stability and parts compatibility. Then there's the issue of board layout: You'll want to make sure that your mobo's components won't physically prevent the installation of particular cooling solutions and add-in cards. And, yeah, it *can* be difficult to choose the best core-logic chipset. Plus, it's sometimes difficult to decide which features should be integrated into the motherboard, and which features separate add-in cards should handle.

So we're back at square one. Picking a mobo can indeed be a wicked, wicked pissa. Thus the purpose of this chapter. It's time to lift the shroud of confusion. We'll start with some general advice, and then get into choosing specific mobos for specific CPU types.

Making the Logical Choice

Your core-logic chipset controls all the data traffic that occurs between different PC subsystems. It's typically defined by two separate chips—a *northbridge* chip and a *southbridge* chip—that are permanently affixed to the motherboard. In general, simplistic terms, the northbridge chip plays traffic cop for all the data that travels between your CPU, main system memory, videocard, and PCI cards. The southbridge chip, meanwhile, handles "lower-level" data traffic—the data that flows to and from hard drives, optical drives, and external peripherals.

Now, of course, this is just the *simple* explanation. In today's modern world of PC design, some "chipsets" are actually consolidated into a single chip, while other chipsets (such as those that support the latest 64-bit Athlon CPUs) actually offload memory traffic control to the processor itself. And, as we've stated before, many modern chipsets have plenty of integrated features, such as support for video, sound, and Ethernet, and even Serial ATA and RAID controllers.

The Asus SK8V sports dual Serial ATA ports, Gigabit Ethernet, and the excellent Athlon 64 VIA K8T800 chipset.

Yes, there's a lot to think about when choosing a chipset, but CPU and memory compatibility should be your most important considerations. Indeed, because each CPU is only compatible with specific motherboard chipsets, it's absolutely vital that your motherboard support your dream CPU. To further complicate matters, if your CPU is newer than your motherboard, your board, while fully compatible, may also require an update to its onboard software (that is, its BIOS) before it will recognize your CPU. To do this BIOS update, you'll need the new CPU installed, so it's for this very reason that we recommend you purchase your motherboard and CPU at the same time and from the same vendor. Most online component stores will actually flash your motherboard with the latest BIOS before it ships the board to you. Just ask them nicely, and they'll probably oblige.

As for formfactor considerations, always remember that your motherboard simply won't fit in a case that's too small. So if you buy a micro-ATX case, make sure you buy a micro-ATX board. You can always fit a micro-ATX mobo into an ATX case, but you can't fit an ATX mobo into a micro-ATX case. From smallest to largest, here are the different ATX size specs: flex-ATX, mini-ATX, micro-ATX, and ATX.

You should also know that with a few exceptions, BTX mobos won't fit into ATX cases, and vice versa. If you've got a jones for a BTX case, you'll need to make certain that you buy a BTX mobo to go with it.

The Pluses and Perils of Integrated Components

Modder alert: If you're going to install a case window, make sure you get a dead sexy motherboard, like DFI's fluorescent LAN Party Pro875.

These days, integration is the name of the motherboard game. In a mad dash to one-up each other, motherboard and chipset manufacturers have started offering all sorts of onboard integrated features that can save you both money and expansion slots. Indeed, only a few years ago, *Maximum PC* editors would debate the relative merits of different Ethernet cards, but in today's age of "onboard everything," those debates seem quaint.

Cost-savings and PCI slot-savings aside, integrated chipset features also pay off in performance dividends. It all has to do with bypassing the troubled, barbiturate-addled PCI bus.

Kick-Ass Construction Tip

Every single dream-worthy motherboard should have these features onboard:

- AGP 8x or PCI Express X16: Without the massive amount of bandwidth that these two buses provide, you won't be able to get the most from your videocard.

- USB 2.0: The most popular connection protocol for PC hardware, from mouse devices to external hard drives, is USB 2.0. Every motherboard should support USB 2.0, or you'll have no place to plug in your peripherals.

- Serial ATA: The biggest, fastest hard drives on the planet only support Serial ATA. Without a Serial ATA controller on your mobo, you could clog your PCI bus with high-speed data transfers.

- FireWire: The second most popular connection for PC hardware, most external hard and optical drives support FireWire in addition to USB 2.0.

- Gigabit Ethernet: This networking protocol is so fast, it can actually send and receive data faster than the PCI bus can cope with it. By integrating Gigabit directly into the chipset, mobo manufacturers can bypass these bandwidth bottlenecks.

Here's the deal: Most PCI add-in cards (and even some controller chips soldered onto the motherboard, but not integrated into the chipset) use the PCI bus to communicate with the rest of the system. But the PCI bus is dog slow—too slow, in fact, to keep pace with many modern PC components. Consider that the maximum bandwidth shared between all PCI devices is only 133MB/sec. That sounds fast, but it's not fast enough for a RAID array of 10,000rpm Serial ATA drives, which can reach sustained transfer rates in excess of 250MB/sec. See the dilemma? If you have a PCI RAID controller directing traffic for a fast RAID array, the PCI bus will bottleneck your drive performance.

Yeah, it all sounds pretty nasty. The drive performance bottleneck is minor, however, compared to all the havoc that your RAID array will impose on *other* PCI components. Your network card's performance will suffer, your soundcard might drop out, and your entire system will perform below its full potential.

And thus we have integration. Chipset vendors now integrate bandwidth-hungry hardware controllers directly into their core-logic, so they can provide high-speed pipelines directly from individual devices to the CPU and system memory. Integration removes layers of abstraction—and every removed abstraction layer can potentially lead to improved performance.

Now, with all that said, some types of integrated hardware are better than others. We'd never recommend using onboard video controllers for anything but 2D desktop work. They just don't offer anything

The Good, Bad, & Ugly of Motherboard Design

When you're picking the perfect motherboard, even the tiniest feature or flaw can separate the unworthy mobos from the righteous elite.

Bad! This board's capacitors are way too close to the AGP slot. Force in a videocard with a large cooling solution and you might break a capacitor off!

Good! The ATX power connector and IDE connector interfaces allow enough room for the easy removal and insertion of each connector type.

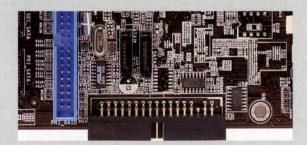

Bad! Putting the IDE connectors on the side of the board seems like a great idea—until you try to plug an unwieldy IDE cable into the mobo while it's in a case.

Good! This board includes internal headers for FireWire and USB 2.0 so you can connect front-mounted USB and FireWire ports internally.

approaching acceptable 3D gaming performance. But we have found that integrated hard drive controllers, network controllers, and FireWire controllers usually outperform otherwise identical PCI peripherals. It's all about the bandwidth, baby!

Almost every motherboard now includes integrated audio support, but it's hard to find a mobo with *quality* integrated audio. In fact, for Pentium 4, Athlon 64, and Athlon FX motherboards, it's almost impossible. So, if sound quality is important to you, we recommend you get an add-in soundcard, like Creative Labs' Audigy 2. The only integrated sound we currently endorse is that offered by nVidia's nForce2 chipset, but the nForce2 only supports old-school Athlon XP processors.

When choosing your mobo, also keep an eye out for cool peripherals—such as remote controls and PC carrying cases—that may come bundled in the box. If you're building a rig with a flashy case window, you might consider a motherboard featuring a wild circuit board color and fluorescent expansion slots. And lastly, don't brush off software bundles. Although most mobos ship with a bunch of trashy programs, some come with useful apps (temperature monitors and virus scanners are always welcome).

Picking the Perfect Pentium 4 Chipset

Before you can begin your search for the perfect Pentium 4 motherboard, you need to know what chipset you want—and there are a lot to choose from. Intel makes the best all-around chipsets for Pentium 4 motherboards. For most uses, we wholeheartedly recommend the Intel 875P chipset. Its combination of pure, unadulterated speed and rich roll call of integrated features make it a tough contender. The 875P supports dual-channel DDR400 memory, the 800MHz front-side bus that the fastest processors require, AGP 8x, and Hyper-Threading.

The MSI 875P Neo sports Intel's top-class 875P chipset, a surefire performer that's absolutely loaded with features.

For a more integrated approach, the ATI Radeon 9100 IGP can't be beat. It also supports all the latest technologies—dual-channel DDR400, 800MHz FSB, AGP 8x, Hyper-Threading—but just so happens to boast a decent integrated graphics controller. Hardcore gamers and true performance enthusiasts will want to buy an add-in graphics card, but if your budget is tight (or if you don't intend to play games that demand a top-class 3D accelerator), the 9100 IGP offers the best integrated graphics of any chipset on the market. It's also the *only* chipset with integrated graphics that offers even rudimentary programmable shader support (For more info on programmable shaders, check out Chapter 8, "Selecting a Videocard.")

We recommend you avoid Pentium 4 chipsets made by SiS and VIA. They're either slower than the chipsets we mentioned above, or sacrifice stability for speed. There will likely be newer, faster, better chipsets available by the time you read this book, so regardless of which Pentium 4 motherboard you buy, just make sure it includes support for dual-channel DDR400 memory, an 800MHz front-side bus, and CPU Hyper-Threading.

What About Athlon XP?

With the release of Athlon 64 and Athlon FX processors, the 32-bit Athlon XP CPUs are last year's news. However, if you don't mind running a slightly slower machine, you can find great deals on older 32-bit Athlon hardware. There are really only two companies making performance chipsets for the Athlon XP platform today: nVidia and VIA. SiS also makes Athlon chipsets, but we recommend you avoid them, as they're targeted at the budget market, and generally aren't as refined or feature-filled as the chipsets from nVidia and VIA.

Picking the Perfect Athlon 64 or Athlon FX Chipset

Picking the right chipset for Athlon 64 processors is considerably more difficult than picking a great Pentium 4 chipset. Because the 64-bit Athlon CPU is so new, its chipset world is still in a state of flux. Both nVidia and VIA have been releasing frequent revisions to their Athlon 64 chipsets, and, as a result, each company has at some time bested the other in respect to benchmark performance and feature offerings.

That said, of all the Athlon 64 chipsets we've tested in the Lab, we recommend the VIA K8T800. Its combination of great integrated features (including support for Gigabit Ethernet and dual Serial ATA) and slightly better benchmark results give it an edge over the original nVidia nForce3 Pro 150 chipset.

As for the updated nForce3 250, it might easily dethrone the VIA K8T800. As of press time, we hadn't yet tested a final shipping, reviewable board, so we can't actually recommend the chipset yet. But beta benchmark results are encouraging, and the 250 version of nForce3 seems to compensate for the failings of the Pro 150 version by adding several key features that no other chipset vendor offers.

The nForce3 250 includes pretty much everything a young lad might need in an Athlon 64 mobo, including support for Serial ATA and Gigabit Ethernet, a RAID controller, and a hyper-fast link between the components that are on the southbridge and northbridge in other chipsets. You see, on the nForce3 250, both the northbridge and southbridge functions are integrated on a single chip. Because each component is directly integrated into the chipset, there is much more bandwidth available than with other architectures. During nForce3 250 testing, we've seen 250Mbit/sec sustained transfer rates from RAID arrays, and Gigabit Ethernet transfer rates that roughly double what one might get from a PCI add-in card. We're also intrigued by the nForce3 250's hardware firewall, which is actually integrated into the chipset's network controller. The nForce3 250 should support existing Socket 754 Athlon 64s and Athlon 64 FX CPUs, as well as new Socket 939 CPUs in late 2004.

Regardless of which Athlon 64 or Athlon FX mobo you buy, just make sure it supports DDR400 memory in dual-channel mode, an 800MHz front-side bus, and Socket 939 CPUs. These are bare-minimum requirements.

Of all the Athlon XP chipsets available, nVidia's nForce2 Ultra earns our highest recommendation. The nForce2 line sports built-in Dolby 5.1 audio, 10/100Mbps Ethernet support, AGP 8x support, a dual-channel DDR400 memory controller for maximum memory bandwidth, and optional GeForce4 MX-level integrated graphics. The Ultra version even adds support for the 400MHz front-side bus (earlier versions of the nForce2 promised this support, but frequently couldn't deliver). If you don't care about 400MHz FSB support, however, any old version of the nForce2 should give you great performance and rock-solid stability.

VIA's KT400A is the other main contender for the Athlon XP chipset throne. It offers DDR400 memory support, but only in single-channel configurations, and also lacks 400MHz FSB support. The KT400A does include built-in networking and AGP 8x capability, but feature-for-feature it's still outclassed by the nForce2 line. The KT600 chipset will soon succeed the KT400A, boasting such amenities as 400MHz FSB support, six-channel audio, and built-in RAID support. Performance-wise, the KT600 could put nVidia and VIA neck and neck. Be forewarned, however, that VIA has a reputation for problems with stability and robustness, both of which are hallmarks of the nForce2.

This MSI mobo uses the Via PT880 chipset, to its detriment. Unlike its Intel 875P-based brother, the PT880 Neo should be avoided because of its poor performance and lack of features.

Ask the Motherboard Doctor

Q: What is overclocking, and should I do it to my computer?

A: Overclocking increases the clock speed of certain key components—namely, the CPU and videocard—beyond manufacturer-recommended settings, resulting in extra performance for free. Unfortunately, overclocking will void your warranty and can, in rare cases, destroy hardware if done improperly. Many people regularly overclock their computers and suffer no ill effects, but it's not for the faint of heart. A good motherboard is crucial to successful CPU overclocking, so we'll talk more about that later.

Estimating Overclockability

Hoping to overclock your system to get the most from your investment? If so, there are a few additional motherboard features you'll want to look out for. For starters, you'll want a motherboard that gives you the ability to adjust front-side bus speeds and clock multipliers through the BIOS. Some mobos still use jumpers or DIP switches for this task, and they're a royal pain in the arse. Even worse, some boards simply don't allow you to change bus and multiplier settings at all—so make sure you're getting the real deal.

Pentium 4 owners don't have as many overclocking options as Athlon owners, simply because the multipliers on a P4 can't be unlocked. Nonetheless, a good P4 motherboard will allow you to make the best of the options you do have. So if you're planning to do any overclocking at all, you'll want a mobo that allows FSB speed adjustments through the BIOS, at the very least. Otherwise, you'll be stuck with the chore of fiddling with hardware jumpers.

Motherboard Connector Guide

The AGP and PCI slots are where you'll connect most add-on hardware. Next-gen boards will also use PCI-Express, which won't be backward-compatible with existing PCI technology.

You'll need to connect your case's power switch, reset switch, power LED, hard drive activity LED, and internal speaker to these color-coded pins. Each mobo is different, so consult your documentation!

Without these internal USB headers, you'll have to run cable to your case's exterior if you want to add front-mounted USB ports to your system.

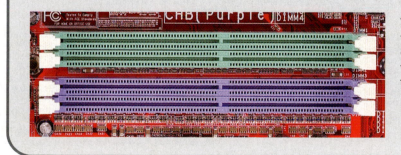

These sockets hold your memory. Make sure you read your motherboard's manual to find out which memory slots you need to place your memory in to get the memory to run in the double-fast dual channel mode.

Anatomy of a Motherboard

Want to know what all those little chips on your mobo do? Here's the inside scoop on the key components soldered onto this MSI 875P Neo motherboard

BIOS: The basic input/output system of your motherboard is contained in a small nonvolatile piece of memory. When you update the BIOS, this is the chip that's reprogrammed. Generally, socketed designs are preferred. If you kill the BIOS during an update or corrupt it with static electricity, you simply pry out the old one and replace it.

Audio CODEC: Most new motherboards feature integrated audio that's quite advanced from stereo output. The Analog Devices chip here supports multichannel output and advanced 3D audio.

Clock generator: The clock generator on a motherboard does what it sounds like—it controls the clock on the PC that determines the clock speed. Don't confuse this with the real-time clock, which controls the time and date stashed in a battery-backed chip called the CMOS.

Northbridge: The northbridge is a single chip that plays traffic cop between the RAM, CPU, and AGP card. It has a high speed interconnect that attaches to the southbridge. Because of the tremendous heat that modern northbridge chips transfer and generate, almost all have heatsinks or fans to keep them cool.

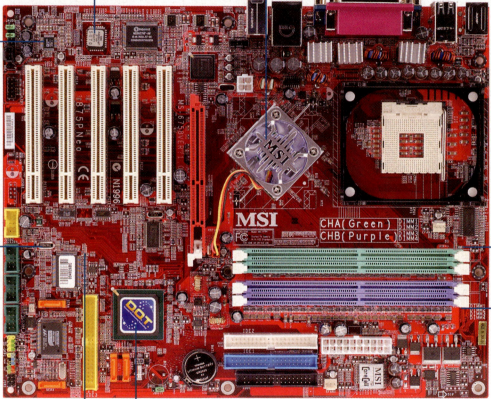

RAID and FireWire: Motherboard manufacturers build features into a motherboard by simply adding additional chips to the PCB, such as the Serial ATA RAID and FireWire A support on this board.

Southbridge: The southbridge controls the unglamorous portions of the PC, such as USB ports, IDE, and PCI slots. The Intel chip here connects to the northbridge at 266MB/s. Other chipsets feature double and quadruple the speeds of the Intel chipset.

RAM slots: The state of the art in motherboard technology is now DDR400 in dual-channels. Don't be confused—dual-channel DDR doesn't require new RAM. If you currently have DDR RAM, you simply get another piece of RAM that matches it in size and speed. By running the RAM in pairs, you greatly increase the memory bandwidth. The notches in the center prevent you from incorrectly inserting the RAM, and the colors indicate corresponding channels that RAM should be paired up in.

The Tyan Thunder K8W is a dual Opteron mobo. Unlike other dualie boards, the K8W actually has a separate memory pool for each processor, which greatly boosts performance over other dual boards that share a single memory pool.

An ideal overclocking board will allow you to set your AGP and PCI bus clocks independently of your front-side bus and/or memory clocks. This is a great win for overclockers. In the past, increasing front-side bus and/or memory bus speeds also increased AGP and PCI bus speeds, and this limited the extent to which a system could be overclocked. But now that AGP and PCI speeds can be locked down, overclockers have much more headroom to play with. So make sure that your motherboard ships with bus lockdown controls, because although your CPU and memory might be ready to run faster than spec, it's unlikely that your PCI and videocards will be so forgiving.

Kick-Ass Construction Tip

Your Athlon FX mobo *must* support this stuff!

- Support for DDR400 in dual-channel mode: Just like the Pentium 4 chipsets, Athlon FX boards can use two DDR400 chips together to make a single double-speed memory channel. If you want to get the most performance from your processor, you need a dual-channel board.

- 800MHz HyperTransport: HyperTransport is the AMD system's pipeline between the chipset's northbridge and southbridge. Older Athlon FX boards only supported a 600MHz HyperTransport link, but we wouldn't settle for anything less than 800MHz these days.

Motherboard Spec Speak

Core-Logic Chipset

The silicon glue that allows the rest of your PC's components to talk to each other. The chipset regulates data traffic between the CPU, memory, AGP card, PCI cards, USB ports, and keyboard and mouse ports.

Northbridge

The northbridge transfers data between the CPU, system memory, AGP card, and southbridge chip. Most modern northbridges run very hot, so they need at least a passive heatsink, and frequently a fan, too!

Southbridge

While the northbridge handles all the glamorous hardware, the southbridge does the grunt work. It connects PCI devices, USB devices, the onboard hard drive controller, and the legacy ports—PS/2, serial, and parallel ports—to the rest of the system. Newer southbridge chips also include integrated audio support, RAID controllers, and Gigabit Ethernet support.

Integrated hardware

Simply put, integrated components are included as part of the motherboard. They can be either soldered directly to the motherboard or be physically integrated into the northbridge or southbridge.

HyperTransport

Really just a fancy name for a fast connection between different chipset components. HyperTransport was developed by AMD, and allows for 400MB/sec transfers between the northbridge and the southbridge.

Dream Machine 2004 Contenders

Here's a look two motherboards—one Athlon FX and one Pentium 4—that are possible contenders for Dream Machine 2004

Tyan Thunder K8W

We've already extolled the virtues of the K8W, but it's clearly the mobo to beat—at least if we decide to go with a dual Opteron rig instead of a single Athlon FX chip.

The Asus P4C800-E Deluxe

The Asus P4C800-E Deluxe is a likely contender for the 2004 Dream Machine. It's not very flashy, but its 875 chipset has features like onboard Serial ATA and integrated FireWire that kick ass.

Chapter Five

Memory

Without it, your system just won't work. If you buy the wrong memory, your computer will be crippled. We're here to help you pick the perfect memory for your Dream Machine

For Dream Machine 2003, we needed at least one gigabyte of overclocking-friendly memory to use in a dual-channel config. One gig of Corsair Micro XMS4000 DDR SDRAM fit the bill perfectly.

RAM. It's short for random-access memory, and you already know the basics: Your system can't run without it; Windows XP should have at least 512MB or more; and faster RAM can improve system performance, but only if your system is designed to use it.

How well do you really *under-stand* memory? It's easy to say "Faster memory can improve system performance," but to understand why, you need to understand how memory works. Only then can we really talk about how your BIOS and chipset combine forces to manage memory access, and the prospects for current and emerging memory technologies, from SDRAM and RDRAM to DDR2.

How RAM Works

Your system sees the available RAM as a sort of giant spreadsheet, with rows and columns of data. However, to understand the process of accessing memory, a second analogy is useful.

Imagine RAM locations as books in a library that uses a ladder attached to the top of the shelves for access. The process of getting a particular book in such a library works like this:

1. Locate the book.
2. Roll the ladder to the correct set of shelves.
3. Go up the ladder to get the book or books on the shelf.
4. Put away any books that go on the shelf.
5. Go down the ladder with the book(s).
6. Give the book(s) to the reader.

Just as the process of retrieving or returning a book involves delays in moving from one set of shelves to another (rolling the ladder) and then reaching the correct shelf containing the book (going up and down the ladder), RAM access is delayed by moving from one row of memory addresses to another, and from locat-

ing the correct row/column address of the information needed from RAM.

And just as the librarian fetches books for the reader, the processor uses the memory controller (usually part of the northbridge or Memory Controller Hub chip) to access memory locations. Newer AMD processors, such as the Opteron, Athlon 64, and 64 FX processors feature built-in memory controllers, but the principle is the same.

With the right motherboard and high-quality memory, you can speed up the "librarian's" movements and thus greatly increase your PC's performance. In fact, many of the BIOS tweaks in Chapter 16, "Tweaking Your BIOS Settings," show you exactly how to tweak your memory settings to improve overall system performance.

If you don't plan to overclock, standard PC3200 DDR SDRAM should work perfectly for your Dream Machine. This matched pair of Kingston PC3200 DDR modules is entirely sufficient.

Current Memory Technologies

The oldest type of memory still in use is PC133 (133MHz) SDRAM (synchronous DRAM). SDRAM performs one operation per clock cycle. SDRAM is in use mainly on very old Pentium III and Athlon systems.

DDR (double data-rate) SDRAM, now the most common type of memory, performs two operations per clock cycle, so it can transfer data much more quickly than SDRAM. For example, DDR400 runs at a clock speed of 200MHz, but with two operations per clock cycle, the effective speed of the memory is 400MHz. DIMM modules that use DDR chips are usually referred to by their throughput. For example, DDR400 memory has a throughput of 3.2MB/s, so memory modules using DDR400 RAM are usually referred to as PC3200 modules. Because of its low price and kick-ass performance, DDR SDRAM is the preferred current memory technology for system builders.

Some Pentium 4 systems use Rambus DRAM (RDRAM) modules (RIMMs). Unlike SDRAM or DDR SDRAM modules, which perform parallel data transfers over a 64-bit data bus, RIMMs perform serial data transfers over a 16-bit data bus. Typical RIMMs contain up to 32 devices (chips), and data transfer takes place from chip to chip within the RIMM. Until recently, the most common RIMM was the RIMM1600 (also called PC800) 16-bit RIMM. However, some recent chipsets, such as those from SiS, support faster and wider RIMMs. Currently, the most popular RIMM runs at 600MHz and combines two channels into a single 32-bit module. It's referred to as RIMM4800 for its 4.8MB/sec throughput.

Although RIMMs have a much faster clock speed than DIMMs, their real-world memory performance is only slightly better in most cases. Because of their lagging speed and the much higher price of RDRAM memory, chipset manufacturers have been moving away from using Rambus RIMMs for their motherboards.

Understanding Banks of Memory

When you add memory to a new motherboard or upgrade an existing system, the memory must be added in *banks*. A memory bank refers to the

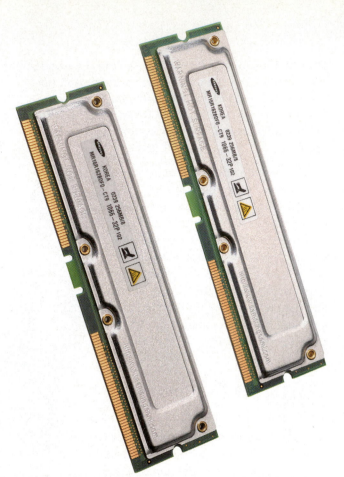

A full gigabyte of RDRAM was the memory config of choice for high-speed Pentium 4 systems until 2003. That's when DDR SDRAM surpassed Rambus in both price and performance.

amount of memory, in bits, that matches the data bus of the processor. SDRAM and DDR DIMM memory modules, regardless of their size, are 64 bits wide, and so is the data bus of Pentium 4, Athlon XP, and Athlon 64 processors. Thus, you can add a single DIMM module at a time to expand the memory of systems using these processors *if* the motherboard uses a conventional single-channel memory controller design.

Single-Bank or Dual-Bank?

A single DIMM can add one bank or two banks of memory to a system. Dual-bank DIMM modules (these often have chips on both sides, and are also referred to as double-sided DIMMs) let you install more memory into a single slot and, in recent tests with high-speed overclocking-friendly memory, improve performance over single-bank modules.

In some rare cases, you might find motherboards with three memory sockets that use chipsets that

How Fast Is Your Memory?

Don't know your PC3200 from 533MHz Rambus? Lucky for you, we're here to help you understand exactly how fast all the different types of memory really are.

RAM Technology	Types	Clock Speed	Form Factor	Maximum Throughput	Notes
SDRAM DIMM	PC66	66MHz	168-pin	533MB/sec	One access per clock cycle
	PC100	100MHz		800MB/sec	
	PC133	133MHz		1.066GB/sec	
DDR SDRAM DIMM	PC2100	100MHz	184-pin	2.1GB/sec	Two accesses per clock cycle
	PC2700	133MHz		2.7GB/sec	
	PC3200	166MHz		3.2GB/sec	
	PC3700	200MHz		3.7GB/sec	
	PC4000	250MHz		4.0GB/sec	
RDRAM RIMM	RIMM1600	400MHz	184-pin	1.6GB/sec	16-bit (single channel)
	RIMM2100	533MHz		2.1GB/sec	
	RIMM2400	600MHz		2.4GB/sec	
	RIMM3200	400MHz	242-pin	3.2GB/sec	32-bit (dual-channel)
	RIMM4200	533MHz		4.2GB/sec	
	RIMM4800	600MHz		4.8GB/sec	

support just four banks of memory. Thus, if two dual-bank/double-sided modules are already installed, you must leave the third socket empty. Some systems support dual-bank modules in slots 1 and 2, but slot 3 can use only single-bank memory.

Older systems designed for use with DDR266 (PC2100) memory might be less stable if you use nonstandard memory timings, but systems designed for DDR333 (PC2700) and faster memory usually work well with either standard or nonstandard memory timings,

regardless of whether the modules are single-bank or dual-bank.

Understanding Dual-Channel Memory

Dual-channel memory designs are now widespread, thanks to chipsets from nVidia (nForce series), Intel (865 and 875 series), VIA (PT880), and the memory controller built into the AMD Athlon 64 FX and Opteron processors. Dual-channel doesn't refer to a

Memory Spec Speak

It's time to master all the lingo you'll find when you go memory shopping

Registered memory

Registered memory redrives memory signals for better reliability—it can't be mixed with standard memory.

Packaging

There are two common types of memory package these days, TSOP and CSP. TSOP (thin small outline package) is an older technology that connects the RAM to the module via a series of leads on two sides of the chip. CSP (chip scale package) is a newer technology that uses a ball-grid array underneath the actual chip to connect it to the module.

Number of banks

RAM modules that have just one bank are known as single-bank modules. If your RAM has two banks, it's called a double-bank module. This is rocket science, eh?

16 × 64

The first number (16) is the size of each memory chip on the module (16Mbit). Multiply this number by 8 to get the size of the module in MB (16 × 8 = 128MB). The second number (64) is the width of the module in bits. A 64-bit wide module has no parity or ECC bits, so it does no error checking or correcting.

ECC

Memory that uses additional bits for error correction; ECC support in the chipset is required. Also sometimes called memory with parity.

Access time

That's the amount of time from when a memory module receives a request for data to the time that data becomes available.

different type of module, but to how memory is accessed.

Although systems with dual-channel chipsets can use just one DDR DIMM, their performance is slower than if you use two identical DIMMs and enable dual-channel mode. Why are dual-channel designs faster? As discussed earlier, the process of accessing a particular row of memory takes several clock cycles from start to finish. A dual-channel design can access each channel as soon as it is ready to provide the memory location desired, which reduces delays.

Although some vendors sell matched modules that have been tested as a unit, you don't need to buy a pair of modules to upgrade an existing dual-channel system that has just one module. You can buy another module with the same size and memory timing parameters (preferably the same brand/model) as your current module. If you don't know the brand and model of the memory in your PC, use a utility such as SiSoftware Sandra (www.sisoftware.co.uk) to determine the brand and model of memory installed.

If you want to add a little functional bling to your case, these Corsair XMS Pro Series modules light up to show memory activity.

Beyond PC3200— Memory That Works for Overclocking

The JEDEC Solid State Technology Association (www.jedec.org) is the organization responsible for establishing memory standards. The fastest DDR SDRAM memory approved by JEDEC is DDR400, which is the memory used in PC3200 memory modules. However, many vendors, including Corsair Memory, Kingston, Muskin, OCZ, and GeIL now offer PC3700 and PC4000 modules. These modules are designed and priced for the overclocker/gamer market. Most of them feature heat spreaders and other features designed to handle the higher heat and voltages used in overclocking. If you're content to run your memory at stock clock speeds and timings, stick with standard modules and spend your money elsewhere. But if the highest clock speeds on the planet are what you're aiming for, PC3700 and PC4000 memory should be on your shopping list.

As memory speeds increase, standard timing settings become more relaxed. For example, instead of the 2-3-2-6 timings typically used with PC3200 memory, PC3700 and PC4000 memory often use timings of 3-4-4-8.

Kick-Ass Construction Tip

When you're assembling your system, make certain that you have memory in the proper slots. If you put your DIMMs in the wrong slots, your motherboard might not be able to run the memory in dual-channel mode, which will effectively half the available memory bandwidth. Check your mobo documentation for optimal positioning guidelines.

Fast Memory Makes for Fast Computers

Your system's memory speed can have a massive impact on your system's performance if you choose poorly. Here's all you need to know.

On a Pentium 4 processor, the front-side bus speed determines your CPU's speed, but your memory doesn't necessarily determine the front-side bus speed.

In the old days of the Pentium III and classic Athlon, there was a direct correlation between the speed of your memory and your processor speed. To determine your clock speed, you'd simply multiply the speed of your memory by the CPU multiplier—a number fixed for each processor at the factory—and the result was your clock speed in MHz. It's not quite so simple anymore, because many motherboard chipsets let you run your memory and the front-side bus—the connection between the CPU and the rest of the system—at different speeds.

If your motherboard doesn't need full-speed memory to run the CPU at maximum speed, you can shave a few bucks off your budget by buying slower, cheaper memory, right? Wrong! Although it is true that your CPU will be running at full speed, your memory's speed has a tremendous impact on your overall system's performance.

The two Pentium 4 2.4GHz processors are a perfect example. The original 2.4GHz processor communicated with memory over a 400MHz bus, but the second version of the 2.4GHz processor communicated over a 533MHz bus. The 533MHz bus version of the 2.4GHz Pentium 4 was significantly faster than the 400MHz version, up to 20% in some benchmarks.

Don't needlessly cripple your CPU. Use the fastest memory that it supports!

Registered Memory and the Athlon 64 FX

T o provide maximum reliability, servers and workstations typically use registered DIMMs instead of the unbuffered DIMMs used in desktop computers. A registered DIMM uses an additional chip mounted horizontally on the DIMM to boost memory signals running to and from the module. This process takes one clock cycle, so registered memory is slightly slower than normal unbuffered memory. Registered memory is also more expensive than unbuffered memory, cannot be mixed with unbuffered memory, and must be supported by the motherboard chipset.

Because servers (which typically use special processors such as the Intel Xeon or AMD Opteron) use registered memory, we weren't surprised that the first motherboards for the AMD Athlon 64 FX also require registered memory. Here's why: The initial versions of the Athlon 64 FX are based on the Opteron server/workstation chip. Newer Athlon 64 CPUs that use Socket 939 do not require registered memory.

DDR2: The Next Wave of Memory

Starting late this year or in early 2005, you will be able to buy systems that use the next generation of DDR memory, DDR2. DDR2, previously known as DDR-II, is designed to solve the shortcomings of current DDR memory:

- *Power:* DDR2 uses less than half the power of DDR memory to help reduce heat buildup and demands on laptop battery power.

We can't imagine that you'd build a system today that used standard single speed SDRAM, but you might run across it if you're ever working on an older rig. These Corsair modules provide 512MB of storage each.

- *High clock speeds:* DDR2 starts at 400MHz effective clock speed and can scale to 800MHz while running the chip core at just a quarter of the effective clock speed.

- *Component density:* DDR2 supports up to 2GB chips, enabling a 2GB module to be supplied as a single-sided module.

- *Chip size:* DDR2 memory chips are half the size of those used by DDR modules.

- *Chip connection technology:* DDR2 memory chips use a *ball grid array (BGA)* connector. Older DDR chips use a less efficient TSOP connector.

Kick-Ass Construction Tip

Today's memory runs at extremely high speeds, and might need extra cooling, especially in older ATX boxes. There are a large number of memory coolers that will attach either directly to the RAM's heat spreader or to the memory socket.

Dream Machine 2004 Contender

Without just the right RAM, our next Dream Machine could end up a nightmare

TwinX 2048RE-3200 DDR SDRAM

Because we're building a gaming machine, we'd prefer to go with the slightly faster non-registered memory—remember that registered DIMMs sacrifice some speed for a little extra stability. However, with the Socket 940 motherboard we've chosen and the current Athlon FX CPUs, we really don't have a choice.

By the time you read this, the Socket 939 Athlon 64s should be available, and Athlon FX and Athlon 64 owners won't be shackled to the more expensive and slower registered RAM anymore!

If you're building an Athlon 64 FX system pre-Socket 939, you'll need the very best registered DDR memory. The TwinX 2048RE-3200 is a matched pair of 1GB DDR modules designed to run well flawlessly with 64-bit Athlons.

Chapter Six

Hard Drives

Bigger, faster, and smarter—meet the new crop of hard drives, and learn how to pick the perfect one for your Dream Machine

The Western Digital 360 Raptor used in the 2003 Dream Machine was so blindingly fast that it destroyed benchmark records set by the fastest 7200rpm hard drives. Its secret wasn't the spiffy new Serial ATA interface, but its astonishing 10,000rpm spindle speed. Naturally, we tossed a pair of them in a striped RAID array for the Dream Machine.

Your CPU and videocard are glamorous components, with impressive-sounding descriptors like "gigahertz," and faster iterations popping up every few months. But it's the hard drive that's the heart of your PC. It's the basket where your PC puts all the goods—your OS, your applications, and, of course, all your valuable data.

Not much more than a decade ago, hard disk storage was expensive and fairly limited in capacity. But today, it's almost an afterthought. A high-performance drive from a major manufacturer such as Western Digital will cost you less than a buck per gigabyte. So it's tempting to just grab the biggest one you can find and assume you're set for a year or so.

Not so fast.

Your hard drive is a mechanical device, and it won't ever challenge solid-state components like your CPU and RAM in the speed category. But it does do its job—keeping your CPU and RAM fed with the data they hunger for—reliably and cheaply. So given that we're stuck with the technology for the time being, we may as well minimize the drag on our system's performance by intelligently selecting the right hard drive (or drives, as the case may be).

A Few Nanoseconds in the Life of a Hard Drive

If you want to understand what makes one hard drive faster than another, well, wouldn't you know, you need to understand a bit about how they work. It's a lot more interesting than you might expect.

Suppose a program is looking for a file. Your operating system and hard drive work together (mediated by a disk controller built into the drive) to find out where the file is physically situated on the disk. Disk addressing is done in terms of tracks and sectors (which can be thought of as rings and points on the rings, respectively). If the data has already been read and stored into a small amount of built-in memory called the *cache*, the data is served up directly from the cache. This would be the case, for example, if you reopened a document that you just closed. If the data isn't there, the drive needs to retrieve the data by moving the read and write heads to the right disk location.

Even though they were astonishingly fast, the mere 72GB of storage afforded by our Raptor RAID array needed augmentation in a bad way. To solve our storage woes, we added a pair of 250GB Western Digital 2500JBs in a second RAID array.

The read and write heads (they are separate) are mounted at the very tip of the arm assembly. The assembly is similar to the arm and stylus of a classic record player, except that instead of being driven by a motor and belt, the arm is moved by a very strong and precise magnet capable of rapidly twitching the arm to and fro. The read and write heads float above the surface of the drive platters, which store digital information in a thin layer of magnetic particles (like cassette tapes).

Once the read head arrives at the correct track, the drive needs to wait for the platter to spin to the correct sector before reading. Once the data is picked up, it is passed to the cache, and then on to the rest of your PC for processing.

Speed Metrics for Power Users

This Seagate Barracuda 7200.7 Serial ATA drive is one of the first non-SCSI drives to support native command queuing for optimal drive access times, even under heavy load!

That's the hyper-simplified, 30-second brief on how hard drives work. Now let's look at the attributes that determine what kind of performance you'll get from your drive. Again, it comes down to the efficiency of physically moving parts.

Rotational speed is the speed at which the spindle motor spins your drive platters. The faster the rotational speed, the less you'll have to deal with the effects of *rotational latency*, which is the time it takes for a disk to spin the right sectors past your drive's read or write head. Think about it like this: Imagine two buses running through the same city loop. One goes 10 miles per hour, while the other runs at 20 m.p.h. Meanwhile, you run to the curb just in time to see both of them drive by. Obviously, the 20 m.p.h. bus will come back your way sooner. Increasing the rotational speed on a hard drive helps with transfer rates the same way, by passing more bits under the head with every rotation. We wouldn't consider a desktop drive that runs at less than 7200rpm, and power users need to take a good look at 10,000rpm drives.

Another number getting a lot of attention in the past few years is the cache size. Western Digital turned over the desktop drive industry with 8MB caches (compared with the then-typical 2MB) and other vendors soon followed suit. A larger cache has more room for stored data, thus increasing cache *hits*, which are successful retrievals from the fast cache instead of

Kick-Ass Construction Tip

Note that putting more than one drive on a single IDE channel *will* affect your performance! Design limitations of the original IDE bus prevent multiple drives from sending or receiving data over the IDE bus simultaneously. The lesson: Always keep your hard drives on separate channels! This won't be a problem much longer, as Serial ATA only allows you to connect one drive per channel, neatly sidestepping the problem.

the relatively pokey drive platters. A 2MB cache is acceptable, but we've observed dramatic improvements in performance with hard drives that utilize the brawnier 8MB cache, and newer drives with whopping 16MB caches are arriving now.

The most misunderstood performance stat is the *interface speed*. Interface speeds such as ATA66, ATA100, ATA133 and SATA150 are, for the most part, much faster than what your desktop drive is able to continuously transfer, and rarely, if ever, constrict your data flow. These standards (representing megabytes per second) are more than capable of handling the 60MB per second or so of traffic that the fastest drives can continuously deliver. To test this, we benchmarked an ATA133-capable drive on both an ATA100 and an ATA133 controller, and came out with identical scores. Even the new SATA150 interface had virtually no performance advantage over an identical drive with an ATA100 interface. You don't need an ATA133 drive if you've already got a fast ATA100 drive. In fact, we question whether buying an ATA133 is wise at all—you'd be better off trading up to a Serial ATA drive (but make sure you get a motherboard or controller card that supports it).

Seek time describes how quickly a drive can move from one place on the drive platter to another. It can be expressed as *average seek time* (meaning how long it takes to go from one random position to another), and *full stroke* (which measures the travel time between the outermost and innermost tracks). Most current drives post average seek times between 8 and 10ms (milliseconds). These numbers are useful, but don't go overboard. For example, some SCSI drives have average seek times as low as 5ms; you'll notice a difference between this and your bread-and-butter 9.5ms desktop drive. Less urgent is the difference between a drive with a 8.5ms and one with a 10ms average seek time—and the lower rated one might be much more expensive. Stick with a high-rpm drive and use common sense. Lower average seek times are better, but you won't want to pay through the nose for a slightly lower figure. If performance is that crucial, consider a RAID setup.

Choosing the Right Interface

L et's take some time to talk interfaces. There are basically three different types of hard drive interface available for PCs today: SCSI, Parallel ATA, and Serial ATA.

If you're building on a budget, you should sacrifice size rather than speed. For less than half the price of a 400GB Deskstar, you can get this 250GB drive and get about the same performance as the bigger drive.

RAID: Is It Right for You?

Setting up a multi-disk array isn't without peril, but if you create a RAID array the right way, you can boost your Dream Machine's performance in a big way

No, this is not a police RAID, so you can put your hands down. *RAID* stands for *Redundant Array of Inexpensive Disks*, and it's a technology that allows multiple hard drives to work together as one big hard drive, with each drive sharing a small part of the workload to boost disk transfer rates, improve reliability, or sometimes both. Think of it as hard drive teamwork. The two most common RAID configurations are *striping*, which involves two drives working in tandem as one big drive, and *mirroring*, which stores one drive's worth of data across two drives. Striping increases your system's performance, whereas mirroring protects your data in case of a hard drive crash. Imagine that—your hard drive crashes and all your data is automatically backed up around the clock, ready to go, just in case! Just for the

record, a striped array is called *RAID 0*, and the mirrored one is known as *RAID 1*. These are known as RAID *levels*, so if you set up a four-disk array that is both mirrored and striped, you would call it a RAID 0+1 array. RAID may seem scary, but it's actually very easy to set up and offers a host of benefits.

There is one catch, though. When you use a single hard drive in your system, there's a very small chance your drive will fail someday and take all your data with it. Realize that in a striped two-drive array, the chance of data loss is effectively doubled. You see, in a striped array, if either drive fails, the whole array will fail. You can offset this danger by mirroring your striped array, but that takes a lot of disks. If you don't mirror your striped array, make sure you back up important data often!

If you want the full scoop on RAID, turn to Chapter 15, "Add RAID to Your Computer," for our complete guide.

SCSI

SCSI, which stands for *Small Computer System Interface*, is a constantly evolving data bus designed for the very fastest components in your system. Currently, the fastest SCSI connections share a whopping 640MB/sec of bandwidth with all the devices on the SCSI bus. SCSI cables come in many different shapes and sizes, from wide ribbon cables to uber-thin fiber optics—it seems like there's a SCSI format in every size and shape. Newer SCSI interfaces let commercial users remove and install drives while the power is on—this is called *hot-swapping*. These features are really designed for higher-demand use than desktop PCs require. Servers and high-powered workstations usually sport SCSI drives, but most desktop PCs do not. Because SCSI hard drives are designed for the server market, they're usually much more expensive than similar Parallel ATA and Serial ATA drives.

If you're looking for a quiet drive, you can't go wrong with this Maxtor DiamondMax Plus 9. It starts out quiet, and you can download a special utility from Maxtor to sacrifice a small amount of performance for even quieter operations.

Parallel ATA

Parallel ATA is the old standby interface for desktop hard drives. Currently the Parallel ATA spec tops out at about 133MB/sec, which is still faster than any Parallel ATA drive we've ever tested. Parallel ATA drives connect to the controller using an unwieldy ribbon cable, and for the most part, they don't support any fancy next-gen features like command queuing or hot-swappability. Parallel ATA is officially a legacy spec now. Although manufacturers will continue to ship drives well into 2006, the future of desktop hard drives is Serial ATA.

All You Need to Know About Fancy IDE Cables

Round, slim, and low-profile—we break down everything that's important to know when purchasing Parallel ATA cables

Ribbon cables are a real pain. They're big, unwieldy, and block all important airflow over your drives and to the rest of your components. Connecting your PC with wide ribbon cables is like putting a windbreak directly in front of a windmill—it just *does not make sense*. However, until Serial ATA optical drives and hard drives become more common, we're stuck with big, wide ribbon cables for at least a couple more years.

Lucky for you, there's an alternative. By bundling the 80 wires that a standard IDE ribbon cable contains into a round bundle, cable manufacturers have shrunk the dreaded ribbon cable into a much more manageable round cable. They work just like normal IDE cables, and they work with normal IDE drives, they're just narrower and don't block airflow as effectively as a standard IDE ribbon cable.

The only real downside to rounded cables comes from the fact that bundling those data lines so closely together can create electromagnetic interference above the tolerance of the drive or the controller, which can lead to slower operation as data is sent and re-sent, or in extreme cases, lost entirely. The best long-term solution to cabling issues is to switch to Serial ATA. SATA cables are substantially smaller and flatter than even the most tightly packed round IDE cable.

Serial ATA

Take a look at a machine equipped with Serial ATA, and the most striking feature will be the skinny data cables. While skinny cables have a positive impact on a case's internal airflow, this isn't the main reason why the PC industry is dropping Parallel ATA and its flat, wide cables for SATA. The main reason is that the current parallel interface is facing a performance wall.

Parallel ATA cables send data along multiple wires. Each piece of data must travel along the length of the familiar ribbon cable and arrive at the same time in order to maintain data integrity. To get more speed from this scheme, the only options are to push the data to higher frequencies, or make the data path wider. That's where the problems lie. Making the data path wider is impractical, as the ribbon cable already includes 80 conductors—adding more would make it even bigger. Increasing speed beyond the current 133MB/sec adds to the likelihood of data corruption.

Because serial interfaces don't have to deal with coordinating multiple lanes of data, we can push them to much higher speeds. SATA is currently rated for 150MB/sec, slightly higher than the 133MB/sec offered by the fastest Parallel ATA spec (which still hasn't been widely adopted). SATA will double to 300MB/sec in late 2004 or 2005, and then again to 600MB/sec by 2007.

Four Tested Hard Drive Configurations

Pick the perfect hard drive configuration for your Dream Machine

Gigantic main drive: This is the preferred drive configuration for the vast majority of PCs. Because the operating system can place files that are important for either fast boot-up times or quick application loading times in optimal portions of the hard drive, using a single large boot-up drive is a clever way to do things. You can even reserve a few gigabytes near the end of the drive for a hidden partition to store your drive images if you want!

Two Drives in RAID—Striped: This is another popular configuration. With a striped array, you pair two identical hard drives with each other and get a single drive with double the capacity of either drive and significantly better burst speeds and access times. The downside is any drive failure will destroy the RAID array and all your data will be lost. For a two-disk array, that statistically doubles your chance of data loss.

Two Drives Striped with a Third Drive: Another popular configuration, by installing Windows and your applications on the striped RAID array, you gain the benefit of the high performance striped RAID array, but you have a single reliable drive that you can use to store backups of your RAID array and mirror any important data directories to safeguard against drive failure. Your third drive won't be protected, but if any important files are stored on both the standalone drive and the RAID array, the chances of losing data are slim.

Two Drives in RAID—Mirrored: This final configuration places two identical hard drives in a mirrored RAID array. Mirrored arrays store every bit of data on the array on both drives, completely protecting from data loss in the event of a single drive failure. There is a slight performance hit from a mirrored RAID array, and the space available on your RAID array equals one-half the capacity of the actual hard drives.

That's not to say that there aren't some problems with Serial ATA. The first SATA implementations on motherboards were kludgey: Serial ATA chips were piped through the PCI bus. This limited the 150MB/sec potential of SATA to PCI's 133MB/sec throughput, and required the loading of drivers just to recognize the chip. But current generation SATA-equipped motherboards should be plug-and-play. In Intel's ICH5 southbridge chip, for example, SATA is native. Plug a SATA hard drive into an Intel 875P motherboard, and you can load Windows XP onto your Serial ATA drive without needing to install any drivers.

Because of their bandwidth needs, hard drives were the first SATA candidates, but we expect to see optical drives with SATA interfaces by the end of 2004. Because of the glut of parallel devices, it'll probably take two to three years for the whole PC industry to drop Parallel ATA entirely, but at this point it's inevitable.

Although current hard drive data rates fall far short of the maximum throughput of even Parallel ATA specs, companies are laying the foundation for the future. You don't, after all, wait for the traffic jam before you try to build the roads (unless of course, you run the state of California).

Like Parallel ATA before it, Serial ATA is a constantly evolving spec. Already, drive and controller manufacturers are working on the next version of the Serial ATA specification, which will not only include faster transfer speeds, but new connectors and more advanced features. Here are the highlights as we went to press.

First, Serial ATA II is twice as fast as Serial ATA. That's 300MB/sec of take-it-to-the-bank hard drive transfer speed. We're already seeing drives that burst at speeds that saturate the SATA bus, so this is definitely a good thing.

Rounded IDE cables like the ones pictured here offer the same performance as standard IDE ribbon cables, but they're much easier to work with and are much less of an airflow problem.

The next version also includes an external spec, which allows users to connect their external hard drives with a special Serial ATA II connector. SATA-II also addresses one of our biggest complaints with SATA[md]that the cables come off too easily. There will be SATA-II cables with locking attachments to more securely hold your cables in place, both on the mobo and on the hard drive.

Kick-Ass Construction Tip

Try to keep old-fashioned IDE hard drives on their own channel. Because only one device at a time can use the IDE channel, isolating drives on their own channel can drastically improve disk-to-disk file transfer performance.

Anatomy of a Hard Drive

Here's what all the hardware inside your hard drive actually does

Voice coil/voice coil magnet: Hidden beneath this curved piece of metal is an extremely strong rare-earth magnet. If you were to look closely underneath the metal shield, you'd just barely see the copper wire coiled beneath. When current is passed through the wire, the resulting electromagnetic field pushes or pulls the drive head assembly across the platters. The drive head assembly can sweep across the platter hundreds of times a second; each sweep causes a faint click that is the sound of a hard drive earning its keep.

Disk media: Modern drives have several platters stacked one on top of the other like a stack of pancakes. Each platter is two-sided, and both sides are used for data storage. On the surface of each platter is an extremely thin layer of magnetic particles. Using a very delicate electromagnetic write head, these particles are organized and reorganized into neat groups that represent either ones or zeros. The read head then reads these "bits" and translates them back into digital data.

Spindle motor: This is the motor that spins the platters of a hard drive. Each platter is supported by ball bearings around the circumference of the spindle motor to prevent excess wobbling. Newer hard drives use fluid dynamic bearings, however, which use a thick oil to stabilize the platters without the whirring racket of ball bearings.

Flex circuit: This thin ribbon provides power to the head assembly. It also has a tiny pre-amp built into it that amplifies the wee signals picked up from the platters.

Read/write head assembly: Like the old cassette recorders of yore, there are two separate heads in a hard drive head assembly for reading and writing data. We're pointing out the "assembly" here because the actual read/write heads could be hidden behind the leg of a gnat. Most modern hard drives employ GMR heads, which, oddly enough, is an acronym for "giant magnetoresistive" heads. Nobody was trying to be funny or ironic; the name comes from the "giant magnetoresistive effect," a sly technique discovered in the 1980s that allows weaker magnetic fields from the disk media to be picked up by the read/write heads. The result is more data packed into less space.

Desktop Versus Server Drives

Hard drives are designed for specific tasks that generally fall into two categories: server and desktop duties. Typically, server drives use ultra-high spindle speeds and connect to your PC using the SCSI bus.

High-end server drives do offer features that most desktop-level drives omit. Features such as command queuing, which lets a high-rpm SCSI drives can optimize disk accesses so it can better handle many simultaneous tasks, are essential for servers that get requests from many different users or processes at the same time. However, most desktop users simply can't multitask efficiently enough to spend much time waiting on their hard drive. When you factor in the extreme price differentials—a 75GB 15,000rpm SCSI drive can cost four times as much as a 75GB 10,000rpm Serial ATA drive—it just doesn't make sense to spend that much money on your hard drives.

Command queuing is coming to the desktop hard drives, though. Newer 10,000rpm Serial ATA drives already support command queuing, but most Serial ATA controllers don't. If you must have command queuing on a budget, you can save a lot of money by picking up the appropriate Serial ATA controller card and a few Raptors.

Ask the Hard Drive Doctor

Q: Whenever I run Scandisk on my computer, it always finds a few bad sectors. Is my drive OK, or do I need to replace it?

A: First you need to back up any important data from that drive, and then you need to replace it ASAP. An occasional bad sector isn't a terrible thing, but if you find more bad sectors every time you run Scandisk—the standard Windows disk-maintenance application—that means that your drive is getting progressively worse, and could conk out once and for all at any time.

Hard Drive Specs

It's time to master all the lingo you'll find on your hard drive's packaging

Capacity

Even a hard drive's advertised size can be misleading. In the hard-drive industry, 1MB is defined as 1 million bytes, not the more technically accurate 1,048,576 bytes. So what does this mean to you at the end of the day? Well, if you're buying a 75GB drive, be aware that if you believe 1MB to be 1,048,576 bytes, your "75GB" hard drive is closer to 72GB. Alternately, you can just get a 200GB drive and not sweat the missing few gigs.

Buffer size

This is the amount of memory, or *cache*, that's used to store recently read data, or buffer data, that's being written to the disk. Many drives today come with a generous 8MB of cache, and some newer drives even sport 16MB caches.

Spindle speed

This describes how quickly a hard drive can spin its disk platters (which are attached to a shaft, or *spindle*), and is measured in revolutions per minute (rpm). Most consumer hard-drive speeds range from 5400rpm to 15,000rpm, with the average performance of an IDE drive ringing in at 7200rpm. A drive's spindle speed and areal density are among the most important specs to consider, because the two combined essentially determine the personality of the drive. A higher spindle speed typically suggests faster drive performance, but not always. To wit, a drive with a high spindle speed and low areal density might actually deliver less throughput than a drive with a low spindle speed and high areal density.

Seek time

Measured in milliseconds (ms) and usually expressed as an average, the seek time tells you how long it takes for a drive's read heads to move back and forth across the platters that actually store the drive's data. Seek time can be an important factor in determining how fast a drive performs, but most modern 7200rpm drives have very similar seek times in the 9ms range.

Interface

The speed of the interface between the hard drive and the rest of the PC, and definitely not to be confused with the actual maximum speed of the drive. Current interfaces are ATA133 on the old Parallel ATA spec, and SATA150 for the new Serial ATA spec. Don't be fooled by big interface numbers. Your drive's areal density, the number of platters, spindle speed, and seek time have a much bigger impact on performance.

Areal density

This defines the amount of data that can be packed onto a square inch of magnetic platter surface. The closer together you can corral your data, the higher the areal density. Usually expressed in gigabits per square inch, higher densities generally indicate faster drives.

Dream Machine 2004 Contenders

Here's a close-up look at the hard drives that might adorn next year's Dream Machine

Western Digital Raptor

For consumer-level hard drives, the speed champion remains the Western Digital 10,000rpm Raptor, and this year the 74GB version is looking like a strong speed contender. Sitting smugly on its Serial ATA interface, the Raptor is the king of desktop hard drives.

Hitachi Deskstar 7K400

With the highest areal density on the market, a tasty 8MB cache, and a whopping 400GB of storage space for any files we might need, the Hitachi Deskstar 7K400 is tough to beat for mass storage.

Chapter Seven

Optical Drives

Your Dream Machine's optical drive is the main conduit for getting software and media in and out of your system—so pay attention!

Last year we said "Burn 'em all and let God sort it out." That's exactly what the Pioneer DVR-A06 does. We take dual-format DVD burners for granted these days, but back then, being able to burn whatever media you tossed at a drive was a rare treat.

The optical drive is frequently overlooked as a key performance component. For most people, such an oversight is a costly mistake. Sure, you might not use your optical drive all that frequently, but when you do, you might rue the day you skimped and bought a $100 DVD burner. After you've burned the third bad DVD in a row, an extra $80 won't seem like too much to pay for a decent drive.

There are several features that define a good optical drive, but before you can understand what makes a good drive, you need to understand a little about how optical discs store data. CDs store data in a single, continuous track that begins at the inner ring of the disc. DVDs work much the same way, but they hold more data by utilizing more of the disk surface, and by using multiple storage layers. The data in any optical disc, CD or DVD, is stored digitally—that is, every bit of text, imagery, or sound is stored as a sequence of 1s and 0s. On a commercially pressed disc, these 1s and 0s are represented by *pits* (areas that have been microscopically indented) and *lands* (areas that have been left flat). When the laser in your optical drive scans a track on a disc and hits a land, the laser beam is reflected to an optical sensor, which registers the hit as a 1. When the laser hits a pit, the light is reflected *away* from the sensor, resulting in a 0.

The CD and DVD burners that we install in our home PCs don't really create pits and lands like commercial CD presses do, but they function in the same manner. Instead of pressing an indentation into a disc's surface, a consumer-level optical drive "burns" a mark into a photosensitive dye on the disc—the dye is protected by a transparent plastic layer. Wherever the disc is left untouched, laser light is reflected and a 1 is registered. Wherever the disc has been burned, the laser light is absorbed and a 0 is registered. When you finish burning a disc, you can actually see the difference between the used and unused portions of a disc—the burned areas are slightly darker. Rewritable media for consumer-level optical drives work similarly, except that the photosensitive layer is replaced by a polymorphous layer. This layer can change from one form to another and back again—from burned to unburned, in other words.

OK, now that you know how optical drives store data, we can talk about the optical drive that you're going to put in your system. For most people, we recommend the optical drive equivalent of a Swiss Army knife: a drive that can read every disc format ever made, and quickly write dozens of CDs and DVDs. This drive must not only be reliable (in that it burns an error-free disc every time), it should also read from and write to all the important optical disc formats: CD-R, CD-RW, DVD-R, DVD-RW, DVD+R, and DVD+RW. Any drive that handles all these formats is called a "dual-format combo drive," and in most cases, this will be the drive you'll want for your Dream Machine. The term *dual-format* refers to the fact that the drive can handle both competing DVD standards (DVD-R/W and DVD+R/W). The term *combo drive* means that the drive can handle both CD- and DVD-related duties.

The secret sauce that powers the 52x Plextor Plexwriter Premium isn't raw speed. No siree…. It's the bevy of fancy features—such as C2 error correction—that made this drive Dream Machine–worthy.

In most retail outlets and online stores, you'll encounter the following types of optical drives:

- CD-RW drives (which can read, write, and rewrite CDs)

- DVD-ROM drives (which read both CDs and DVDs, but don't do any writing)

- Single-format CD/DVD combo burners (which can read and write CDs, as well as read and write to only *one* of the two DVD formats)

- Dual-format CD/DVD combo burners (which can do everything under the sun)

Other optical drives with different levels of functionality do exist, but they're so rare, they're not worth mentioning here.

As we stated before, most people should opt for a dual-format combo burner. If you go this route, you'll only have to spend money on a single drive—a single optical device that can do it all. However (and this is a big however), some people might want to spend more money on *two* drives to avoid the compromises made

by dual-format combo burners. To wit, when we were configuring our own Dream Machine 2003 creation, we teamed up a kick-ass DVD burner with an equally kick-ass CD-RW drive. Why? Because the CD-RW drive offered digital-audio extraction performance that well exceeded the capabilities of any then-available DVD burner. In a nutshell, we wanted it all: DVD playback and recording was a must, but we didn't want to compromise our audio CD ripping performance. Thus the purchase of two optical drives.

Now, it's our opinion at *Maximum PC* that everyone needs a PC with that can read DVDs. No, not because you'll need to play DVD movies on your computer, but because the day has come when large games—think *Unreal Tournament 2004*—ship on DVD-ROMs. (You can still buy *UT2004* as a six-CD set, but who really wants to feed that many discs into their computer?) That said, we don't necessarily think everyone needs to *burn* DVDs. Sure, if you want to make your own DVD movies or back up gigantic amounts of data, a DVD burner is a must-have. But not everyone has these needs. If you're one of these people, you can consider pairing an inexpensive DVD-ROM drive with a top-shelf CD-RW drive.

So what makes for a killer CD-RW drive? We suggest you pay attention to four key qualities: reliability, compatibility, speed, and loudness. Read on for details!

Kick-Ass Construction Tip

Make absolutely certain that your optical drive's jumpers are properly set before you mount the drive in your case. Each parallel ATA optical drive's position on the IDE channel needs to be set to either master or slave. If you have multiple devices that share the IDE channel, you need to set one to master and the other to slave. Alternatively, you can set both devices to "cable select," which determines their master/slave setting based on the drive's position on the IDE cable. Note that Serial ATA drives don't have master and slave settings, but they're not in very wide circulation yet. We don't expect to see Serial ATA dominate the optical market until well into 2005.

The Lite-On 52X kicked ass for two reasons—52× CD burning and 32× CD-RW burning. You can fill an entire CD-RW in less than three minutes, easing the CD-R burden of landfills everywhere.

Understanding Error Correction

You might think that a multi-format DVD burner would actually surpass dedicated CD burners on all fronts, but you'd be mistaken. A good stand-alone CD burner will not only burn CDs faster than a multi-format DVD burner, it will also provide the improved digital audio extraction discussed above. The secret to reliable audio ripping lies in *error correction*. In other words, when an optical drive is reading a music CD, extracting its audio data bit by bit (for later conversion to MP3), it uses error-correction strategies to mitigate the problems incurred by scratches on the disc surface. Error correction is imperative because the CD Audio specification with which we're all familiar (known as "Red Book") was designed for fault-tolerant playback, not flawless audio extraction.

The pits and lands that represent digital information on an audio CD are microscopic, so even a teeny-tiny scratch on the disc surface will obliterate a few bits of data. The first (and most simple) error-correction scheme designed to deal with these scratches is called C1 correction. In this scheme, the audio data on the CD is surrounded by a matrix of confirmation bits, which are referenced by your optical drive when data is obscured. It works a lot like algebra: When you see the equation $9 + x = 10$, you know x has to represent the number 1, even though the middle digit is missing.

By the same token, if 9 is the available audio data, and 10 is the confirmation bit, your CD ripper's error-correction scheme knows the missing audio data is 1.

The second error-correction scheme, C2, is far more advanced. With C2, one block of audio information is interleaved with information from many other blocks. This way, a surface scratch will affect only small parts of many blocks, instead of a large part of one block. (For this very reason, you should never clean a CD by wiping in a circular motion; you're far more likely to scratch several contiguous blocks this way.)

Here's another way to look at C2 error correction: It's fairly easy to guess the evenly distributed missing letters in "M_XIMU_ PC MAG_ZIN_" but it's much more difficult to reach a definitive conclusion with a contiguous missing block such as "M____UM PC MAG-AZINE." (After all, the full spelling could be "MINI-MUM PC MAGAZINE," which is just plain wrong.) C2 error correction performs an analysis similar to C1 error correction, but across many interleaved frames instead of within just one.

The Panasonic MultiDrive II was a dual-format burner—from a certain perspective. It could burn both DVD-R discs and DVD-RAM media. DVD-RAM was stillborn in the consumer market because its media was so fragile it required a protective caddy.

Why Your Disc Media Matters

How a particular CD burner interacts with a particular type of disc media is called its *write strategy*. Believe it or not, optical drive manufacturers tailor the strength of their lasers to the dye formulations applied to different kinds of media. These write strategies are stored in firmware—rewritable, nonvolatile memory chips found in all optical burners.

When you pop in a disc, your optical drive reads information imprinted in a small area of the disc called the ATIP and adjusts itself accordingly. High-quality drive manufacturers such as Plextor and Lite-On constantly update their firmware to work with new, better, and different kinds of media, implementing new write strategies as disc media evolves. No-name manufacturers are more apt to let their

firmware updates slide, and as a result, consumers who own no-name optical drives suffer slower performance and even compatibility problems.

At *Maximum PC*, we think it's worth paying a premium for a quality drive and brand-name media. Those extra dollars today will pay big dividends when you burn CDs six months from now. Plus, the price difference is negligible after you factor in the cost of all the coasters created because of outdated firmware and unreliable media. You'll find that manufacturers such as Verbatim and Memorex consistently deliver more reliable media. They use higher-quality dyes that not only provide higher reflectivity, but last longer as well.

If both C1 and C2 error correction somehow fails during the ripping process, your optical drive will attempt to hide the glitch by essentially guessing at what an audio value should have been. It does this by referencing the information in nearby blocks. The process is called *interpolation*, and it results in signal degradation and distortion. Even worse, during the ripping process, your optical drive might just skip errant blocks altogether, resulting in clicks, pops, and dropouts.

Now, keep in mind, these two error-correction schemes were designed to produce great-sounding music during playback, not necessarily during audio extraction. But they do indeed come into play when you're ripping tracks from an audio CD. If audio extraction is important to you, your best defense against clicks, pops, and dropouts is to get an optical drive with good hardware error correction. This means you need a drive that's capable of reporting C2 error information to your PC.

Our favorite drives for digital audio extraction are made by Plextor. This manufacturer's drives are legendary for their digital audio extraction and reliability. They offer optimized circuits for "cleaner power" and come with black CD trays that supposedly absorb laser light, which purportedly reduces disc errors caused by stray bits of light.

Must... Burn... Faster

OK, let's assume you don't give jack-doodly about digital audio extraction. What you *really* care about is basic CD writing—how long it takes to burn a 650MB data disc. So, you mostly pay attention to optical drive performance ratings. That 52× burner sure does sound fast, doesn't it?

Well, 52× sounds much sexier than 40×, no doubt about it. But the actual real-world difference between the two performance ratings is negligible. At most, a 52× burner will save you about 45 seconds over a 40× drive, and you'll only realize that advantage when writing a full 700MB disc. Why? Because the top burning speed of the drive—that 52× performance rating—is only reached during the last 100MB or so of the burn, when the laser is writing to the outer extremities of a disc. This is where the track circumferences are longer and the data rate increases.

The Sony DRU-510A is the followup to the original dual-format DVD-burner from Sony. Its 24× CD-burning speed wasn't anything to sneeze at, either.

If you've already got a 32× drive or higher and are happy with its features, there's no compelling argument to upgrade to a drive with faster performance ratings. Of course, optical drive prices are so low these days that you might not have to pay much more simply to have 52× bragging rights. Just be aware that 32× burning is well within acceptable *Maximum PC* standards.

Performance ratings aside, you absolutely must own an optical drive that offers some kind of buffer-underrun protection. A *buffer underrun* occurs when your PC can't feed data to your CD burner fast enough—in other words, the drive's onboard memory chip (its buffer) is starved of data. When this happens, the CD-writing process seizes to a halt, and the end result is an unreadable disc (otherwise known as a "coaster"). It's a regrettable occurrence, but it's easy to avoid: Buffer-underrun protection pauses the CD burning process until the depleted buffer is replenished with more data, and then resumes burning chores right where it left off.

Different drive manufacturers have various names for the buffer-underrun protection technology, but each scheme works essentially the same way, and all are equally effective.

Make sure your optical drive supports either SafeBurn, JustLink, or BurnProof. Our guess is that your "slow" 32× CD-RW already supports one of these buffer-underrun schemes, because they've all been around for quite a while.

Five Tested Optical Drive Configurations

Modern PC motherboards have several IDE adapters, which makes the configuration of traditional IDE drives quite perplexing. Here are the five most common IDE configurations for optical and hard drives, along with the pros and cons for each one.

HD and Optical Drives Sharing the Primary Channel

You can consider this configuration when interior case space is limited, or when it's inconvenient to run more than one cable between the motherboard and your drives (a frequent problem in small formfactor systems). Obviously, your HD takes the master position, while your optical drive plays slave. Please note, however, that this config will present dilemmas: Because only one device can use the single IDE channel at a time, your hard drive will be unable to read or write data directly to the optical drive.

Single Optical on Secondary IDE Channel

This is probably the most common configuration. Your hard drive and optical drive each assume the master position of a single, independent channel, which means that they can transfer data simultaneously. The performance difference is especially apparent when you're copying large volumes of data from the optical drive to the hard drive.

Two Opticals on the Secondary Channel

This setup places your hard drive as the master on the primary channel, while two optical drives share the secondary IDE channel. This setup provides great optical drive-to-hard drive performance for either optical drive, but is practically useless for optical-to-optical copying, because both optical drives share the same channel.

One Optical Drive on Each Channel

This is an ideal setup, especially if your machine has limited IDE channels. If you make your fastest optical drive the master of the secondary channel and let your slower optical drive play slave on the primary channel, you'll get fast optical-to-optical copying, as well as great optical-to-HD transfer speeds for your faster optical drive (the one by itself on the secondary channel). You just need to remember which optical drive is residing where when you install, and everything will be cool.

Each Drive on Its Own Channel

In a perfect world—a world in which your PC has extra IDE channels cared for by an IDE controller connected directly to your motherboard's chipset—you'll isolate every hard drive and optical drive on its own IDE channel. In this setup, all drives can work simultaneously, preventing any confusing situations in which you might use one optical drive for CD copying, but the other for disk-to-disk copies because of IDE channel concerns.

Picking the Perfect DVD Burner

There are various reasons why your dream PC should be outfitted with a DVD burner: You might want back up gigantic amounts of data (each standard single-layer DVD data disc can hold 4.7GB, although there are new dual-layer burners coming out at the end of 2004 that can hold a whopping 8.5GB!). You might want to create your own home movie discs. You might want to create backup replicas of commercial DVD movie discs (assuming they haven't been copy-protected). And, of course, if you want to use your PC to play DVD movies, you'll need an optical drive with DVD playback functionality.

So, assuming that you will indeed be installing a DVD burner, you'll want to pay attention to both speed and features. You'll need to decide which format (or formats) you want your burner to support, and you'll have to factor in whether you'll also be buying a standalone CD burner for improved audio CD ripping.

Despite boasting an 8× rating, the TDK Indi burner was a tad slow in our benchmarks. However, it was the first drive we tested that could burn at 8× speeds to much cheaper 4× media.

First let's talk about the two current recordable DVD specs. The 4.7GB, write-once DVD-R format (pronounced "DVD dash R") was introduced by Pioneer Electronics in 2000, and has the distinction of being the first format to offer some compatibility with set-top DVD movie players and DVD-ROM drives. We use the phrase "some compatibility" because not all DVD readers could resolve the subtle differences between commercially "stamped" DVD movies and DVD-ROMs and the less-reflective DVD-R discs. Indeed, the first and second generations of DVD playback devices rarely play DVD media recorded on a PC.

Pioneer introduced rewritable DVD-RW discs two years after it launched DVD-R. Unfortunately, the thrill of reusing media was mitigated by DVD-RW's much poorer compatibility with set-top players and DVD-ROM drives.

Nonetheless, Pioneer's DVD-R/W technology worked fairly well as a solution for backing up large amounts of PC data. The *real* problem with the technology was licensing: Pioneer's competitors balked at paying licensing fees to Pioneer for every drive they produced and sold. So, a cadre of companies including Sony, Philips, and Hewlett-Packard got together and created

Kick-Ass Construction Tip

Serial ATA optical drives first became available in 2004. Optical drives don't need a fast Serial ATA connection for performance reasons (parallel ATA is fast enough), but when routing drive cables through a computer case, it's much easier to work with thin Serial ATA cables than unwieldy parallel ATA ribbon cables. We don't recommend shelling out any additional money for a Serial ATA optical drive—it won't net you any performance gain—but if your motherboard has Serial ATA ports aplenty, you won't regret getting a Serial ATA version of your optical drive.

their own format—DVD+RW (pronounced "DVD plus RW"). The first DVD+RW drives appeared in March 2001, accompanied by a huge marketing push that touted the technical advantages of the format, such as "lossless linking" and "defect management." But sadly, the 4.7GB DVD+RW discs had an even *lower* rate of compatibility with set-top players and DVD-ROM drives than did DVD-RW.

Getting to Know Your Optical Drive

Plug the right connectors into the right ports, or you'll have problems pulling data from your drive

This big momma is the IDE connector. It's the main way your optical drive transmits data to the rest of your PC. It only fits one way though, so make sure it's connected correctly!

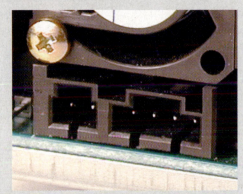

In the bad old days, you had to use either the analog audio output or the digital S/PDIF output to extract audio from your optical drive. Luckily, most drives can extract music from audio CDs as data and transfer it back to the PC over the IDE cable—a far superior technique, so these ports are rarely used anymore.

You must configure every drive on an IDE chain as either master, slave, or cable select using jumper blocks just like these. Remember, if you choose cable select, you need to set every device on the chain to cable select!

Without this little four-pin power connector, your optical drive won't have enough juice to rip track one. Always make sure your optical drives are plugged into the power supply if they misbehave.

The write-once DVD+R format was released in late 2001. Although DVD+R offered greater compatibility with other playback devices, many early adopters of recordable DVD drives were surprised to find that their drives weren't upgradeable to the new format, even though some manufacturers suggested they would be able to do just that. Thus the DVD+R/W consortium suffered much bad press.

Now, as I explained above, -R/W and +R/W are the two current standards you'll find in today's recordable DVD drives. But what of DVD-RAM, you ask? Well, DVD-RAM was indeed the first recordable, rewritable DVD standard introduced to consumers. DVD-RAM discs hold up to 4.7GB per side, and double-sided discs can hold up to 9.4GB. That's the good news—but it all goes downhill from there. Although the discs themselves resemble typical DVDs, they are encased in cartridges to protect their delicate surface. That's an awkward curiosity, but the real bad news is that DVD-RAM disks were never designed to be compatible with set-top DVD players, so you can't use a DVD-RAM drive to author your own home videos to play in the living room.

Although you can remove DVD-RAM discs from the cartridges, you would never want to because only a scant few DVD-ROM drives can read the discs (they have to support the MultiRead2 spec). What's more, even the tiniest scratch on a DVD-RAM disc will destroy your precious data.

The format lives on today as a storage/backup solution for businesses. In this regard, the cartridges are an effective deterrent against wear and tear. But for home use, there isn't much argument for DVD-RAM.

No matter what format you buy, make sure that your drive supports some sort of buffer underrun protection. There's nothing that sucks more than waiting fifteen minutes for a full DVD to finish burning, and then coasterizing the disk when your antivirus software fires up for its weekly scan at the two seconds-to-go mark of your DVD burn.

Different vendors call their buffer underrun prevention technology different things. Some especially cheap drives will support buffer underrun protection on the CD-burning portion of the drive, but not on the DVD-burning portion. Buyer beware!

Optical Drive Spec Speak

It's time to master the lingo you'll find on your optical drive's box

Write/rewrite/read speed

Optical drives capable of burning to CD-R and CD-RW always indicate speeds in the AxBxCx format (DVD burners don't use a standard format, you'll just have to read the box closely), in which A describes the maximum write speed to CD-R, B describes the maximum write speed to CD-RW, and C describes the drive's maximum data read speed. For CDs, a speed of 1× is 150KB/sec (for DVDs it's 1350KB/sec) so data rates higher than this are multiples of this base figure. Needless to say, higher numbers are better across the board. Note that the maximum speed a drive can actually hit before physics begins to upset the process is between 52× and 56×.

Data buffer size

Data buffers are crucial to preventing the buffer underruns that cause you to burn coasters instead of usable CDs. Buffers essentially ensure that a constant stream of information is available to your burner's laser. If the data buffer runs dry during the burning process, the laser stops recording, and the disc is ruined. When writing at 16× speed, a data-starved 2MB buffer can survive for just under a second before it drains completely. Buffer-under-run protection technology (such as Burn Proof) can eliminate the consequences of this problem.

Seek time

This is the amount of time it takes a drive to locate and deliver information. The lower the number, the faster the drive should be. But don't make this the determining factor in selecting a drive. Although most optical drives claim an access time of around 150 milliseconds, there really aren't any specific standards for measuring this type of performance.

DAE speed

Digital audio extraction (DAE) indicates how fast an optical drive can extract tracks from an audio CD using the 1× = 150KB/sec ratio. Again, higher numbers are better. DAE times tend to be slower than general read times because audio tracks on compact discs are recorded differently than files recorded on a hard disk.

So, What to Buy: DVD-RW or DVD+RW?

After a confusing VHS versus Betamax–style standards slugout, the solution to the "plus or dash?" question presented itself: The hardware industry introduced dual-format DVD burners that can burn both DVD-R/RW disks *and* DVD+R/RW disks.

Sony was the first to bite the bullet with the DRU-500A, a sparkling, silvery beauty that wrote to both DVD formats. As such, it was the first DVD burner to allow consumers to experiment with different types of media to figure out which format was most compatible with their particular playback devices. Today's dual-format DVD burners are ringing in at less than $300, and 16× versions should be available before the ink dries on this page.

Having access to a burner that can burn both DVD- and DVD+ disks is handy, but don't even think of sacrificing burn speed for ever-so-slightly greater compatibility. After all, most DVD players—set-top and DVD-ROM drives—will read either DVD+ or DVD-. Some players can play one format but not the other, but most players that fail to play one format won't be able to play the other, either.

On the other hand, speed is crucial. Spending money on a faster DVD burner pays off every single time you sit down to burn a CD or even rip audio from a CD. Because we value our time, we'd take a fast single-format burner over a slower dual-format burner any day.

What's the Deal with Dual-Layer DVDs?

Double-sided DVD-RAM discs can hold up to 9.4GB of data and video, but you have to literally flip the disc over to access the second half of all that information. Commercial DVDs can also hold up to 9.4GB of data and video, but disc-flipping is unnecessary. That's because these mass-stamped discs have two layers: When the end of one layer is reached, the reading laser adjusts its focus to zoom onto the second layer of the disc. That's why with some very long DVD movies, you'll notice a brief pause or stuttering as the laser adjusts itself to read the second layer. In *Titanic*, this happens just after Leonardo de Caprio is hauled away for stealing the necklace.

Home DVD burners can read dual-layer discs, but they can't create them. In 2003, drive manufacturers announced newer burners capable of burning dual-layer disks, but as we sent this book to press, we hadn't yet tested one in the *Maximum PC* Lab. Dual-layer discs will let you burn two layers of data—a whopping 8.5GB—to a single side of one disk. This means that one could burn even the longest of Hollywood movies to a single side of a disc. We fully expect a dual-format, dual-layer DVD burner to be in the Dream Machine 2004.

Now that the format issue is essentially moot, you need only pick among different manufacturers' products. Unless your budget has no wiggle room at all, we recommend getting a burner that records DVDs at a rate of at least 8×. And of course, you should also pay close attention to a DVD burner's CD-burning and audio-extraction speeds as well. Some cheaper 12× and 16× dual-format combo drives skimp on their CD-related duties, so that "faster" 16× DVD burner might actually end up being slower than an 8× burner when it comes to everyday tasks. To wit, the minimum audio-extraction and CD-burning speed you should settle for is 40×. Any slower, and you'll just spend too much time waiting on your drive.

Dream Machine 2004 Contenders

This dynamic twosome could very well handle the optical drive chores in our upcoming Dream Machine

Plextor 712A

This is hands down the best dual-format DVD burner we've ever tested. Not only does it burn DVDs at 8×, it also can rip CD audio at a whopping 40× and burn normal CDs at 40×. The are only two key features this baby lacks: 16× DVD burning and support for dual-layer burning. Hmmm… Maybe a more advanced DVD burner will eclipse the 712A before Dream Machine judgment day arrives.

PlexWriter Premium

When we first tested the 52× PlexWriter Premium, it demolished all our CD-burning speed records. It's undoubtedly the fastest CD burner we've ever tested, burning 700MB of data in under 90 seconds and ripping an 80-minute CD in under two minutes—and with crystal-clear results to boot. Do you really need a standalone CD burner? No. Does the Premium offer better CD-related features than a DVD combo burner? Undoubtedly. This would be a "price is no object" Dream Machine add-on, make no mistake.

Chapter Eight

Videocards

Your videocard contains the secret sauce that separates a Dream Machine from a mere PC

The GeForce 5900 Ultra was the pixel-pushing heart of the 2003 Dream Machine. With a whopping 256MB of onboard memory, uber-high core clock speeds, and super-fast DDR 2 memory, it couldn't be beat.

The single most important PC component for gamers—trumping even the almighty CPU—is the videocard. The videocard is responsible for drawing every polygon, texture, and particle effect in every game you play. A fast videocard will carry you into videogame nirvana, where everything runs at 60 frames per second and graphic detail is set to Maximum. A slow videocard will doom you to frame rate hell, where your games will look like a slideshow.

For the uninitiated, reading the specs of a typical videocard can be a terrifying experience. But you don't have to be cowed into picking up the most expensive card on the shelf and hoping for the best. We're going to explain everything you need to know about buying the right graphics accelerator for your PC, whether you're a gamer, a graphic artist, or an evil genius. And by the time we're done, you'll know everything we know. (At least until the next generation of videocards arrives.)

The Basics

At the heart of every videocard is a chip called a *graphics processing unit*, or *GPU*. Two major players design most of the GPUs suitable for gaming 3D accelerators: ATI and nVidia. Both companies sell their chips—which are significantly more complex than CPUs—to other companies, which then build the actual videocards you buy at Ye Olde Videocard Shoppe. These boards are generally labeled with either the ATI or nVidia logo. (ATI also sells its own ATI-branded boards.)

If somebody tells you that one company's GPU is superior, take that advice with a big fat grain of salt, because the technologies that each company deploy are leapfrogging each other constantly. It's such fierce competition that ATI and nVidia release new versions of existing chips at least every six months, and entirely new chip designs appear every year to 18 months. As a result of these grueling product cycles, the fastest

card can change three, four, or even more times a year.

There are three different types of videocard interfaces you need to know about these days, although your PC will probably only support two of them. The accelerated graphics port (AGP) was designed specifically for 3D accelerators, which require massive data transfers between the videocard and the rest of the system; however, AGP is on the way out in favor of the newer, faster PCI Express technology. PCI Express provides double the bandwidth of AGP 8×, and it also allows much faster connections from the videocard to the CPU than AGP does. This is especially important if you want to perform high-bandwidth tasks, like editing high-definition video.

The other interface is a standard PCI slot, just like your other cards use (soundcard, network adapter, and so on). Because the PCI bus is much slower than even the AGP bus, you'll want to avoid buying a PCI videocard unless it's absolutely necessary. Your motherboard, for instance, might have a videocard built into it with no AGP slot at all. If your mobo doesn't have an AGP slot, you should seriously consider upgrading to a better motherboard.

If you're looking for a good performer at a decent price, the Radeon 9600 XT should be available for less than $200. It only has four pipelines, but its 500MHz+ clock speeds counteract the crippled core.

Depending on your needs, you might not even need to pay for a rudimentary 3D accelerator. In fact, a card that specializes in 2D performance might be better for you, especially if you need highly specialized features—like quad-display support or hardware compressed video editing. Make sure you know what you're going to use your machine for before you shell out big bucks for a videocard with fancy features that you don't need and will never use.

Regular or Extra Strength?

There is a wide price range for videocards. As a general rule, all the cards from the same vendor (ATI or nVidia, for example) use the same basic chip, but performance-enhancing functions are disabled on the cheaper cards. The highest-end cards are priced between $400 and $500, and have more memory and higher clock speeds than anything else on the market. (We'll talk about what those specs mean in the next section.) These are the brawniest of the videocards, capable of drawing more polygons at higher resolutions and higher frame rates than anything else—even professional-level cards!

In the $300 range, the boards are generally based on the same basic chip as the hyper-expensive cards, but have less onboard memory or some features intentionally disabled to slow them down. Videocards priced in the $200 range generally have less memory and are even more crippled than the $300 cards, but still include the same basic functionality as the $500 cards. Generally cards under $200 are either one generation old, or they're so slow that they can't actually use the advanced features their chipsets support because of pathetic frame rates.

The nVidia-powered counterpart to the Radeon 9600 XT, the 5700 Ultra left a lot to be desired in the performance category. Don't skimp on your videocard if you intend to play games.

Ask the Videocard Doctor

Q: Frequently when I play games, my system crashes to the desktop. What's happening with my rig?

A: Your symptoms are almost always indicative of a problem with drivers, but it's not always a problem with your videocard's drivers. Equally important to your performance in games are your motherboard's chipset drivers, which control how the card accesses the AGP interface. You should download and install the latest chipset drivers from your motherboard manufacturer and the latest drivers from your videocard chipset's manufacturer, and then install them.

What you sacrifice by purchasing a $200 card versus a $500 card varies from manufacturer to manufacturer, but speed is virtually always the first victim. We'll explain why in the next section.

Clock Speeds

Just about every component in your PC has a "clock" speed, including your videocard. In fact, there are two different clocks on the videocard. One controls the speed of the GPU, while the other sets the speed of the memory. The GPU clock is called the *core clock*,

The Good, Bad, and Ugly of Videocard Design

Don't buy the wrong videocard! Here are four things you should look out for when you're purchasing a new videocard

This GeForce FX 5800 generated so much heat that it required a massive two-slot cooling rig. *Maximum PC* doesn't recommend any two-slot solution, unless it's by far the fastest videocard you can buy.

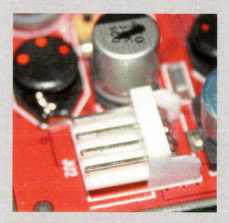

We've resigned ourselves to the fact that modern 3D accelerators require extra power from internal power supply connectors, but we prefer they use full-size Molex connectors, not the easily damaged mini-Molex connectors that floppy drives and internal USB hubs use.

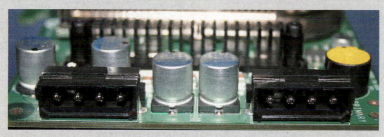

Whoopsie! nVidia's GeForce 6800 Ultra is such a power-hungry beast that it needs to draw power from two power leads, and the card requires a 480W power supply! If your machine doesn't have a beefy enough power supply, you'll need to purchase one before you can use a 6800 Ultra.

This old Matrox G220 is pretty useless as a 3D accelerator, but because it doesn't require a fan to keep cool, it's perfect for use in a computer you want to keep quiet. It's increasingly difficult to find fanless videocards, but you can usually find them in the value bin at computer shows.

Memory Bandwidth

The amount of data your card can move between the GPU and the videocard's onboard memory (called *memory bandwidth*) is the biggest bottleneck on the videocard. Three things control the memory bandwidth, the memory clock, the size of each "chunk" of data transferred every clock cycle, and the number of chunks of data transferred each cycle.

The GPU reads and writes small chunks of data to the memory almost a billion times per second. Right now, most videocards use *double data rate (DDR)* memory. DDR memory can transfer two chunks of data every clock cycle instead of just one. (The type of memory a board supports is configured at the chip level, and it's not user-configurable.) In addition to original DDR memory, which is in wide use now, there are also newer DDR-II and G-DDR3 memory specs. DDR-II is designed to run at much higher clock speeds than vanilla DDR and is used for main system memory and some videocards. G-DDR3 (or graphics DDR3) memory is designed specifically for videocards, and

and the other is called the *memory clock*. Increasing the core clock ups the number of calculations the GPU can do every second, while adjusting the memory clock changes the bandwidth, or amount of data the memory can transfer to the GPU every second. If everything else is equal, a card with faster core and memory clocks will be faster than a card with slower clocks.

Even though high-end videocards use the same basic core as cheap videocards, GPU cores that will run at the requisite super-high speeds are rare. Only a small percentage of GPUs can run at the 500MHz+ speeds required by a high-end videocard. Memory is much the same. System memory that's in most PCs runs somewhere between 100MHz and 200MHz—one MHz, or megahertz, is one million memory transfers per second. The memory on high-end videocards runs at 500MHz. Memory this fast doesn't come cheap.

The easiest way for a GPU manufacturer to slow down a videocard is to lower the core and memory clocks. The default clocks for each card are programmed on a BIOS chip that's soldered to the motherboard, but those clock speeds are easy to adjust by an adventuresome end user. Using an application like Powerstrip (www.entech.co.tw), it's easy to overclock most videocards' GPU and memory. However, overclocking isn't for everyone. It can create heat-related visual glitches in your games, jeopardize your machine's stability, or even permanently damage your videocard if it isn't properly cooled. You've been warned.

Long the choice of *Maximum PC*, the R300-based Radeon 9800 XT has been supplanted in every way by the R420-based Radeon X800 XT.

has just come into use on higher-end systems. Check out the "Committing Memory Types to Memory" sidebar for more info on the different memory types found on videocards. We don't expect to see any videocards equipped with anything other than one of the flavors of DDR memory going forward.

GPU manufacturers design their chips to accommodate specific-size chunks of data; this isn't user-configurable either. The size of the data chunks is also referred to as the width of the memory pipeline. A wider pipeline means more memory bandwidth for the GPU. Most high-end cards today transfer 256-bit chunks of data at a time, while budget boards transfer just 128-bit or 64-bit chunks. It's always best to get a card with the widest pipeline possible. You can always overclock your memory to make it faster, but you can't adjust the width of the memory pipeline on most cards. There are some hardware hacks that enable wider pipelines on some videocards, but this is the exception, not the norm. Because memory bandwidth is one of the main performance-limiting factors on today's videocards, we wouldn't consider a card without a 256-bit pipeline.

Memory Size

The fastest memory in the world won't do you any good if there's not enough of it to hold all the data your games and applications will toss at it. The two things that absorb the most memory on your videocard are the textures that give your game's surfaces a realistic look and the vertex information that shapes the in-game world. Even crappy-looking old games can fill a 64MB card's onboard RAM, and when that happens, the game will have to store its data in

Kick-Ass Construction Tip

Most motherboards' AGP slot has a retaining clip, which prevents the sometimes heavy AGP card from falling out of the slot when you move your PC. If you ever need to remove the AGP card from the slot, make absolutely certain that you unlatch the retaining clip (it's usually at the end of the AGP slot away from the back of the case) before you start tugging on the board.

Get to Know Your Ins and Outs

Here's the breakdown of all the different connectors you might encounter on a modern videocard

Nearly every videocard made in the last ten years includes a DB-15 port just like this one. It carries a standard analog signal from your PC to your monitor from your PC's videocard.

Flat-panel displays require a digital signal from your videocard for optimal image quality. The DVI connector is the modern standard for native output to digital flat panels. You can also use a small DVI-to-DB-15 adapter to connect a DVI port on a videocard to an analog monitor.

Many high-end videocards also offer TV-output in the form of an S-Video output. Note that the S-Video output is only good up to standard NTSC TV resolutions, not higher-res HDTV resolutions.

Videocards with integrated TV tuners—such as the All-in-Wonder series—usually have large coaxial connectors like this one. You can connect either an over-the-air antenna or a cable TV signal to this box.

your significantly slower system memory. As a result, your frame rates will tank.

Games use onboard memory to store both the textures and models that make up a 3D scene, and the work in progress as an image is rendered. Modern GPUs read and write to video memory just like a CPU does with system memory, but video memory is an order of magnitude faster than the memory the CPU has to work with. Where even the fastest system memory can only transfer 2GB/sec, video memory on a high-end card can transfer more than 20GB/sec of data.

We recommend a minimum of 128MB of RAM for optimum results in most games. People who primarily favor single-player games can probably get by with 64MB, but online multiplayer gamers need as much video memory as possible. Even 256MB isn't out of the question. Consider going with less than 64MB of RAM only if you don't intend to play any (recent) games at all.

GPU Architecture

Memory bandwidth is an important part of the videocard speed equation, but the inner workings of the GPU have a lot to do with it, too. To understand how GPU architecture affects performance, you need to understand a bit about how 3D accelerators work.

The fourth-generation GeForce 6800 Ultra is two times as fast as the fastest previous generation 3D accelerators in game benchmarks. Its only fault is the whopping 480W power supply requirement.

The image displayed on your monitor is made up of many tiny dots of color called *pixels*. The 3D accelerator has to draw each pixel and form them into a single frame, which is then displayed on the monitor. The entire screen must be redrawn at least 30 times a second to create the illusion of motion.

Drawing individual pixels isn't a simple process. To draw a 3D scene, the game first describes the shape of the world to the videocard, and then it draws wireframes out of polygons. At this point, the hardware T&L engine converts the polygon-based wireframes into individual pixels that make up the scene. After that, textures are applied to each pixel. For example, a wall might get a stone texture applied to it, whereas a human model will get a skin texture. More advanced techniques such as bump maps are then applied to the textures to make them look less flat and more real (a bump map would help the stone wall look rougher, more dimensional, and realistic). If the pixel being drawn is behind glass or fog, those effects are blended in, too. Finally, any lighting calculations are performed and applied to the texture. In today's games, each pixel can sometimes have twelve or more effects applied to it!

To speed up this process, modern 3D accelerators process more than one pixel at a time. High-end 3D cards sport 8 or even 16 pipelines capable of applying one texture or effect to a pixel per clock cycle. Because 3D accelerators perform the same functions over and over for millions of pixels each frame, adding extra pipelines makes them significantly faster. Whereas high-end cards can have up to 16 pipelines, budget boards usually just have 4 or 8, which severely affects performance.

Tech Talk: Committing Memory Types to Memory

Everything you really need to know about the different types of video RAM your card might be equipped with

DDR SD-RAM, short for Double Data Rate Synchronous Dynamic Random Access Memory, can transfer two chunks of data between the videocard memory and GPU every clock cycle, giving it effectively double the performance of standard SD-RAM. DDR memory doesn't run well beyond 500MHz, and has largely fallen out of use for videocards.

DDR 2 SD-RAM isn't twice as fast as DDR memory, it's just improved DDR. The improvements allow it to run at higher clock speeds, but it's usefulness as video-card memory is again limited by clock speed limitations.

The hottest memory for high-end videocards right now is G-DDR3 memory. DDR3 was designed specifically for graphics cards and can run much cooler at higher clock speeds than even DDR 2 RAM.

Programmable Shaders

An important feature of the last two generations of videocards are programmable *shader units*, which let developers create much better looking games. Before programmable shader cards were introduced, the fixed-function 3D pipeline was highly specialized. Although it worked much faster than a more general-purpose processor, such as a CPU, it was also extremely inflexible.

Programmable shader units make GPUs more CPU-like. In addition to the basic 3D tasks that fixed-function cards perform, shader units can execute shader programs that run complex algorithms on pixels, which are similar to regular computer programs. These shader programs can be thousands of instructions long and calculate everything from the lighting for an entire scene to the reflections in a simple mirror to the way light hitting skin scatters just beneath the surface.

Like everything else we've talked about, high-end videocards will have the most powerful, most flexible shader units. Don't fret, budget buyers! These days, even sub-$200 videocards can run rudimentary shader programs, even for demanding upcoming games (such as *Half-Life 2* and *Doom 3*) that make very heavy use of programmable shader technology.

Kick-Ass Construction Tip

Overclocking your videocard is easy and reasonably safe. You can use an app such as Powerstrip (www.entech-taiwan.com) to crank up the core and memory clock speeds for better performance in games. As always, overclocking your hardware voids your warranty, so if you choose to tweak your clocks, do so in small increments, or you risk permanent damage to your videocard.

TV Tuners, Inputs, and Outputs

Now you know what you need to look for to get the best performance for your 3D games, what other potentially important features do you need to keep an eye out for when you're purchasing a videocard? We love to see a videocard with dual-DVI outputs. It's super-easy to convert a DVI output to a standard analog output, but it's impossible to convert an analog signal into the pure digital signal that you really need for LCD flat-panel monitors.

We're also big fans of basic video-in/video-out (VIVO) functionality, which lets you connect normal S-Video consumer electronics devices to your PC, either to capture video on the PC, or to record video from the PC. Taking the power of VIVO one step further are videocards that also integrate fully featured TV tuners—such as the All-in-Wonder series of cards from ATI. All you need to convert your PC into an idiot box is one of these cards and a standard TV antenna.

If you're looking for a videocard to make the perfect living room PC in a small formfactor box, purchasing a videocard with an integrated TV tuner is a great way to save a slot.

Anyone building a home entertainment PC should take a close look at the All-in-Wonder series of cards. This one—based on the Radeon 9800 Pro—includes top-class 3D acceleration and a kick-ass TV tuner to boot!

Q: The fan on my videocard stopped working. Can I replace it?

A: Assuming the videocard heatsink isn't glued to your GPU, GPU coolers are generally fairly easy to replace. There are several sites that offer replacement aftermarket GPU coolers, including PC Toys (www.pctoys.com). You'll need to make certain that you purchase a cooler designed for your videocard. Different board vendors use different ways to secure heavy GPU coolers.

General Buying Guidelines

We can't give hard and fast rules for videocard purchases because the market changes so quickly, but we can give soft and slow suggestions to help you make a more informed decision.

For gamers who infrequently upgrade their videocard, it makes sense to spend the money for a high-end videocard. A $400 investment now gets you a card that's damn fast and will continue to perform acceptably for two or more years. As a general rule, high-end boards don't overclock terribly well, though. Overclockers can find great deals in the $150 price range, if they don't mind slightly more frequent upgrades. Non-gamers needn't shell out the big bucks for great 2D performance. There's no reason to pay big for all that 3D research and development if you don't play PC games, and even the cheapest 3D cards are extremely fast 2D accelerators.

The videocard is probably the one area that you should not follow the "buy generation-old hardware" philosophy, even if you're on a tight budget. Well, you can still buy generation-old hardware, but you need to keep your eyes open.

Videocard Specs

Master the lingo you'll find on your videocard's packaging

RAMDAC speed

Usually measured in megahertz (MHz) the RAMDAC converts the digital signal your videocard outputs into an analog signal that old-fashioned CRT monitors can understand. RAMDAC speed is directly tied to the maximum resolution your videocard supports; however, it's only important if you want to use an ultra-high resolution above 1600×1200. Even the cheapest cards RAMDAC supports can handle 1600×1200 and lower resolutions.

Core clock

The speed at which the GPU core runs. The faster the core clock speed, the better your card's performance will be.

Memory type

There are several different types of memory in use on videocards today. For more info on the different types of videocard memory available, turn to the "Committing Memory Types to Memory" sidebar earlier in this chapter.

Memory clock

The speed at which memory runs, usually measured in megahertz (MHz). Because your videocard's memory bandwidth limits the performance of most games, even small increases in memory speed can yield big improvements.

GPU core

The manufacturer and model number of the graphics processing unit that powers your videocard. Your GPU determines which advanced features your videocard supports.

Like many other things in computer hardware, videocard GPUs go through major revisions and minor revisions. The performance differences between a minor rev of a GPU and the previous version can be miniscule—as little as 10 percent. However, the difference between an old GPU design and a brand-new generation of GPUs can be huge.

If you're purchasing a new videocard and the top-of-the-line videocard uses an entirely new GPU, it may behoove you to save up for the new card. To wit: The new Radeon X800 XT is more than twice as fast as the previous speed champ, the Radeon 9800 XT.

We're starting to see some specialty cards designed for people who spend a lot of time manipulating large digital images. Creative Labs announced a new Graphics Blaster Picture Perfect board based on a 3dlabs workstation chip that claims to be significantly faster than a standard videocard when manipulating large image files. The board is available for about $150. We think the image manipulation sounds cool, but we're concerned that these cards won't be able to handle even minor 3D applications.

The GeForce 5950 Ultra suffered many of the flaws of nVidia's other third generation cards, but its high clock speeds partially made up for them. Still, it's a card to be avoided for future-looking gamers.

Big Videocards in Small Boxes: What You Must Know

So you want it all, eh? Big performance in a tiny box used to be a pipe dream, but with today's beefy small formfactor boxes, you can actually run a top-class videocard in a small formfactor case without a problem.

You need to keep a few things in mind, though. First, many small formfactor boxes' power supplies don't supply enough juice for a videocard above 500MHz. Space and heat are also major concerns. Many top-of-the-line video-cards—newer GeForce cards in particular—are too big to fit into any small formfactor case. Even if your card fits, is the airflow near the AGP slot strong enough to keep a hot card cool? It's easy enough to find this out, if you do your research.

Many small formfactor vendors keep a list of supported videocards on their websites. If your videocard appears on the list, you can rest assured that it will work in the listed small formfactor cases. If the card you want to buy doesn't appear on the supported list, you'll need to either consider a different case or get a new videocard. Trying to fit a large, power-hungry videocard into a small formfactor that can't handle it is like trying to fit a square peg into a round hole—it just won't work.

Dream Machine 2004 Contender

Only a worthy card can power the Dream Machine 2004

Radeon X800 XT Platinum Edition

The Radeon X800 XT Platinum Edition is truly an astounding performer. It's almost twice as fast as the previous-generation of hardware thanks to its 16 pipeline design. With a single slot design and power sipping circuitry, we could even put this board into a small formfactor box with nary a problem.

The only real question is whether the X800 XT Platinum Edition be replaced by an even faster PCI Express card! You'll just have to wait and see!

Chapter Nine

Soundcards

Picking the perfect soundcard is a journey fraught with peril. Let Maximum PC be your chaperone through the mire

The Dream Machine 2003's soundcard was the Audigy 2. Unlike other cards, it handles all your audio processing on its onboard DSP, instead of dumping extra work on the CPU.

Qualitative testing of soundcards is notoriously difficult. Our on-staff soundcard expert's favorite parable about sound tests says it better than we can: If you show an audience a movie with a busted speaker running in mono, and then you show them exactly the same movie running with state-of-the-art surround-sound speakers, viewers will say the second movie *looked* better.

In the early days of the PC, PC audio was the red-headed stepchild of the computer. In 1994, most computers shipped with CD-ROMs, but very few shipped with even rudimentary soundcards. Megahertz, pixels, and gigabytes are more important to most enthusiasts than getting quality sound from their PCs.

We've come a long way since the days of scratchy hissing sounds emanating from the PC speaker. Today's PCs sing in better-than-CD-quality surround sound, and produce advanced 3D audio that can fool you into believing that sounds are coming at you from every angle. And much of this spectacular sound quality can occur even if you're running a simple two-speaker rig or a pair of headphones.

We're getting ahead of ourselves, though. First let's discuss the job description of a soundcard installed in a modern PC. Most consumer-level cards really only do three basic things: output stereo sound, output 3D sound, and record sound from a variety of sources. Stereo sound is what you hear from the radio, a Walkman, or pretty much any home stereo system that was made before 1990. Most music and voice recordings are recorded in stereo, as are the beeps and whistles your PC makes.

3D sound, on the other hand, creates a vibrant sound field that attempts to provide audible cues about *where* the action is happening in a game or movie. You've surely heard these surround-sound effects in your local movie theater: You're watching the latest action flick and suddenly a helicopter sound erupts behind you, pans to your right, then it's booming in front of you, and finally pans to your left—all while the actual *visual* of the helicopter moves accordingly onscreen. Well, the same surround-sound effects

can be heard while you're playing games or DVD movies on your PC. You simply need the right soundcard hooked up to the right speaker set.

As for recording sounds on your computer, any soundcard can execute this basic function. However, if you intend to record and mix pro-level audio, you need to consider buying a relatively high-end soundcard. As is the case with many other PC components, choosing the right soundcard depends on what you want to use your PC for. Good pro-level recording cards usually aren't worth a damn for gaming, and even the best consumer-level soundcards might not be good enough for music mixing.

The M-Audio Revolution 7.1 supports 24-bi/96KHz recording and offers Audigy 2-level playback quality, but it comes with a frame rate penalty in games because of the work it offloads on the CPU.

Confusing, huh? Well, stay tuned because we're about to show you what you do and don't need in the perfect soundcard for your dream machine.

Where Did Stereo Go?

Standard stereo sound is old hat these days. Soundcards have been producing CD-quality stereo for more than 10 years. That said, there's a big difference between the stereo sound quality produced by old ISA bus-based soundcards and modern PCI- and PCI Express-based soundcards. Modern soundcards have much higher-quality digital-to-analog converters (otherwise known as *DACs*). Compared to an old-school DAC, a high-quality modern DAC will convert a greater portion of the digital signal your computer produces into the analog signal your speakers require. In a nutshell, the modern DAC will output a greater dynamic range, resulting in clearer, cleaner lows, mids, and highs.

And we're not just talking about higher-fidelity stereo sound. Almost any soundcard you'll find available for retail will be able to output multi-channel surround sound. So how many sound channels does one really need? Well, only you can answer the first question. Many people are quite happy to play games and music with simple stereo speakers—they find the left/right dimensionality to be quite sufficient, and don't want a bunch of speakers (and speaker wire) cluttering up their room. Other enthusiasts, meanwhile, want it all—support for the greatest number of discrete sound channels possible. At *Maximum PC*, we recommend that if you're a price-is-no-object gamer or DVD movie buff, you invest in a soundcard that can support the greatest number of separate channels, if for no other reason to be prepared for future upgrades. Right now, this means buying a soundcard that supports a "7.1" speaker rig.

Before you make any purchase, you need to make very certain that your soundcard and your speaker rig are compatible, especially if you're considering a rig with more than five satellites. Stereo, Quadraphonic, and 5.1 rigs use very well defined connection schemes, but beyond that, things get murky—very murky. For example, many Cambridge Soundworks PC speakers require a Creative Labs soundcard to connect the sixth and seventh channels.

Confused by sound specs like 7.1? Here's a quick cheat sheet:

- **Stereo:** Outputs two channels only. Stereo rigs may or may not include a subwoofer, but if they do, the sub doesn't have its own channel. An analog signal is passed from the PC to the speakers via a single headphone-type wire.

- **Quadraphonic:** Sometimes called 4.1, although this is technically incorrect. A quadraphonic rig sports four channels: front right, front left, rear right, and rear left. Quadraphonic speaker rigs usually include a subwoofer, but the subwoofer just plays the low-frequency sounds that the soundcard sends to each satellite. The sub does *not* have its own channel. In a quadraphonic rig, the analog signal moves from the soundcard to the speakers over two headphone-type cables.

- **5.1:** This config includes channels for five satellites plus a discrete, fully independent low-frequency channel to be played on a subwoofer. Signal passes from the PC to the speakers using either three analog headphone cables or a single digital connection (either a Toslink optical cable or a mono RCA cable). In the most common speaker arrangement, two satellites are positioned on either side of the monitor, on top of the monitor, and two behind the listener on either side.

Like the M-Audio Revolution, the Prodigy 7.1 uses Via's Envy24HT sound chip, and like the M-Audio card, the Prodigy also offloads sound processing to the CPU, which can affect your in-game frame rates.

- **6.1 and 7.1:** Like 5.1 rigs, these speaker sets include six or seven discrete satellite channels and a separate discrete subwoofer channel. 6.1 and 7.1 rigs usually connect via multiple analog cables instead of a single digital cable. There's an industry-standard spec for 5.1 analog connections, but there's no such spec for 6.1 and 7.1 rigs. Before you purchase a 6.1 or 7.1 speaker setup, make sure that your soundcard actually supports the exact type of speakers you plan to buy!

Ask the Soundcard Doctor

Q: My audio CDs won't play on my CD-RW or DVD-ROM drives! Both drives can see the audio files on my CDs, and I can even extract the files as WAV or MP3 files and they'll play fine through Winamp or any other app, but no CDs will play!

A: You need to enable Digital CD Playback. Right-click on your optical drive in My Computer and select Properties. Then go to the Hardware tab and double-click on your optical drive. Go to the Properties tab and check Enable Digital CD Audio For This CD-ROM Device. This option sends the audio stream through the same IDE cable that everything else uses and should give you better quality audio.

Soundcard Anatomy: Getting to Know Your Connectors

Don't know a line-in from an unamplified output? We'll help you discern the difference

This is the connector plate of an Audigy 2 ZS soundcard. From left to right, here are the assorted inputs and outputs and what you'll use them for.

1. Digital Output—Using an adapter that comes with your Audigy 2, you'll be able to pipe pure digital sound from your soundcard to a digital home theater rig or multimedia speaker rig.

2. Line In—An unamplified input, the line in is a perfect way to pipe tunes from your MP3 player, phonograph, or other source directly into the PC.

3. Microphone—The amplified microphone input lets you use a standard PC mic for voice recognition, voice-over-IP calling, or voice chat in games.

4. Front Speakers—Plug your 2.1 speaker rig in here. If your rig sports more than two satellites, you'll plug the two front channels in here.

5. Rear Speakers—In a 4.1 or higher rig, you'll plug your rear channel speakers into this output. If you're just using a 2.1 rig, this output will lie fallow.

6. Center/Subwoofer—This output provides discrete channels for the front center speaker and the sub-woofer. A discrete channel to the subwoofer lets you more accurately control the bass level your speakers output.

7. FireWire—Not all soundcards have FireWire ports, and it's definitely not a required feature, but a FireWire port is handy, especially if your mobo doesn't come with built-in FireWire.

The Audigy 2 ZS's breakout box includes MIDI inputs and outputs, which let you connect basic MIDI peripherals such as keyboards and guitars to your PC.

There are two basic ways to digitally connect audio components to your computer. This Toslink port lets you create a S/PDIF connection using fiber optics for a clean, clear signal.

The Toslink connector might use a nifty fiber optic cable, but those cables are damn expensive! If you demand a S/PDIF connection but don't want to pay for fiber, coaxial digital input and outputs work nearly as well, at a fraction of the cost.

If your soundcard includes support for one of the surround-sound modes, it will also support all the surround-sound specs beneath that mode as well. In other words, a 6.1 soundcard should also support 5.1 and quadraphonic rigs. Now, with all that said, if you intend to simply listen to music on your PC—and you have no interest in games or DVD movies—you should only invest in a high-quality, two-channel system. Yes, there are "solutions" for hearing multi-channel surround sound from regular old music (namely DVD-Audio and SACD), but we feel they're not ready for prime time.

On the other hand, if you plan on watching DVD movies or playing games, you can definitely benefit from a multi-channel soundcard and speaker rig. A good soundcard and a 5.1 speaker rig can create a sound field that will suck you right into the action, be it *Doom 3* or a rollicking war movie. And if you're *really* into multiplayer games—especially shooters where you need to remain aware of your surroundings at all times—a 5.1, 6.1, or 7.1 setup can actually improve your chances for victory.

There are actually two ways that your soundcard can improve your deathmatching skills. First, a good soundcard can assume some of the audio-processing chores that your PC's CPU would otherwise execute, and this in turn should improve your frame rates in 3D games. A higher frame rate is always an advantage in multiplayer games, because there's simply no way you can frag the baddies if your system is lagging behind the systems of everyone you're fighting.

Your soundcard can also help you get a quick drop on the enemy. Indeed, when you're running a system with multi-channel positional sound, you'll be able to tell whether the noise your enemy is making came from ahead, behind, to the left, or to the right. You'll gain an extra second or two of sensory warning, allowing you to turn and fight (or turn and flee) before your enemy is even ready to battle. By the same token, if you're the aggressor, hearing the location of a cowering enemy's footsteps will allow you to chase him down even quicker.

For less than $50, you can buy the Mad Dog Entertainer 7.1. It's not really 24-bit audio, but it sounds better than most budget solutions.

Which 3D Sound Specs Must Your Card Support?

At this point, you should have already decided whether you want to be running stereo sound or more complex multi-channel surround sound. Right? Good. Assuming that you're going the surround-sound route, it's important to become familiar with the different audio specs any soundcard might support, as there are a variety of different formats in which positional 3D sound can be mastered.

Ideally, your soundcard of choice should support all the specs you need—most of today's premium soundcards do. However, many sound solutions integrated into motherboards, and even some budget soundcards, lack support for either DirectSound3D for 3D in-game surround sound, or they lack the capability to decode the Dolby Digital 5.1 and DTS signals used for DVD movies into something playable with analog speakers.

The formats you'll want your card to support are really dependent on what you intend to use your soundcard for, so in this section we'll be listing and explaining the most important formats. Some are

exclusively real-time formats, used for games and other interactive media. Others are designed for pre-mastered audio—like DVD movies. Here's the rundown:

Ask the Soundcard Doctor

Q: Is it possible to run two soundcards simultaneously in Windows? Can I run a high-end card for digital recording and a SoundBlaster Audigy for gaming?

A: Unfortunately, Windows makes using two soundcards difficult. If your editing app won't let you specify the soundcard you want to use, the process is an annoyance. To change between the two cards, you have to open the Sounds and Audio Devices control panel and change the "preferred device" any time you need to switch cards. There's no easy way to assign all games to the Audigy and all audio-editing apps to the high-end card.

Pro-Level Soundcards: Do You Need One?

With the introduction of the Audigy 2 ZS line of soundcards, the difference between pro-level soundcards and consumer-level soundcards became nearly indistinguishable. The three main differences between consumer- and studio-level soundcards needs are frequency response, signal-to-noise ratio, latency, and I/O options. These features are really only necessary for high-end studio work, not shade-tree audio mixing. The Audigy 2 ZS boasts a nearly studio-quality signal-to-noise ratio, decent latency, and enough I/O ports for any casual mixer. Best of all is its price: At $200 with an internal breakout box or $250 for an external breakout box, the Audigy 2 ZS Platinum is half the price of a cheap pro-level card.

The Echo Audio Gina 24 provides 24-bit/96KHz audio recording with much lower distortion and a higher dynamic range than consumer-level cards.

There are also a couple of big negatives to using a pro-level card for day-to-day computing. First, very few pro-level cards have DirectX sound drivers. That means that you don't get any 3D positional sound in games, and some cards won't produce any sound in games at all. You will also experience playback problems with DVD movies and any other programs that use DirectX to output sound. The other big problem with professional cards is the price. Pro-level cards start at $500 for a basic four-channel card and go up from there. The more channels and features you add, the higher the price.

Don't get us wrong. An Audigy 2 ZS card is not a professional-level card, and it isn't suitable for high-quality work in a studio setting. It is, however, perfectly acceptable for people who want to dabble with mixing their garage band's tracks in their home or to try out basic sound editing and mixing.

Soundcard Spec Speak

Master the lingo you'll find on your soundcard's box

Audio DSP chipset

The digital signal processing (DSP) chip determines the basic features of a soundcard.

Hardware voices/hardware audio channels

This is the number of audio streams that a soundcard can play back simultaneously. A single audio stream can be anything from a sound effect, to a character vocalization in a game, to individual musical notes in a MIDI synthesizer. Most soundcards support 64 hardware voices, which means they can play up to 64 different sounds at one time.

3D audio formats

When attached to a set of PC speakers that includes at least four speaker boxes, most soundcards can render 3D or "positional" audio, which generates sounds from any direction around a listener.

ADC/DAC resolution and sampling frequency

Even if you create music on your PC and play it through digital speakers, all audio must at some point be converted to analog for you to hear it. All soundcards support signal conversion, both analog-to-digital (ADC) and digital-to-analog (DAC), but not all have the same resolution and sampling frequency, which are measured in bit rate and Hertz, respectively. The higher the resolution and sampling frequency your soundcard offers, the more precise your PC can be in audio reproduction. Accept nothing less than CD quality in these categories: 16-bit resolution, and a 44.1KHz sampling frequency.

- **DirectSound3D:** The premiere format for 3D positional sound in Windows-based software. Your soundcard must support DirectSound3D if you want to get the most from your multi-channel

The **Philips Aurilium** is another kick-ass external soundcard. Most people building their own PC will probably eschew external sound, but if you have a single-slot, small formfactor PC, an external soundcard like the Aurilium is the perfect way to make the jump to 24-bit audio.

speaker rig in games, but we've never heard of any *applications* that use DirectSound3D. Most consumer-level soundcards support DirectSound3D, but many pro-level cards designed for studio recording and mixing do not.

- **OpenAL:** A cross-platform competitor to DirectSound3D. OpenAL was created by an open standards body so that Linux and Mac users could get the same nifty positional sound effects that Windows users enjoy. Most consumer-level soundcards support OpenAL.

- **EAX:** This spec is Creative Labs's extension to DirectSound3D and OpenAL, and adds more realistic audio modeling to in-game sounds. By adding effects such as reverb, occlusion, and reflections, EAX helps the audio in 3D games sound more life-like. For example, gunshots in caverns will echo more than they would in carpeted hallways, and glass windows will block certain sound frequencies, but let other frequencies through seamlessly. Only Creative Labs soundcards support the latest 3.0 revision of EAX.

- **Dolby Digital 5.1:** This format, also known as AC-3, is the predominant spec for multi-channel audio in DVD movies. By default, Dolby Digital 5.1 provides five channels of surround sound and a low-frequency channel for subwoofer data. The new Dolby Digital Surround EX spec adds another channel, the rear center. Most soundcards can decode Dolby Digital 5.1 from DVD movies and output the sound to multi-channel analog speakers. Some soundcards can even encode real-time formats to Dolby Digital 5.1 for output to digital decoders.

The Good, Bad, and Ugly of Soundcard Design

Watch your step, or your new soundcard could degrade system performance!

The Audigy 2's onboard DSP can handle most of the audio processing needed for your day-to-day computing without bothering the CPU. This lets you enable advanced features—like 3D audio in games—without suffering a performance penalty.

We really dig the onboard FireWire header that the Audigy 2 ZS provides. Because it uses a standard interface, you can plug your front-panel connectors into it if your mobo lacks onboard FireWire.

The biggest flaw with today's budget soundcards is that they're lazy! Instead of using an onboard processor to handle your computer's audio, the Mad Dog—and many other cards—expect the CPU to pick up their slack!

- **DTS:** Like Dolby Digital, DTS is used primarily in prerecorded material such as DVD movies and music. DTS claims to offer better channel separation and sound quality than Dolby Digital, but it's difficult to compare the two. Regardless, you'll want your soundcard to support DTS decoding if you plan to use your PC to watch movies.

- **DVD-Audio:** The latest 3D positional sound spec, DVD-Audio is mainly targeted at music playback devices. The format provides true multi-channel music to audiophiles who've only listened to stereo for years, and some of the newer soundcards can decode this emerging audio format. The main hurdle to adoption on the PC front isn't technical. Rather, the slow adoption is because of draconian anti-piracy features that are required for DVD-Audio playback support. DVD-Audio playback is a nice bonus if your soundcard supports it, but we feel it's definitely not a must-have feature because record companies are producing so few DVD-Audio discs, and consumers just don't want to trade the ability to rip their music to MP3 for marginally higher sound quality.

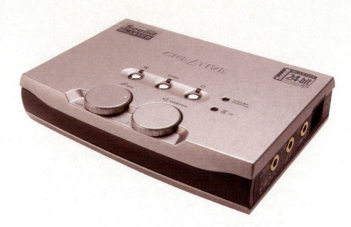

This high-speed USB 2.0-compliant Sound Blaster external soundcard is the perfect solution for any PC that doesn't have enough space in the case.

What's the Big Deal About 24-bit Audio?

Until the launch of the original Audigy, all PC audio was manipulated in a 16-bit, CD-quality format. The original Audigy offered limited 24-bit audio support, and it sounded head and shoulders above the Sound Blaster Live! and the majority of other consumer PC soundcards. The big difference is that 24-bit audio simply packs in more audio information than 16-bit audio.

If you imagine a sound file as a gentle curve, 16-bit is a jagged stair-step approximation of that curve. By increasing it to 24-bit, the jaggedness is reduced significantly and the sound is smoother and richer. Increasing the amount of information used to store data is always a good thing, right? Sometimes.

The real problem with higher resolution audio is the lack of source material. Because the majority of PC audio is 16-bit (audio CDs are 16-bit as well), the benefit of 24-bit isn't as noticeable for most uses. The reason 24-bit cards sound better than older 16-bit cards, even when playing older 16-bit MP3s or CDs, isn't the processor, but the digital-to-analog converter, also known as the DAC. Because 24-bit soundcards generally use higher quality digital audio converters and codecs, even 16-bit audio source material can sound improved when compared to playback on a garden variety 16-bit soundcard.

Creative Labs has been the sole retailer of consumer-level 24-bit audio cards for the last few years (as opposed to brawny-but-expensive professional audio soundcards), but the competition is heating up. AudioTrak and M-Audio are among several vendors that also offer affordable multi-channel 24-bit products. Heck, Intel's newer chipsets even support 24-bit audio on the onboard sound solution!

Make Sure You Have Enough Inputs and Outputs!

Pay attention here, kids, this is important. The only way to upgrade the number of inputs and outputs your card has is to replace the card. For that reason alone, you'll want to make absolutely certain that your soundcard has as many inputs and outputs as you'll ever need. What do you really need, what is unnecessary, and what ices our cake? We'll tell you what to look for!

All that most people will ever need are the basic outputs and a single input. For a gaming rig, that means a multi-analog connector for a good set of gaming speakers, a microphone input, and not much else. We don't get terribly excited about any kind of digital

S/PDIF outputs because most cards will only output a digitally encoded stereo signal over the digital output. (The one exception to this rule is the nForce2's integrated sound solution.) We also like to see internal headers on the soundcard for any headphone and mic jacks mounted on the front of the case. No one wants to crawl behind their PC to use a pair of headphones, do they?

If you plan on doing anything more complex than playing games and listening to music, you'll need more inputs. You can make high-quality rips of old vinyl albums using a cheap consumer soundcard, if you have enough inputs. The more expensive cards include loads of extra inputs and outputs on separate breakout boxes, which can be mounted either inside or outside your computer's case. Breakout boxes provide easy access to anyone who frequently needs to change their inputs and outputs. Your breakout box also provides access to MIDI ports, if you want to use a MIDI device such as a keyboard to manipulate music.

While consumer-level cards like the SoundBlaster Audigy 2 ZS don't have a low enough signal-to-noise ratio for real studio work, a consumer card is more than sufficient for you to do quick and dirty work for a demo CD or a for-fun project.

Is Onboard Audio Good Enough?

Just as soundcards have evolved, so has the audio on motherboards. Years ago, motherboard makers simply bought audio chips such as a Sound Blaster and embedded it onto their boards. Onboard audio offered few frills then, but today onboard audio provides an amazing amount of functionality, such as multi-channel, coax, and optical digital links for truly finicky audiophiles, and even the capability to sense whether a microphone is plugged into a speaker jack. The overwhelming majority of today's onboard audio, however, relies on the CPU and drivers to do most of the heavy lifting. We remain suspicious of onboard audio, not so much because of the hardware, but because on many motherboards we've reviewed, the audio hardware might be good, but the audio software is usually poorly implemented.

Among the most popular onboard vendors are Analog Devices and its SoundMAX, C-Media, Via's Envy, RealTek,

and nVidia. nVidia's nForce2 MCP-T audio solution is fairly unique in the audio space. Unlike the other onboard competitors, the nForce2 MCP-T is an audio "accelerator," and just like a graphic accelerator, it offloads processing of audio from the CPU. The nForce2 is also unique because it can encode audio in real time to Dolby Digital. Hook any of the other audio solutions to a home entertainment system's Dolby Digital decoder and all you will get is DVD audio or stereo for games. Because the nForce2 MCP-T uses technology developed for the Xbox, it can output games in multi-channel to a decoder.

Although onboard audio is clearly becoming increasingly sophisticated, we still prefer the feature orgy associated with add-in cards. The Audigy 2, for example, does 24-bit audio, offers a multitude of I/O options (including a FireWire port), and is unique in its capability to play DVD-Audio discs (in the event you happen to have one of those lying around).

Dream Machine 2004 Contender

We'd give better than even odds that this soundcard will show up as part of this year's Dream Machine!

Audigy 2 ZS Platinum Pro

The Audigy 2 ZS Platinum Pro has everything a consumer needs to make (or play) music. It supports 24-bit audio on all seven channels and brings the signal-to-noise ratio on the satellite channels to unheard of lows. The breakout box includes MIDI in/out, coaxial, and optical S/PDIF in/out, and even a pair of FireWire ports for easy connection to audio devices from DAT players to an iPod.

Chapter Ten

Monitors

Choosing the right monitor is especially important when you realize that you'll probably keep the display you choose for more than one upgrade cycle

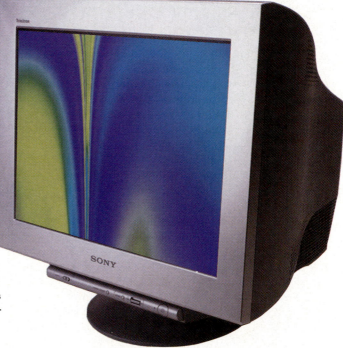

The venerable Sony F520 has been the *Maximum PC* CRT of choice for the last several years because of its insanely low pixel resolution and phenomenal brightness.

Many of the same rules for case shopping also apply to monitors. Like your case, you'll probably keep your new monitor for several years, upgrading the rest of your system around it. If you purchase a good monitor, it will serve you well for many years, giving you thousands of hours of eyestrain-free computing. On the other hand, if you buy a low-quality monitor, you'd best stock up on Advil at the same time, unless of course you have a high tolerance for splitting headaches.

Before you can select a monitor, you first need to decide whether you want the convenient size and weight of a flat-panel LCD or the pixel-perfect image quality of a high-end CRT. Both types of displays have pros and cons, so you'll need to fully consider each before you can make an informed decision. Lucky for you, there's an entire section on the next page that should answer all your questions about the choice between an LCD and a CRT. Go ahead and turn the page to read it. We'll still be here.

Now you should have a pretty good idea what type of display you want for your Dream Machine. There is one more thing you must keep in mind before you go monitor shopping. It's super-easy to do intermediate upgrades on *some* PC components. The monitor is not one of them. You can easily add 1GB of memory to most systems, but we've never seen a 17-inch monitor you can upgrade to a 21-incher without replacing it. Buy the biggest, best monitor you can afford when you're building your rig, even if it means you have to scrimp on another component. It's better to buy the big monitor now and suffer with a small hard drive for a few months than suffer for two years with a pathetic 17-inch monitor. Remember that compared to a basic 17-inch monitor, 19- and 21-inch displays offer 34 and 64 percent more screen real estate, respectively!

Ready to get started? Let's take a look at what makes a CRT Dream Machine-worthy.

Choosing Your CRT

There are two basic types of technologies used to display images on a CRT today: shadow mask and

aperture grille. The two wildly different technologies perform the same function—direct a series of electrons onto a thick piece of glass covered with phosphors. Shadow mask monitors use a perforated sheet of metal (a "mask" if you will), while aperture grille displays utilize a series of narrow, vertical metal strips (a grille, by any other name). Shadow masks and aperture grilles help confine a CRT's electron beam, ensuring that the beam triggers only the red, green, or blue phosphor dots that need to be illuminated (these dots are arranged in triangular arrangements called *triads*). After a phosphor dot is triggered, it glows with color, and, voilà, you have a screen image. This is a gross simplification, of course, and we wish we had enough space to explain how CRTs *actually* work. But for the purpose of this article, we'll simply explain the pluses and minuses of each approach.

We chose the Sharp LL-T2020B LCD display to add the multi- to the first multi-monitor display seen in one of our Dream Machines. Its 20.1-inch diagonal screen offers more screen real estate than the F520, and more visible colors than any LCD we'd tested before.

- **Shadow Mask:** Shadow mask CRTs tend to be less expensive than aperture grilles. They also lack the faint horizontal lines that span the screens of aperture grille CRTs. The shadow mask prevents poorly aimed electrons from hitting the wrong phosphors in each pixel triad, but the mask also blocks some electrons that should hit the display. This means that shadow mask CRTs usually offer dimmer, less vibrant screens than those with aperture grilles, and they typically don't match their cousins' fine detail reproduction.

- **Aperture Grille:** Every CRT monitor company's highest-quality, pro-level offering uses aperture grille display technology—does that give you an idea of which approach is superior? The aperture grille technology uses precisely placed vertical wires to ensure the electrons hit the correct pixels in each triad. The grille lets more electrons pass than a shadow mask does, which excites more phosphors, and thus creates more light. This fosters a brighter, more brilliant screen image for aperture grille CRTs. The best aperture grille CRTs also boast the finest pitches.

The one minor objection some people have to aperture grille monitors is that the shadow the guide wires, which hold the grille in place, cast shows up on your display. The upshot is that aperture grille displays have two very faint horizontal lines across the screen. They're only really obvious when you're looking at a light colored object onscreen, although most people don't notice them at all. The improved image quality for the other 99.99% of the screen is enough for us to overlook the nearly imperceptible lines.

Separating CRT Fact from Fiction

B uying a monitor based on its advertised specs is always a dubious proposition. Still, the specs you see on CRT cartons do mean something, so let's get to the bottom of them:

- **Size/viewing area:** You've probably already figured out that a "19-inch" monitor doesn't offer 19 diagonal inches of screen real estate—it actually comes in at around 18 inches. Then you have the problem of 21- and 22-inch monitors essentially falling into the same size category. Sony specs its best 21-inch CRT at 19.8 viewable inches, while NEC specs its primo-grande 22-inch CRT as having 20.0 viewable inches. NEC's viewable diagonal is just 0.2 inches longer than

The Samsung SyncMaster 172X's brushed-aluminum shell looks sophisticated, and its image quality matches more expensive monitors. We especially like that Samsung's included cable management gadgets.

Sony's, but box advertising would suggest a full inch of difference. Buyer beware.

Our overall advice is to pay closest attention to actual visible viewing area specs, and always purchase the largest, most brilliant CRT that your desk (and budget) can support. Actual visual quality is very important, yes, but we'd still rather have a 21-inch CRT with "good" visual quality over a 17-inch CRT with "category-leading" visual quality. There's just no replacement for screen real estate.

- **Dot and grille pitch:** A CRT's sharpness can be directly related to its dot or grille pitch. Technically, *dot pitch* applies to shadow mask displays, and *grille pitch* to aperture grille displays, but the terms are frequently interchanged. In simple terms, a monitor's pitch describes the distance between one of its phosphor dots and the next closest dot of exactly the same color. The CRT industry doesn't use a standard method to measure this distance, but in general,

Kick-Ass Construction Tip

Unless you enjoy splitting headaches and blurry vision, make sure you choose the correct position for your monitor. It should be away from any windows, between 18 and 24 inches from your face, and the top of the screen should be just below eye level.

regardless of which type of CRT you buy, you'll want to go with the lowest pitch spec possible. For example, Sony's 0.22mm grille pitch CRT is preferred over its 0.24mm pitch CRT. The smaller the pitch, the finer your screen pixels, and thus the sharper your overall image.

With some aperture grille monitors, you'll see a grille pitch spec that describes a range; for example, "0.25mm–0.27mm." This means that the pixels in the center of the display are sharper than the pixels on the display perimeter—they ramp from a 0.25mm pitch to a 0.27mm pitch. Is the gradation noticeable? We don't think so.

However, you should be concerned with shadow mask specs that describe a "horizontal dot pitch" of a super-low figure like 0.22mm. Shadow mask vendors have traditionally quoted diagonal pitch specs, despite the fact that diagonal pitch numbers never look as attractive on a spec sheet. To

If you're shopping for an LCD on a budget, you can't go wrong with the Planar PL170. Despite its budget price, this display manages to put on an impressive show.

CRT or LCD—What's the Diff, and Which One Is Best?

Very few power users consider the CRT monitor to be a glamour component. After all, cathode ray tube displays are based on essentially the same technology found in common TV sets—that old-school technology was invented way, way back in the 1920s. (The date of television's official birth is open to debate, but that's another story altogether.)

Yes, CRTs are completely "yestertech" compared with videocards and optical drives, which seem to be reinvented every six months, but they cannot—must not—be underestimated. Think about it: A good CRT can potentially be a system's most expensive component. Even more importantly, CRT life cycles are relatively long, so the monitor you buy this year will likely be the same one you're using in 2007. Think you'll be running the same CPU, hard drives, and videocard in 2007? For the sake of your games and applications, we certainly hope not. But you'll probably be running the same CRT, so you'd best take your CRT purchasing decision seriously.

CRTs offer a few key benefits over flat-panel LCDs: In most cases, they offer more square inches of screen real estate for every dollar spent. They can display quick-moving

video and 3D gaming content without any hint of streaking and trailing whatsoever. They can display every single color a videocard can produce—no excuses, ifs, ands, or buts. They can display multiple resolutions, from 640×480 to 1600×1200 and beyond. LCDs have only one "native" resolution, which can lead to problems.

But CRTs are not without their foibles: Compared to LCDs, they're heavy as all get-out, emit more heat, and consume much more desk space. Their screen image is more prone to geometric distortion. Bad CRTs can exhibit a fuzzy picture.

Maximum PC prefers CRTs over LCDs for gaming and image-editing work. A flat-panel LCD is easier to transport to LAN parties, but we are loath to give up native support for multiple game resolutions. As for image editing, very few LCDs can accurately display the full range of color and grayscale gradation in continuous-tone images. That said, if you're only going to be typing and web surfing on your new computer, we think that high-quality, high-resolution LCDs are hard to beat.

wit, a CRT's horizontal dot pitch equals 0.866 times its diagonal dot pitch. The upshot is that a 0.22mm horizontal dot pitch offers the same level of screen sharpness as a 0.25mm diagonal dot pitch.

- **Resolutions/refresh rates:** Every CRT displays a matrix of dots to describe whatever image is being presented onscreen. This matrix is called its *resolution*. The lowest standard resolution you'll ever see supported is 640×480 (480 lines of 640 individual dots), but the best consumer CRTs can display 2048×1536. The higher your resolution, the more visual information that can be displayed on your screen. Do you really need a 2048×1536 display? Probably not, unless you're doing high-end graphic design. Still, support for high resolutions indicates that the display will also be able to display lower resolutions at a great refresh rate.

A monitor's refresh rate is directly related to its resolution. In simple terms, the refresh rate describes how many times per second a CRT redraws its screen. But here's the catch: The higher the resolution setting, the more difficult it is to redraw the screen. Thus, as resolutions go up, refresh rates go down. This is true for all CRTs. The key is finding a CRT that can maintain high refresh rates (75Hz and above) at high resolutions.

We suggest that you avoid any CRT that can't maintain a refresh rate of at least 85Hz at 1600×1200. A refresh rate under 75Hz will give you eyestrain, and any rate above 85Hz could possibly lead to blurry content.

Ain't LCDs Good for Nothing?

Flat-panel LCDs are seemingly taking over the PC market. But are they really the best choice? First, let's consider their pluses: They're light and easy to carry, they don't take up much physical desk space, and they don't consume much electricity or emit much heat. Because LCD pixels are arranged on a fixed, physical grid, geometric distortion is an impossibility. They offer a sharp, crystal-clear image when running in their native resolution.

The successor to our all-time favorite monitor, the Sony GDM-C520 falls slightly short of the mark set by its predecessor. We'd recommend you pick up an older F520 instead of this bad boy.

Everything You Need to Know to Run Multiple Monitors

The best way to increase your screen real estate is to add a second monitor. Here's our quick-n'-dirty guide

There are really only three ways to increase the amount of space you have to work with when you're using your computer: You can either buy a bigger monitor, run your current monitor at an eye-bleedingly high resolution, or add another monitor to your existing display. Most modern videocards ship with support for multiple monitors out of the box, so most likely, all you'll need is a second monitor. Let's get started.

1. Connect Your Second Display

Whether it's a flat-panel or a CRT, your second display needs to be connected to your videocard or it just won't work. If you're connecting a second analog display to your machine, you'll probably need a DVI-to-DB-15 adapter—it should have been included with your videocard.

2. Enable the Secondary Display

Now that your second monitor is connected, you need to enable it in the videocard drivers. Right-click on an empty place on your Desktop and select Properties. Go to the Advanced tab. You should see something that looks like the image included here. Right-click on the secondary, grayed-out display and select Attached and click the Apply button.

3. Get the Settings Right

Now that your second monitor is turned on and displaying your desktop, you need to adjust some settings. First, you need to make the position of the monitors on the screen

A dual- or even tri-monitor rig is easy to set up, if you have the right hardware and a big enough desk.

match the way they're arranged on your desktop. Once you've done that, click Apply. You'll also need to adjust the refresh rate for your new monitor to minimize flicker. Right-click on the secondary display and select Properties. Go to the Monitor tab and increase the refresh rate to a more ergonomic setting.

4. Set the Primary Monitor

Your multimon setup is almost complete. The last thing you need to do is set the primary monitor. When you open applications and games, they'll initially open on the primary monitor, so we generally recommend setting your best CRT to be the primary display. Do this by right-clicking on the appropriate display and selecting Primary. Click Apply, and you're all done!

Sounds like one big pixel-loving party, right? Well, LCDs also have their problems: They still cost more than CRTs, screen sizes being equal. Some can't display fast-moving video and games without streaking (for example, a quick-moving hockey puck might look like a comet with a tail). They don't have the color accuracy of CRTs, so they're not ideal for image-editing work. When running in their non-native resolution, they must "interpolate" pixels, and this leads to horribly degraded visual quality.

OK, so let's say you're copacetic with the inherent weaknesses of LCDs. It's now time to deconstruct their specs.

- **Viewing area:** When an LCD is marketed as a 17-inch display, you really do get 17 diagonal inches of screen real estate. More is better—buy as much screen as you can possibly afford.

- **Pixel pitch:** A smaller pitch is better, and will provide a sharper screen image. And unlike CRTs, all LCD pixel pitches are measured in a consistent manner. So when comparing flat-panels, you

How-To: Calibrate Your Monitor Like a Professional

Every monitor needs to be calibrated. Follow our simple seven-step plan to get your display looking its best

Setting up a monitor isn't as simple as plugging it in and switching the power on. To get a pixel-perfect display, you need to take a few minutes to calibrate the onscreen image. Our favorite tool for monitor calibration is DisplayMate—it guides you through a number of different test patterns, explains what to look for at each pattern, and explains how to correct any problems in simple and easy-to-understand English. You can download a demo version of DisplayMate at www.maximumpc.com/images/dmw_demo.exe.

Here's a quick and dirty guide that will help you perform basic monitor calibration using the demo. If you want to get the best image quality possible, you should get the full version of DisplayMate from www.displaymate.com. Before you begin, you should let your monitor warm up for at least 30 minutes.

1. Set Your Refresh Rate

Set the refresh rate to the lowest rate that doesn't produce any sensation of flicker. For CRTs, this is usually 75Hz, but LCD displays usually only require a 60Hz setting. Setting it lower than this value is not recommended. Setting the refresh rate higher than necessary will needlessly degrade image sharpness as a result of video bandwidth effects because the pixel clock rate increases with the refresh rate.

2. Degauss the Screen

All CRT color monitors are affected by the earth's magnetic field, and need to be regularly degaussed. Monitors automatically do this when they are turned on. (That's the source of the buzzing sound.) Many CRT monitors have a front panel Degauss button or a menu option to do this manually. If you keep your monitor on all the time, you should hit the button periodically.

3. Initial Settings

Record all the initial monitor control values: If your control settings show digital values, record them so that you can restore the values in case you need to later on.

4. First Pass

The settings for most of the controls interact to varying degrees, so you might need to go through this setup procedure more than one time. For starters, familiarize yourself with all the available user controls for your monitor by

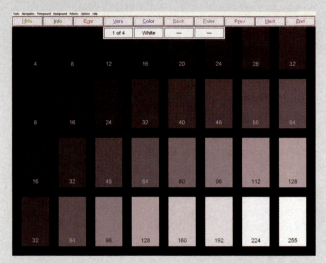

DisplayMate is designed specifically to help you calibrate your computer monitor, whether it's a CRT, LCD, or projector. This test pattern helps you determine the proper contrast and brightness for your display.

either reading the manual or systematically going through all the onscreen menus and controls. For a quick first pass, roughly set the Brightness, Contrast, Size, and Position controls so they look about right. We will set each one carefully in turn in the following steps.

5. Brightness Control

The Brightness control is poorly named because it has very little effect on the screen brightness. It's used to adjust the black level of the monitor so that the dark end of the grayscale is properly reproduced. If it's set too low, the darkest grays are reproduced as black instead of gray. If it's set too high, black is reproduced as dark gray. It is important that this never happen because losing the capability to produce black significantly reduces the contrast capability of the monitor.

Accurately setting the Brightness control is the single most important adjustment on any display. DisplayMate includes a number of test patterns that help you accurately set the black level of the monitor. The first screen in the DisplayMate demo, Brightness and Contrast Adjustment, includes dark gray, light gray, and peak white text that tell you onscreen how to make the initial adjustments of both the Brightness and Contrast controls.

Increase the Brightness control until the screen background just becomes visible. Then decrease it until the background just becomes black again. The second test pattern in the Demo, Extreme Gray-Scale, will guide you in making a more accurate setting for the Brightness control. Look at the top row of dark blocks, labeled 4 to 32. Adjust the Brightness control so that you can just see the 8 Block, but the 4 Block is indistinguishable from the black background.

6. Contrast Control

The Contrast control sets the monitor's peak brightness. It controls the white level, but has little effect on the black level. If the monitor appears too bright to you, use the Contrast control to lower the brightness to a more comfortable level. On the flip side, you have to be careful about turning up the Contrast control too high because the image can degrade substantially.

On the Demo test pattern Extreme Gray-Scale, increase the Contrast control until the 251 or 253 blocks are indistinguishable from the white background. Then back it off until they just reappear. On some monitors, you might reach the maximum limit for the control before this happens. Don't worry, that's perfectly fine.

If the image is now too bright for comfort, decrease the Contrast control until the screen looks good to you.

7. Framing the Image: Size and Position

Now that we've gotten the grayscale properly set up, the next step is to carefully frame the image on the screen. Adjust the Horizontal and Vertical Size and Position controls to fill the screen almost to the outer edge. Leave one or two millimeters of border space to allow for some variation and drift in the image. If the monitor is not performing well, it might be best to restrict the image size and stay away from the edges of the screen. Use the DisplayMate Screen Framing and Aspect Ratio test pattern for the adjustments. This pattern is also available in the DisplayMate Demo.

might as well opt for those with the smallest pitch specs.

- **Resolution:** Because your LCD will essentially be fixed at a single resolution, you better make sure it's the right resolution for your screen size. For 17- and 18-inch LCDs, we prefer 1280×1024. For larger monitors, 1600×1200 is preferred. Of course, this also means that you'll need to have a videocard capable of delivering playable frame rates at your display's native resolution. You should also be aware that some (usually older) games just don't support resolutions above 800×600, so you'll be forced to use interpolation for those games. (Note: LCDs don't have refresh rates, per se, so don't be worried if you see that an LCD is preset to run at a low 60Hz or 75Hz.)

- **Pixel response:** This spec, expressed in milliseconds (ms), refers to the speed at which the LCD's pixels can change color. Speed is important because if the pixels can't switch quickly enough, fast-moving screen content will exhibit streaking. Generally speaking, any LCD with a pixel response spec of 25ms or faster should be problem-free. That said, just because an LCD has a 25ms spec doesn't mean it can switch at 25ms, so buyer beware. It always pays to run some content on the LCD before purchasing. But for what it's worth, even today's lamest LCDs can switch pretty damn quickly, and we haven't seen streaking problems in a while, even in budget models.

Kick-Ass Construction Tip

If you're in an area with lots of ambient light that creates annoying glare, you can easily make a hood to protect your screen from a few pieces of Velcro and an old cardboard box—the one your monitor came in should work perfectly. To make the glare shield, cut the cardboard into a trapezoidal shape—it will look like a long rectangle with a triangle attached to both ends. The length of the short parallel segment should be equal to the width of your monitor, and the length of the long parallel segment should be equal to the width of the monitor plus two times the height of your monitor. Attach the Velcro to the long side of the trapezoid and the top and sides of your monitor, and your $5 glare shield is complete!

This screenshot is from one of our editor's tri-monitor rigs. The center screen runs at a beautiful 1600×1200, while the secondary and tertiary monitors on either side are set to 1280×1024. The benefit of this rig is that the editor never needs to Alt-Tab between applications.

- **Brightness:** This spec is expressed in candelas per square foot or meter (a *candela* is the total amount of a light emitted by a single, standard candle). For example, a particular Sharp LCD can display 200cd/m^2—200 candles per square meter. Higher brightness specs are preferred.

Display Dos and Don'ts

Now you know the technology, you've decided whether your Dream Machine should include a CRT, LCD, or maybe even both types of display, and you're ready to go shopping. What else do you need to know?

- **Don't** purchase your monitor online. You'll save some money on sales tax, but it will cost you a bundle on shipping, especially if you need the monitor in a hurry.

- **Do** buy your display with a liberal 30-day return policy. Odds are, if your monitor is going to fail in the first year, it will die less than a month after you bought it.

- **Do** test your monitor before it's too late to return it, especially if you bought an LCD. Look for dead pixels that don't work, and hot pixels that are stuck on.

- **Don't** buy a monitor without at least a three-year warranty. This is the one component you'll probably keep through multiple upgrades.

Monitor Spec Speak

It's time to master all the lingo you'll find on monitor boxes

Dot or Pixel Pitch

The distance between same-color pixels on a CRT or LCD. The smaller the pitch, the finer your screen's pixels will be, and the sharper your image will be.

Size

The diagonal size of the tube or LCD panel in your display. On LCDs, the size is usually the same as the viewable area, but CRTs usually have at least an extra inch or two of tube hidden behind the monitor's bezel.

Viewable Area

The a ctual maximum size of an image your monitor can display onscreen. This is the number to pay attention to on CRTs. Frequently different sizes of monitors will have practically the same viewable area.

Resolution

On CRTs, this will be the maximum resolution that the display supports. For LCDs, it actually represents the number of pixels on your screen. Because LCD displays only support one resolution natively, it's vital that your display have a high enough resolution for the work you're going to do.

Refresh rate

For CRTs, this is the number of times your display updates itself per second at the maximum resolution. Because LCDs don't need to update the entire screen multiple times a second, they're generally fixed at 60Hz.

Pixel Response

The speed, in milliseconds, at which an LCD's pixels can change color. A lower pixel response is better—we wouldn't use a flat-panel with a pixel response above 25ms.

Interface

Most CRTs use the standard analog DB-15 connector that PC monitors have used for the last 15 years. Higher quality LCD displays use the newer digital DVI as well as a standard analog connection. DVI is a must-have feature for modern flat-panels.

Dream Machine 2004 Contenders

Here's a close-up look at the odds-on favorite monitors for next year's Dream Machine

NEC FE2111

A likely contender for the Dream Machine 2004's CRT is the NEC FE2111. It clocks in a little cheaper than the comparably sized Sony GDM-C520, but offers truly astounding image quality, courtesy of its .24mm grille pitch aperture grille display.

Dell UltraSharp 2100FP

When we first laid eyes on the Dell UltraSharp 2001FP, we were flabbergasted. Its 20.1-inch viewable area and 1600×1200 native resolution display are housed within a handsome midnight-gray enclosure. Best of all, this LCD is great for all PC-related tasks, whether you're gaming, editing video, or just browsing the Web.

Chapter Eleven

Speakers

That little tinny speaker built into your case or mobo just won't do. We're going to show you how to pick out speakers so powerful you have to call them a rig!

The Logitech Z-680s provide 5.1 channels of kick-ass sound using an unconventional single-driver, phase-plug design for the satellites. The design may be unconventional, but the Z-680s produce bowel-loosening bass, crystal-clear highs, and everything in between!

Odds are, all the computer speakers you've ever seen are crap. Most computer manufacturers—there are a few exceptions—ship speakers so weak that you shouldn't even play bad music on them. So, what exactly makes a good set of PC speakers? Like everything else, it really depends on what you intend to use your PC for. Gamers have different requirements than movie aficionados, movie aficionados have different requirements than musicians, and musicians have different requirements than gamers.

Now there's no need to buy multiple sets of speakers if you want to listen to music and play games with your computer. That's just crazy talk. But if you're going to listen to music, you'd be much better off spending your speaker budget on a high-quality 2.1 than a more expensive pair of 5.1 speakers. Likewise, a gamer is much better off buying a good 5.1 speaker rig than spending money on an expensive set of reference speakers.

Before we go any further, you need to decide exactly what you're going to use your PC for. If you keep your ultimate goals in mind, it's fairly easy to choose the proper speakers for your Dream Machine. Before we get started, let's talk a bit about how speakers work.

How Speakers Work

Speakers produce sound by moving a rigid surface quickly enough to produce vibrations. But what tells the speaker how fast to vibrate? That's the soundcard's job. The PC speaker rig receives a signal from your computer's soundcard in either analog or digital format, which it then runs through a series of sound processors and amplifiers. Once the signal is through the amps, it goes directly to the speakers in analog format. That signal controls the movement of powerful electromagnets, which in turn moves the surface that produces the sound. Like different size chimes produce different tones, smaller speaker surfaces produce higher-pitched sounds, while larger speaker surfaces can produce lower-pitched sounds.

But of course, there's a trick. To produce the low-frequency bass sounds that give rocket explosions and Def Leppard tracks their punch, you need at least one very large speaker. This speaker, frequently called a *subwoofer*, only outputs the low-frequency sounds near the bottom of the human range of perception. Because the human ear can't precisely tell which direction low-frequency sounds come from, speaker manufacturers can create large, standalone subwoofer boxes that can be hidden out of sight and still produce loud, punchy bass.

With a whopping seven, the Creative Gigaworks S750 has more satellites than Mars! A 7.1 rig definitely isn't for everyone, but for a gamer, it can mean the difference between life and death.

If the subwoofer handles low-frequency sounds, what takes care of the high- and mid-range sounds? These are the purview of the satellite speakers. These much smaller speakers—called *satellites*—include one or two speakers that specialize in producing mid- to high-frequency sounds. Speaker rigs can have anywhere from two to seven of these satellites to create a sound field that envelops your room. Because the human ear can easily determine what direction sounds in this frequency range come from, it's important that the satellite speakers are put in the right places.

There are three basic satellite designs available today. The standard satellite speaker features a mid-range driver and a *tweeter*, which specializes in high-frequency sounds. Recently, Logitech has begun manufacturing speakers that use a single driver and forsake the tweeter. We've also seen flat speakers that vibrate a flat sheet of plastic instead of a more traditional cone shaped object. We were very impressed with Logitech's tweeterless design—high-frequency sounds don't suffer at all, and the overall sound quality is excellent. The flat-panel speakers are very cool to look at, but for the most part, they just can't produce enough sound to satisfy…well, anyone. They just don't get loud.

The only other confusing thing about purchasing a speaker rig is figuring out what interface to use: digital or analog. Most modern soundcards offer both analog and digital interfaces, but unlike almost every connection in your PC, in this instance the digital connection is inferior because of a limitation with most soundcards. Very few can actually convert the 3D positional DirectSound3D sound stream into a format your speakers can understand. Instead, they down-mix your 3D signal into a standard two-channel PCM audio stream. There are a few exceptions—check out Chapter 9, "Soundcards," for the full scoop on soundcards. Whenever possible, unless you're using a soundcard that can convert DirectSound3D streams to Dolby Digital 5.1, you should use the analog inputs for your speakers.

Do I Need Reference Speakers?

Unless you're an audio professional building a home studio, you definitely don't need or want reference-quality speakers. When confronted with the flat audio curve that a good set of reference speakers produces, most casual listeners complain that reference speakers sound less vibrant than normal speakers.

Like its big brother, the Logitech Z-2200 provides ass-kickin' bass, but the Z-2200s come in a convenient 2.1 package perfect for music listening!

Dig: The amplifier and electronics in a normal speaker rig designed for home listening plays some tricks with the signal it receives to tweak the sound for that particular speaker design. This gives music and dialog in movies a warmer feel that people have come to expect from their speakers. In contrast, reference speakers try to play the sound exactly as it is received from your soundcard, with no psychoacoustic tweaks or any other shenanigans. This is very important when you're listening to recordings destined for the CD mastering plant, but it's not cool for home users.

If you're not setting up a home recording studio, there's absolutely no reason to shell out extra cash for reference speakers.

Separating the Good from the Bad

Building a speaker that produces sound isn't really that difficult, but building one that produces sound good enough for a Dream Machine is no easy task. Whenever we get a new set of speakers we run a series of tests so torturous that some inferior speaker rigs didn't survive. We listen for five main criteria: distortion, high-end/low-end response, crossover, volume, and usability. To receive a Kick-Ass award, a

Ask the Speaker Doctor

Q: I have a 5.1 soundcard and speakers, but I only hear sounds from the rear channels when I'm watching a DVD. What's wrong with my setup?

A: This is actually a fairly common problem. Odds are, you've connected your speakers to your PC using the digital connection rather than the analog connection. Many PC soundcards—most notably all the Creative Labs cards—are unable to send an encoded 5.1 digital signal to speakers with a digital decoder. To get 5.1 positional sound in games, you'll need to use your speaker's analog inputs instead.

Good, Bad, and Ugly of Speaker Control Pod Design

Make sure your speaker's control pod is worthy! The control pod can mean the difference between a Dream Machine-worthy speaker rig and all the rest

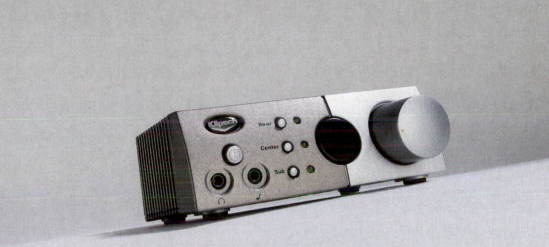

The latest control pod from Klipsch does it all right. It includes an easy-to-read display, a power button, a line input for your MP3 player, and a headphone jack complete with separate volume control.

The Z-680's control pod is another winner. It includes comprehensive audio tweaking controls, a great big volume knob, and a backlit display. Heck, it even includes a remote!

This control pod leaves a lot to be desired. The controls are unwieldy, you have to look at the pod to make even the most minor change, and it takes up a whole lot of desk space.

Ever so simple, the Z-2200's control pod is nothing more than a volume knob. Twist to the right, and the volume goes up. Turn it left and the volume goes down. It's that simple!

speaker rig must receive high marks in all five categories now. Let's talk a bit more about each test category.

Distortion

This one is an easy test. A good speaker rig should be able to reproduce sounds accurately and crisply at all volumes. We listen to reference-quality music in several genres for any missed notes or audio artifacts. Then we fire up subwoofer-killing games, such as *Quake 3 Arena* and *Unreal Tournament 2004* to see whether the sub can handle constant rocket explosions and shotgun blasts without distortion.

A good set of speakers will reproduce every sound perfectly at minimum volume, maximum volume, and everywhere in between. A bad speaker will distort sounds at high or low volumes.

High- and Low-End Response

Next up, we listen to an audio file we've hand crafted to cripple crappy speakers. It's a simple audio sweep that covers the entire range of human hearing, from just under 20Hz to a "only dogs can hear this" 22KHz. We run the sweep at low volume to see whether the speakers are capable of producing sounds throughout the entire range of human hearing. Then we crank the volume to maximum and run the sweep again.

Good speakers handle the sweep exactly the same way at both ends of the audio spectrum, without cutting out or flattening out sounds at the high or low ends. Bad speakers have actually caught fire during this test, so we recommend against trying it at home.

Crossover

To test the crossover, we once again fire up our 20Hz-to-22KHz sweep. This time we run the sweep at maximum volume and listen for the point at which the sub-woofer fades out and the satellites kick in. If the system has a tweeter, we also listen for the crossover from the mid-range driver to the tweeter. A good crossover will be virtually undetectable. A bad crossover will make an audible click or pop.

Volume

This category is really more important for gamers than musicians or movie aficionados. Deathmatches demand a certain level of volume that many lesser speaker rigs just can't match. To test speaker volume, we put on our ear protection, turn the volume to 11, and play the loudest music we can find, frequently Mötley Crüe. If the accountants next door to the *Maximum PC* lab don't complain before the lyrics to "Dr. Feelgood" start, the speakers are not worthy of a kick-ass rating.

Gamers beware—the Klipsch GMX D-5.1s only produce true 5.1 positional sound when attached to a digital output. But because most soundcards can't convert the 3D sound format used in games into Dolby Digital 5.1, GMX D-5.1 owners will miss out on 3D sound.

Usability

The final category encompasses a lot of ground. Usability includes not only the ergonomics of the speaker's control pod, it also covers the quality of the wire that the manufacturer provides between the satellites and the subwoofers, overall speaker construction, and the inclusion of any extra inputs (such as a line-in for your MP3 player) or outputs (a headphone jack is a big bonus) on the control pod. We also deduct points if the wires are physically attached to the satellites or use some sort of proprietary connector at one or both ends. Bonus points are given for digital inputs, but points are not subtracted if a speaker rig omits them, because the digital input is useless when used with most PCs.

Closing Thoughts

Really the only way to tell whether a speaker rig is good or not is to listen to it. That's why we recommend you purchase your speakers from a local store where you can listen to them before you buy—of course, the high cost of shipping heavy speakers has an impact, too.

Before you go to the store, it's probably a good idea to call ahead and ask if it's OK to do listening tests with your own tunes. We've not found any big chains that consistently let you listen to whatever music you want—it usually varies on a store-by-store basis. Make sure you write down the name of the person you spoke with—it always helps to be armed with a name.

Kick-Ass Construction Tip

Positioning your rear channel speakers can also be tricky, especially in a small room. We've found that you can sometimes get the best rear-channel sound by pointing the rear satellites away from the listening spot into the top rear corners of the room. The corners extend the distance from the listening point to the speaker, and also tend to diffuse the sound some, which makes the ambient noises the rear-channels are used for sound better.

Buying the Perfect Headphones

If you're not interested in a 500W speaker rig, or live someplace where you just can't get noisy, you need a set of headphones. We're not talking about those goofy yellow jobs that came with your Walkman in 1987, and we wouldn't even look at the craptacular 'phones they sell at Wal-Mart. If you're interested in a high-quality set of headphones, you have basically two options: closed-ear 'phones or in-ear 'phones like the Sony Earbuds. There are problems with both, so pay attention.

A good set of headphones can actually sound better than the best speaker system in the world, and at a fraction of the cost. These Shure E2C earbuds provide stunning audio fidelity for about $100.

Nothing sounds better than a good set of closed-ear headphones. A top-of-the-line set of Sennheiser headphones are significantly more expensive than Wal-Mart headphones (the HD580s cost between $150 and $200), but they create the type of rich, vibrant sound field that you'd have to spend thousands of dollars and customize a room to duplicate with speakers. A good set of closed-ear headphones doesn't travel well, though. They're definitely too big to fit in your carry-on!

If the HD580s are outside your budget, consider a quality pair of earbuds. The Shure E2C 'buds fit snugly in your ear to block any external noises and deliver thumping bass and crystalline highs. They're still expensive at $100, but are in a class by themselves. The Sony Fontopia in-ear 'phones sound just as good as the Shure's, but are not as comfortable, especially over long periods of time.

Speaker Spec Speak

It's time to master the lingo you'll find on your speaker's packaging

Frequency response

The sensitivity of the human ear ranges from 20Hz to 22KHz, and most speaker systems closely approximate that range. Good speaker rigs usually come with satellites that boast a frequency response of 150MHz to 250MHz—which is just fine, because the subwoofer takes care of everything below this range.

Maximum output

Audio volume is stated in decibels, a figure that's calculated with a complex formula that takes into account the distance between the audio source and where the decibel reading was recorded. That's why manufacturers often include a distance in the maximum output rating, as in "110dB (decibels) at 10 feet." For reference, dance clubs usually average between 100 and 110dB.

Power per channel

Often, a speaker system's power per channel (reported in watts) has more to do with marketing than audio quality. Producing bass frequencies always requires more power than producing treble frequencies, which is why subwoofers might draw 65W, whereas satellites might draw only 25W. All of these variables should tell you that the power-per-channel spec is a vague measure of speaker quality at best.

Input connectors

PC speakers are usually equipped with 1/8-inch "mini" plugs that connect directly into the jacks of your soundcard.

We recommend that you take several pieces of music with which you are extremely familiar. Make sure you mix the genres up a bit. Some speakers will do very well at bass-heavy hip hop songs, but completely choke on the strings common in classical music. We highly recommend firing up a little Blue Oyster Cult, as well. You definitely don't want any speakers that fail the "cowbell" test.

Don't be afraid to ask someone for help setting up an audio test. Most stores use complex signal splitters to power all the speakers on the shelf from one source. These setups make doing A/B testing super-easy, but sometimes it's difficult to find that one source.

If you're going to use the speakers primarily for gaming, pay extra attention to the bass reproduction of all the speakers you listen to. The booming explosions common to most of today's ultra-violent videogames will really stress your subwoofer. If the sub can't handle the stress at high volumes, you'll hear belching noises or just static instead of thumping bass.

Ask the Speaker Doctor

Q: My speakers produce a low hum all the time. What could be wrong with them?

A: Low humming is usually a sign of a grounding problem, not a faulty speaker. Assuming all your power strips and cords are intact—no one removed the round ground prong—then all you need to do to remedy the problem is plug the speakers into the same power strip that your PC is plugged into. This will close the ground loop, and remove the hum.

How-to Properly Place Your 5.1 Speaker Rig

Take note! Our four case studies can teach you how to create the perfect sound field in your living room

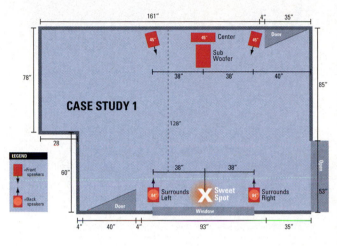

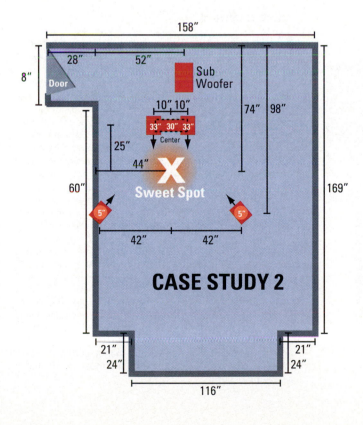

CASE STUDY 1

A Living Room from "L"

Over the next three pages we'll show you how to deal with quandaries ranging from bass traps to rooms with excessive echo. Of course, these are just guidelines. Unless you have rooms that are identical to these, you'll need to set up your speakers, then tweak their orientation.

The worst listening environments are perfectly square rooms and rectangular rooms where the long dimension is twice as long as the short dimension. Both spaces are highly prone to generating "room modes" or "standing waves," which emphasize certain frequencies, diminish others, and generally shoot to hell the smooth frequency response of a good set of speakers. The slightly L-shaped space of our first case study—a living room in a modern apartment—has characteristics of both these troublesome models. Even worse, our intended sweet spot abuts the rear wall, which meant we had limited options for positioning the rear speakers.

Front speaker and sub placement was relatively straightforward. The front speakers were placed far apart and angled slightly inward to provide a wide sound field at the sweet spot and still give some positional cues. We placed the subwoofer directly in front of the PC.

Placement of the rear surround speakers proved more challenging. Aiming the rear speakers directly inward at the listening position sounded too harsh, but turning them outward caused uneven reflected sound. When turned outward, away from the sweet spot, the rear left sounded great, because it reflected off a nearby wall. The rear right, however, aimed directly into another room, and long reverberations from the open space made for lopsided surround effects, especially when paired with the crisp-sounding, quick reflection from the left. The best-sounding solution was to mount the speakers high on the rear wall (roughly three feet above the sweet spot) and directly in line with the front left and front right speakers. Tilted toward the ground at a 45-degree angle, the rear speakers then delivered an enveloping surround-sound effect.

CASE STUDY 2

The DVD Desktop

We were pleasantly surprised by how easy it was to fine-tune this small listening space—a computer den with the floor space of a two-car garage. Our biggest problem wasn't even related to acoustics; it had more to do with cramming so many speakers into such a small area. The whole system—speakers and all—had to fit into an area about three feet wide.

Because the desktop space was so narrow, we had little opportunity to do anything more than position the front speakers on either side of the PC monitor and place the center speaker on the tabletop between the front edge of the monitor and the back edge of the keyboard. We turned up the center speaker volume by 2dB to account for its occlusion by the keyboard.

By using our subwoofer test, we found two spots underneath the desk that were good for the sub. To keep the subwoofer close to our PC and minimize wire-runs, we sacrificed leg room and put the subwoofer directly beneath the PC monitor.

Typically, the optimal placement of rear speakers is directly aside the listening position, aimed inward, and a little higher than head-level to soften the directionality of the surround speakers. By placing the rear left and rear right on the floor, we got close to this optimal placement, though our speakers ended up below head level. The result, however, was the most convincing surround sound of all our case studies.

Corner Pocket

Take the tight configuration of a desktop space, then cram it in the corner of a large room. Can you still have a great PC theater? In our third case study—a game testing room at our publishing company—a corner workstation configuration forced us to make an extra effort to get our rear speakers positioned and balanced. A low ceiling and asymmetric room shape only compounded our difficulties, as did the occupant of an adjoining workstation, who didn't like the idea of a rear speaker planted on his desk.

Limited corner desktop space forced us to make a trade-off between the spread of the front speakers and desktop workspace. If we set up the front left and right for a wider spread, then positioning the center-channel speaker to be in line with them would use up all of our available desktop space. So we compromised by going with an arrangement that gave us roughly four feet of separation between the front left and front right speakers, and about two square feet of desktop space in front of the center speaker.

Positioning the rear speakers was more of a challenge, because of the presence of another workstation. Eventually, we created tiny shelves for our speakers, placed them slightly higher than head-level, and aimed the speakers directly inward. The vast spread between the two rear surround speakers worked well to create a cocoon of sound—even though both speakers were angled directly at our listening position. For subwoofer placement, we determined that a spot three feet to the left of the corner offered the tightest sound (direct corner placement was too loud and boomy). To fine-tune the subwoofer, we boosted its volume by 6dB to compensate for the fact that our workstation's desktop occluded earshot to the subwoofer from the listening position.

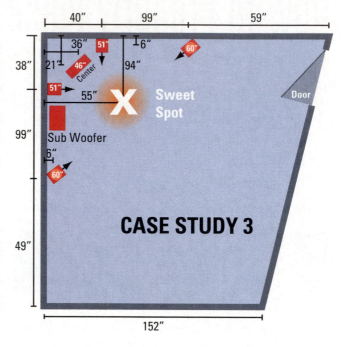

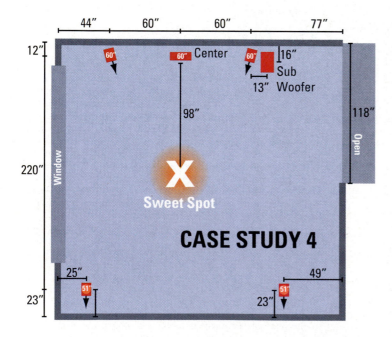

Space, the Final Frontier

A gorgeous picture window that takes up one full wall. Brand-new hardwood floors. A ceiling two floors high. All of these factors made us think we'd have a tough time getting our second living-room case study to do more than echo-echo-echo when we cranked up our PC theater rig. However, in the end, the wide-open space and reflective surfaces allowed us to set up our 5.1 speakers almost exactly to the recommended configuration, with great results.

With plenty of room to spread out, we placed the front left and front right speakers a whopping five feet from the center channel on either side. This gave us a wide sweet spot. We positioned our subwoofer in the front of the room, near the right speaker. The space to the right of the subwoofer—a small alcove with a low ceiling—turned out to be quite a nifty bass trap. It reinforced low frequencies and added a massive presence to the gunfire, explosions, and thumping techno soundtrack of *The Matrix*.

Aiming the rear speakers directly at the sweet spot created sound cues that were a bit too direct. We remedied this situation by turning the surrounds backward and adding a 3dB boost in volume. The final effect wasn't as clear and precise as the close-in desktop theater configuration of Case Study 1, but it did provide the most convincing sensation of depth.

Dream Machine 2004 Contender

Klipsch ProMedia 5.1 Ultra

The Klipsch ProMedia 5.1 Ultras are an audiophile's dream come true. The Klipsch's satellites provide crystal-clear mids and highs, and the sub's side-firing 8-inch woofers crank the bass like you wouldn't believe. You'd better warn the neighbors before you crank these puppies up.

Chapter Twelve

External Storage

Kiss your floppy drive goodbye! Every Dream Machine needs a way to take data on the road

The Mercury On-The-Go may be the ultimate pocket-sized hard drive. It sports dual FireWire and USB 2.0 interfaces and packs a no-excuses 60GB 7200rpm hard drive into its clear plastic shell.

Once upon a time, there was a universal removable storage format for PCs—the floppy disk. Sure, its slower-than-molasses speeds and pathetic 1.44MB size limit eventually made the floppy useless, but for more than a decade it was the ubiquitous form of external storage for PCs around the world. Now the floppy disk is all but gone, and in its place is a wide variety of storage options. From the increasingly popular USB flash drives to external hard drives of many sizes and shapes, consumers today are faced with an intimidating variety of external storage options.

The different types of external storage can be divided into two basic types: pocket-sized devices and standard external drives. Pocket-sized devices include tiny USB dongles, basic flash memory, pocket-sized hard drives, and even some hard drive-based MP3 players. There are also a wide variety of external devices that are not designed to be portable, but can be shared between computers. These fixed external devices include optical drives and hard drives. Let's look at each type of external storage a little more closely.

USB Flash Drives

The flash-based USB drive—also called a USB key—is the first really true floppy disk replacement. Unlike older disk-based solutions, USB keys work in nearly every computer made in the last five years, and they're big enough to use for everything from Word documents to video clips and MP3s.

Typically, USB keys contain between 16MB and 512MB of flash memory—although we have seen models that hold a whopping 2GB of data! Their pocket-sized plastic shell also holds a basic USB hard drive controller and a USB plug. To access the data on your USB key, plug it into a free USB port and access it like any other removable device in the Windows My Computer folder. Modern USB keys should work without drivers on any Windows Me, Windows 2000, or Windows XP machine.

In addition to simply carrying files, more advanced USB keys offer hardware-based encryption, automatic synchronization of certain folders, and compression utilities. These are great bonus features, but when we're purchasing a USB key, the main criteria we consider are capacity and construction.

You definitely want your USB key to have enough storage space to tote any files you might need. However, we don't recommend spending an untoward amount of money on a USB key. Because they're so small and you'll carry a USB key with you everywhere, they can be easily lost. The sweet spot lies squarely between 128MB models and 256MB models. Although sizes range up to 2GB, pricing beyond 512MB becomes prohibitive. A 512MB model usually costs about $130, but the 2GB model costs a whopping $600!

It's an oldie, but a goodie. The original Disk-on-Key delivered pocket-sized storage for the first time. This particular key holds 1GB of data.

We really consider a decent sized (read: greater than 128MB of storage) USB key to be a vital accessory for every PC enthusiast. When you need to take a file someplace—be it a 25KB Word document or a 250MB game demo—a USB key makes it easy to access your file on just about any computer built since 1996.

Flash Memory

Flash memory comes in a nearly a half dozen different formats, is extremely affordable, reasonably fast, and features massive capacities. The most common types of flash memory—Compact Flash, SD Cards, and Sony's Memory Stick—are commonly used for digital cameras and even some MP3 players. The problem with flash memory is compatibility. Very few computers actually include readers for even the most common types of flash memory. For that reason alone, we can't recommend flash memory for day-to-day use.

Another flash memory-esque option is the micro-sized hard drive. Several companies, including Toshiba and Hitachi, make itsy-bitsy hard drives that are small enough to fit into the slightly larger Type II Compact Flash slot. These drives hold more data than a flash-based CF card can, and cost much less than comparably sized flash cards. However, CF-sized hard drives are much slower than even the slowest flash-based memory, so avoid these tiny hard drives if speed is important to you.

Pocket-Size Hard Drives

Over the last year, we've seen dozens of these handy devices spring up. Your typical pocket-sized hard drive is nothing more complex than a notebook hard drive in a ruggedized enclosure with either a USB 2.0 or FireWire interface. Like USB flash drives, you simply plug these devices in and they work with no questions asked. The result is a drive that will comfortably fit in your pocket, holds more than 50GB of data, and isn't terribly expensive.

Depending on the notebook drive inside the enclosure, these external drives can be fast enough to use for just about any task, including performance-intensive tasks such as digital video editing and capture. If you're planning on using your pocket drive for demanding tasks, make absolutely certain that it's a 7200rpm hard drive. You don't want to settle for a puny 5400rpm drive, or even worse—a 4200rpm drive. Although a 5400rpm drive is probably acceptable for your grandmother, it's really too slow for anything more strenuous than file copying, and 4200rpm drives are insultingly slow. When you're purchasing a pocket-size hard drive, make sure you find out what kind of drive is inside the box.

The Western Digital 250GB Media Center is more than just a backup drive. It also includes an 8-in-1 media reader and a single USB port for easy USB flash drive access. Very nice!

Ask the External Storage Doctor

Q: Do I need to have a floppy drive?

A: Depending on the hardware in your rig, you might. If you want to install Windows on a hard drive that's plugged into a hard drive controller that the basic Windows installer doesn't support, you'll need a floppy drive so you can install the drivers to install Windows. Most standard IDE controllers are well supported, but you should have a floppy drive handy if you want to install Windows on a Serial ATA drive or a RAID array. Of course, after you're done with that, you can most certainly remove the floppy drive and stow it someplace where no one will see.

Want to know something really cool? Some of these drives are even bus-powered. This means that they only require the tiny amount of electricity that your FireWire or USB ports provide. This is really a damn good thing—after all, having a pocket-sized hard drive really does no good at all if you have to tote a giant power brick with you everywhere you go. Make sure that your external drive operates on bus power alone.

We touched on interfaces before, but it's worth mentioning again. Virtually every PC built in the last two years includes USB 2.0 ports, and many high-end machines also sport FireWire ports. Under no circumstances should you consider purchasing a USB 1.0 or 1.1 external drive. The original USB bus is just too damn slow to be useful for a hard drive. On the other hand, the original FireWire bus is more than sufficient for disk transfers. Which interface should you choose? Ideally, you'll be able to find a drive with both types of ports. If you can't, choose the universal High-Speed USB 2.0 over FireWire. Don't be fooled by the much slower Full-Speed USB devices whose communication is capped at 12Mbit/sec versus 480Mbits/sec for High-Speed devices.

The Many Faces of External Storage

Dozens of different types of external storage can confuse even an expert. Here's a quick primer on outside-the-box storage

A full-sized external hard drive, such as this 160GB Seagate backup drive, operates just like the internal hard drives inside your computer. You can use an external drive for easy-to-add storage, or even more performance intensive tasks such as video capture. You can buy external drives in sizes ranging from 60GB to 400GB!

Pocket-sized hard drives toe the line between USB flash drives and full-blown external drives. They usually use low-power notebook hard drives, and many will run using only the power provided by your FireWire or USB port. The bus-powered Pockey shown here holds 80GB, but pocket hard drives range between 10GB and 100GB.

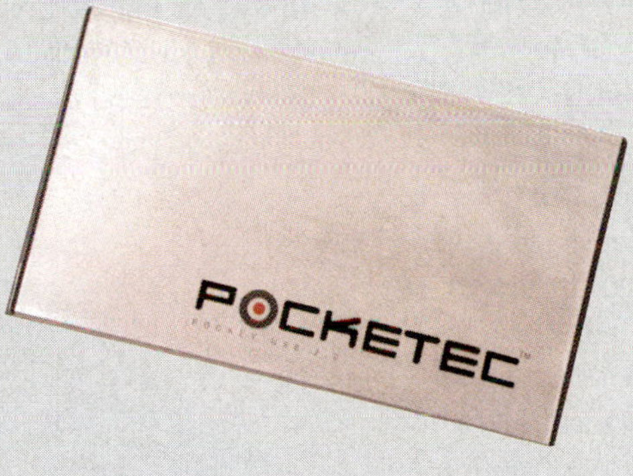

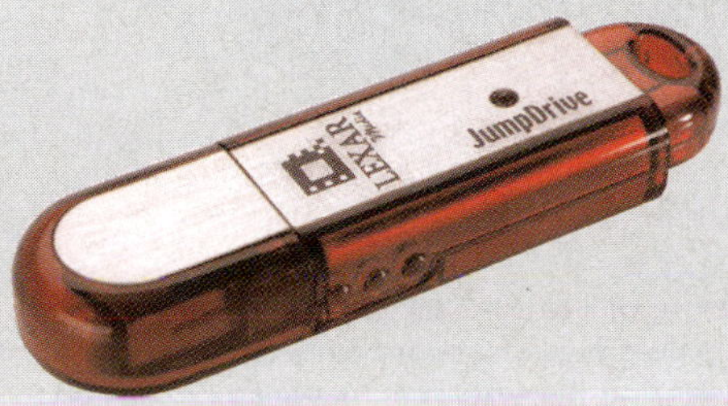

A good USB flash drive—like the JumpDrive pictured—is indispensable today. We use these small drives to store everything from frequently used benchmark files to crucial system drivers. Most USB flash drives range in size from 16MB to an unbelievable 2GB!

Portable MP3 players, like the iPod Mini shown here, can also double as portable storage. The Mini splits its 4GB of available storage between your tunes and the files you store on it, but other hard drive-based MP3 players can have drives up to 40GB!

Not everyone needs a pocket-sized hard drive, but if you frequently find yourself burning full DVDs to tote files to and fro, you might want to consider investing a few hundred dollars in a small drive.

Full-Size External Hard Drives

If you're building a brand-spanking new system, why would you need to consider external drives? That's easy: If you're building a small formfactor box, you might easily need the extra storage that external drives provide. Unlike pocket-sized hard drives, which are designed to be portable, external drives are not meant to be moved around frequently. Instead of ruggedized laptop hard drives, they usually use more fragile desktop drives.

The main benefits to using a desktop hard drive is that they're bigger and faster than laptop hard drives. With more platters, larger cache sizes, and no worries about power consumption, it's easy to see how a desktop drive can be faster than a notebook drive. Of course, this extra power comes with a price. All the external hard drives that use desktop drives require an external power supply—the USB and FireWire buses simply don't provide enough juice for those big drives.

Just like the pocket-sized drives, you'll want high-capacity, fast drives. The price difference between a 7200rpm drive and a comparable size 5400rpm drive is negligible, so don't short yourself.

You'll see a little more variety in interface options with full-size external drives than with pocket-sized drives. In addition to the standard USB 2.0 and FireWire options, you might also see SCSI and external Serial ATA. For most users, SCSI is simply overkill, especially when you consider the truly astounding price difference between external SCSI and external FireWire and USB 2.0 drives. We've only tested one external Serial ATA drive, and it left a lot to be desired. Instead of using a defined external Serial ATA spec, it used a pass-through port to connect to one of your internal Serial ATA ports. Because it just uses the flimsy and insecure internal Serial ATA connectors, we were afraid that the drive would be very easy to inadvertently disconnect. Not good. We've heard rumblings that there is a real external Serial ATA spec in development now, so we'd recommend avoiding external Serial ATA drives until that spec hits. Until then, you should stick with USB 2.0 and FireWire interfaces. Ideally, a full-size external drive should support both interfaces.

One other feature to look out for is included backup software. Many full-size external drives are labeled as "backup drives." In addition to the software, these drives usually include a one-touch backup button that automatically starts the backup process. You aren't limited to using these drives for backup purposes only. When you plug them in, they'll show up exactly like any other hard drive.

This 250GB Maxtor one-touch backup drive hides a 7200rpm hard disk just itching to protect your data. Backing up your files is as easy as installing the software, running a wizard, and pressing that big shiny button on the front bezel.

External Optical Drives

Admittedly a niche product, an external DVD burner is a viable alternative to an internal drive, especially if you want to share a single burner with a couple of computers or supplement burning capacity to your rig.

Use the same criteria to choose an external optical drive that you would to select an internal drive. Burn speeds, compatibility with different recordable DVD formats, and read speeds should all factor into your decision. You'll also want to purchase a drive that uses the interface your computer has the best support for. Unlike external hard drives, external optical drives rarely have both USB 2.0 and FireWire ports.

MP3 Players

This might sound a little kooky, but if you're looking for portable external storage, you should take a close look at MP3 players. Most newer MP3 players also let you use their onboard storage to tote your files. All of the modern iPods will let you use a portion of the integrated hard drive to store files, notes, contacts, or even an appointment list. Although the iPod isn't as versatile as a PDA—its lack of a touch screen makes it very difficult to input data—the iPod is smaller and has a longer battery life.

Kick-Ass Construction Tip

Before you assemble your new machine, take a few minutes and round up all the latest drivers and crucial Windows updates for your new computer, then save them to your USB key or external drive. We recommend saving your chipset drivers, videocard drivers, network card drivers, and the latest Service Pack for Windows.

Three Interfaces for External Drives

Here's a breakdown of the different connectors you may encounter on a modern drive

USB 2.0 provides a tiny trickle of power, and a whopping 480Mbits/sec data transfer rate. USB 2.0 is also suitable for hard drives and optical drives, and should be standard on any computer built after 2003.

The original FireWire spec is still entirely sufficient for most people's external storage needs. It delivers a peppy 400Mbits/sec connection between the host PC and external devices. FireWire connections are sometimes also called iLink or IEEE 1394.

The newest version of FireWire doubles the original spec's speed limit, cranking performance up to a whopping 800Mbit/sec. Although the original FireWire port is fairly common, FireWire-B is still a rarity.

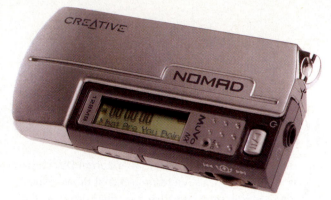

External Storage Spec Speak

It's time to master all the lingo you'll find on product packaging

Interface

There are too many interfaces used for external storage devices than we can keep track of, but the main ones you need to know about are USB 2.0 and FireWire. There are several different flavors of USB, but you want nothing less than the 480Mbits/sec that USB 2.0, also known as High-Speed USB, provides. Don't confuse High-Speed USB with Full-Speed USB, which only runs at 12Mbit/sec and isn't fast enough for use with external storage devices.

FireWire-A and FireWire-B both provide more than enough bandwidth for external drives, so both make fine interfaces. FireWire-A is fairly common, but FireWire-B is still rare, and most PCs simply don't have the ports. For that reason, make sure any FireWire-B device you buy also supports FireWire-A.

Capacity

This is pretty simple. It's the amount of storage an external device provides, and is measured either in megabytes (MB) or gigabytes (GB). Remember when you're comparing devices that 1GB equals 1000MB. The least storage we'd consider for a USB flash drive these days is 64MB, and the smallest external hard drive we'd fool with is 40GB. Memory and hard drive space is so plentiful and cheap these days that there's just no reason to settle for anything less.

Media Type

This is the actual type of medium that your external device stores data on. It could be standard flash memory for USB drives and some MP3 players, CF-formfactor or notebook-sized hard drives for MP3 players or pocket-sized hard drives, or standard-size hard drives for full-size external hard drives. If you're buying an external DVD burner, make sure you consider the formats it can burn to, just as you would for an internal drive.

The Creative Labs MuVo is a combination USB flash drive and MP3 player. Putting music (or data) on the drive is as simple as dragging and dropping files into a removable disk. This NX model holds 256MB of songs or data.

In addition to the well-known hard drive-based iPods, the Creative Labs MuVo is one of the best flash-based MP3 players we've tested. And if you remove it from its battery cradle, it works just like a USB hard drive! You see, it plays any MP3 files you store on it, but ignores any normal files you store on the drive. Best of all, the 256MB model only costs slightly more than a 256MB USB hard drive.

Ask the External Storage Doctor

Q: All the data on my USB key occasionally gets lost. Why does this happen?

A: Unless you have a defective key, your drive has write cache enabled, and you're unplugging the drive before your computer is done writing to it. Disabling write cache is easy, and it shouldn't affect performance for most people. Right-click on the drive in My Computer, go to Properties, then click on the Hardware tab. Double-click the drive in that window and make sure Optimize For Quick Removal is checked.

Dream Machine 2004 Contenders

Here's a close-up look at the odds-on favorite external storage devices for next year's Dream Machine

ComboGB

The Wiebetech ComboGB is everything you need in a pocket-sized hard drive. The enclosure provides full support for FireWire (A *and* B) and USB 2.0. Its svelte metal case hides a high-powered Hitachi Travelstar hard drive, in your choice of sizes up to 80GB.

Disk-on-Key

The folks at M-Systems sure know how to make a portable USB drive. This second generation Disk-on-Key gives you up to 1GB with a super-speedy USB 2.0 interface!

Chapter Thirteen

Buying Hardware Online Safely

Purchasing hardware on the Net is as safe as safe can be, if you know the potential pitfalls

Pricewatch.com can be your best friend when you're buying online. The search engine lists the inventories of thousands of computer parts stores that are dying to get your business, but beware! There are some unscrupulous vendors out there who will overcharge or outright steal from you.

After you've selected all the key components for your Dream Machine, it's time to open up your wallet and make your purchases. But where to buy? You have several options, ranging from traditional brick-and-mortar establishments such as CompUSA and (to a lesser extent) Best Buy, to local screwdriver shops, and to online search engines such as Pricewatch and Froogle. What's best for you? What should you do to protect yourself no matter where you end up making your purchases? Where can you get the best deals? Here's everything you need to know to buy the perfect parts for your Dream Machine, without worrying about getting screwed by unscrupulous online stores.

There are good and bad things about each type of store. For example, you can usually save a bunch of money by buying your components online, but you need to be careful about things like restocking fees, shipping charges, and other hidden costs. If you buy your parts from a local computer shop, along with your purchase, you'll be able to talk to an actual person who has probably built hundreds of PCs—definitely a big plus if this is the first computer you've built and you don't know anyone else who can help you. Somewhere in between those two extremes lie stores like CompUSA and Fry's Electronics. Their prices aren't as good as online wholesalers, and if you've read this book, odds are that you know more about computers than one of the employees at these stores, but the prices are very good, the stores are usually convenient, and they almost always have very liberal return policies for hardware.

To save the most money, we recommend *Maximum PC* readers buy expensive-yet-easily shipped components from online vendors—motherboards, CPUs, videocards, memory, and soundcards are the usual suspects—and the rest from local shops. You should try to avoid mail-ordering bulky or heavy items such as speakers and monitors, and to a lesser extent cases. The money you save by purchasing online will be frittered away on shipping surcharges. Sometimes it's difficult to find exactly the case you want at CompUSA or your local screwdriver shop, so you might be forced to order it online.

You especially don't want to buy displays online. If your monitor has a bad pixel or a glitch, it will cost you a ton to ship the defective monitor back to the online shop. On the other hand, returning a dud display to CompUSA is as easy as carrying it into the store and saying it just didn't look as good as you thought, if you keep your receipt.

Pricewatch can be a little scary, but if you pair it up with the consumer-protection power of ResellerRatings.com, you can protect yourself. Before you purchase anything from a vendor you've never used from Pricewatch, run its name through ResellerRatings and see how other people have fared.

What about those other components, such as optical drives, hard drives, fans, power supplies, and premium cables? We prefer to buy retail hard drives because they're usually packaged much better than the OEM products you buy online. On the other hand, it's safe to buy optical drives online. They're much sturdier than hard drives.

For the rest, it really depends on your area. In many parts of the country, it's difficult to find anything but the most generic parts in local shops. Whether you're looking for just the right illuminated fan or a power supply that's powerful enough to drive a GeForce 6800 Ultra, but still virtually silent, you might have to order specialty parts online. Heck, if you want to buy an expensive aluminum case or a high-end small formfactor box, you'll probably have to buy them online, as well.

No matter where you buy your hardware, make absolutely certain that you save all your receipts. You'll need them should something go wrong and you have to exchange dead hardware for something that actually works. Before you make a purchase, make sure you understand exactly how long you have to return it, and whether there are restocking fees.

Buying from brick-and-mortar is easy, but if you want to protect yourself when you're purchasing gear online, you should turn the page.

10 Steps, No Regrets

Essential buying tips for the ultra-defensive online shopper

1. Choose the product, make, and model

Let's say you want to buy speakers like, for instance, that nice Dolby Digital 11.1 Acme system you saw reviewed in *Maximum PC*. Make sure you note the specific model number of the system, and check out what other people who already bought the speaker systems are saying at www. epinions.com. You'll find a lot of extremely bitter ranting there, and an equal number of suspiciously exuberant product endorsements as well. Avoid basing your decision on any one review from any one source. Also consider other options available from a single company's cornucopia. For example, you probably don't need to spend $600 on Photoshop when Adobe's $150 Photoshop Elements has everything you need.

2. Check for the lowest prices

When hunting for bargains, the first place *Maximum PC* editors go is www. pricewatch.com. There you'll find the absolute lowest prices for PC components sold online. Just be aware that the cheapest offer isn't always the best bargain. The most inexpensive deals are usually for OEM or "white box" versions of popular retail products. These parts are intended to be sold to system vendors, not individuals, and often don't include a warranty. Nonetheless, searching Pricewatch.com will give you a good idea of the going street prices and how they compare to MSRPs.

3. Pick a retailer, any retailer

This part is easy. Do you want to buy your component online, where you might score a great deal, or would you rather go for instant gratification at Best Buy or maybe a mom-and-pop computer store down the road? Big chains might be able to give you a good price, but you might have to face clueless, semi-conscious employees. The little shops, meanwhile, will almost always be able to help you with advice. And, of course, if you do decide to buy at a brick-and-mortar retailer, you can execute returns in a matter of minutes. Whereas, if you decide to go online…

4. Check out the reseller ratings sites

Everyone knows about Amazon .com—it's probably one of the safest online retailers you'll ever do business with. But what about Happy PC Trader, Inc., or Gorgonzola Bros. Component Supply? You can learn details about their business practices at www. resellerratings.com. Just remember to look for *patterns*, and don't give too much credence to any single individual review. Do people consistently complain about getting screwed over, or are they positively aglow about friendly service? Let general trends be your guide.

5. Check for gotchas

Everyone knows to be wary of hidden fees when shopping online. Here's a checklist to consider before actually *buying* the contents of your shopping cart:

- Are the shipping prices reasonable?

- Does the retailer charge a restocking fee for returns? How much?

- What's the return policy? For example, can you send back an opened videocard box in the event the card's drivers won't cooperate with your system?

- If a product needs to be repaired, does the retailer pay for shipping one way, or both? If the product needs to be replaced, will you get a new one, or a refurbished product?

- Does the retailer have a customer service number? Dealing with email support can be a time-consuming nightmare. At many sites, a customer service number can be harder to spot than the Loch Ness Monster. (Amazon's service number, by the way, is 800-201-7575.)

If you can't glean the answers to all these questions from the vendor's website or over the phone, we say: Avoid at all costs (literally).

6. Check the company's privacy policy

Virtually every online retailer wants an email address in order to contact you if something isn't in stock, for example, or to offer you promotions or discounts in the future. But before you give up your addy, check the site's privacy policy. Does the site "share" (read: sell) your email address and/or purchasing information with others? Can you "opt out"—in other words, decline to have your email address and demographic information given away to others?

Never give *any* retailer your top-level email address, if you have more than one. (And you should have more than one.) If you give away a top-level email address, your mailbox might soon be littered with crap that increases logarithmically as your email address is sold from one marketer to another.

Pricewatch.com lets you find the very best prices for your Dream Machine's hardware.

7. Check for site security

Before you submit any personal or credit card information, look at the bottom of your browser window. Do you see a lock or unbroken key at the bottom of your browser, with the "https://" prefix in the address? This indicates the site is using a SSL (Secure Sockets Layer) connection, which encrypts data going to and from the retailer's servers.

We think the hysteria over using a credit card online is exaggerated. Frankly, we're far more fearful of gas station carbon receipts. But if a company can't be bothered to initiate a secure connection, well, it shouldn't be taking your money.

8. Use a credit card

Remember that many debit cards double as credit cards—what you really want to use is a pure credit card. Not only do credit cards tend to limit your liability in cases of fraud, they also sometimes offer extended warranty protections. Plus, if something goes awry and Chechen rebels begin siphoning your account for fun money, wouldn't you rather have them drawing from a large credit institution instead of your personal checking account?

American Express card holders can also take advantage of Private Payments, which generates a unique number every time you shop. All you have to do is visit AmEx's website first. Like Kleenex, these numbers are for one-time use only.

Visa cardholders have a free program called "Verified by Visa" that allows you to select a "personal message" and a password for your card. Each time you enter your credit card number while shopping with a participating retailer, you'll see a dialog box with your personal message, which confirms that the site is authentic, rather than just a dummy site created to gather passwords. After you acknowledge the "personal message" you signed up with, you enter your password for authentication.

Today's banks and credit institutions are in fierce competition, so check with yours. You might be surprised at the protections you already have as a member.

9. Print out receipt with order number

Sure, you're shopping at a virtual store, but you should treat it like a real one. No one would walk away from a real store without a receipt. Online prices can fluctuate, so having a printed receipt provides proof of the purchase price you agreed to.

10. If you get the shaft, let the bank fight it out

Check the contents of your package immediately after receiving it, preferably before FedEx even leaves. Photograph damage, if any. And if you never receive what you paid for, or it's been more than a month with no message or refund from the retailer, call your credit card company immediately and talk about your options. Your card company can act as an intermediary. Until you've paid your balance, it's their money on the line, and they can "charge back" the amount to the retailer if you can prove fraud.

At ResellerRatings.com you can separate the trustworthy hardware resellers from those that will take your money but forget your precious hardware.

Chapter Fourteen

Building Your PC

Picking the perfect components is the really difficult part. Putting it all together is an easy task for a Saturday afternoon

This empty Antec Sonata case will be the basis for our Dream Machine. Its design gives you easy access to most of your components, and it's one of the quietest cases we've ever used.

Now that you've selected the parts for your Dream Machine, it's time to assemble *your* Dream Machine. When your machine is completely built, you'll experience the singular satisfaction of making something from disparate parts. But we're skipping ahead—before you can get started assembling, you need to prepare.

The first thing you'll need is time. If this is the first computer you've built, plan to spend at least half a day putting the hardware together, and another few hours installing Windows, your drivers and all the Windows updates, and your software. This might seem like a long time, but it will take you a while to wrap your head around the way that the different components actually go together. If you plan to spend a Saturday putting your first PC together, you'll probably finish with enough time to enjoy a frosty beverage and a deathmatch before it's time to eat dinner.

OK, you've set aside enough time—now you need to prepare your workspace and collect the tools you'll need. You really don't need anything fancy, just a good Phillips screwdriver (a slightly magnetic one is even OK, as the magnet in a screwdriver really isn't powerful enough to bork a hard drive or mess up memory), a pair of needlenose pliers, an antistatic wristband, and a small bowl to hold any parts that are small and easy to lose. It's also handy to have a small flashlight and a sturdy pair of tweezers—especially if you have meaty hands. It's dark in the recesses of your case, and there are lots of small pieces you'll need to get in place.

As for your workplace, you really need a large flat surface in a well-lit area. If you have a big dining room table, that's perfect, but a linoleum or hardwood floor in a low-traffic area of the house is also acceptable. You really need a place where you won't be disturbed for a few hours. Note: Neither the thick shag carpet in your den nor the wool rug in your living room are smart places to build a PC. Moving on carpet creates component-killing static electricity, so avoid it!

Let's talk about static electricity a bit. You can follow a few simple rules to minimize the chance of static electricity damage.

- Always wear your antistatic wristband, and always keep it attached to the frame of your case.

- Before you work on your PC, first clip your anti-static wristband onto the case and then unplug the case from the wall.

- Never work on your PC while it's plugged into the wall. Even if the computer is off, a small amount of electricity moves from the power supply into the motherboard and other components.

- Never, ever touch the gold or silver contacts on a memory chip, or any kind of add-in card—we're talking about PCI, AGP, and PCI Express here. And never, ever, ever touch the pins on the bottom of the CPU!

Follow those four simple rules and you should be safe from static. Now, let's go over a few last dos and don'ts:

- **Do:** Check to make sure that you're putting the right part in the right place.

- **Do:** Consult your hardware's manuals if you have questions. New hardware comes out all the time, and we can't cover every variable in this book.

- **Don't:** Use excessive force. There are only a couple of components that require more than a feathery touch to install. We'll let you know what those are in the text.

- **Don't:** Get nervous if everything doesn't work the first time. Even experienced PC builders at *Maximum PC* occasionally have machines that refuse to boot or experience other random problems early on.

- **Do:** Read this entire chapter before you start building your machine. If you read the entire thing before you take out your screwdriver, you can avoid some common pitfalls.

- **Do:** Recruit a friend who knows more about computers to come help you out. Having an excellent book on-hand is great, but having another set of hands with first-hand experience building PCs is *very* helpful.

That about covers the preliminaries. Now, turn the page and let's get started.

Making a List and Checking It Twice

Before you begin, make sure you have all the parts and tools you'll need

There's nothing worse than finding yourself without a key part or tool right in the middle of a PC building project. The following is a complete inventory of everything you'll need to build your PC. We've included the components and tools we used, along with blank spaces to jot down your own inventory items. Use a pencil! You never know when your design vision will change.

Once you get everything filled out and your parts are within easy reach on your workbench, commence with step one and have at it!

Phillips screwdriver

Our Pick: Any $2 hardware store screwdriver will do

Your Pick:_____

Needlenose pliers and/or sturdy tweezers

Our Pick: Generic needlenose pliers and tweezers

Your Pick:_____

Disposable antistatic wristband

Our Pick: 3M 2209 disposable wristband

Your Pick:_____

A small flashlight

Our Pick: Sure-Fire Executive, but any light will do

Your Pick:_____

A clean, flat, well-lit area

Our Pick: Our workbench

Your Pick:_____

A small bowl (to hold loose screws and jumpers)

Our Pick: Any bowl will do

Your Pick:_____

Thermal paste

Our Pick: Arctic Silver

Your Pick:_____

PC case, with assorted screws and hardware

Our Pick: Antec Sonata

Your Pick:_____

Power supply

Our Pick: Antec True 380S

Your Pick:_____

Motherboard

Our Pick: MSI K8T Neo

Your Pick:_____

Memory

Our Pick: 1GB Corsair XMS 3200 DDR SDRAM

Your Pick:_____

CPU

Our Pick: Athlon 64 3700

Your Pick:_____

CPU heatsink

Our Pick: Thermaltake Venus 12

Your Pick:_____

Videocard

Our Pick: ATI Radeon X800 XT Platinum Edition

Your Pick:_____

Soundcard

Our Pick: SoundBlaster Audigy 2 ZS

Your Pick:_____

Hard drive(s)

Our Pick: 2× Western Digital Raptor 740

Your Pick:_____

Optical Drives

Our Pick: Plextor PX-708A and Plextor PlexWriter Premium

Your Pick:_____

Parallel and/or Serial ATA cables

Our Pick: Generic cables

Your Pick:_____

Floppy drive (if you're going to use RAID)

Our Pick: Floppy drive from old computer

Your Pick:_____

Monitor

Our Pick: NEC FE2111 and Dell UltraSharp 2001FP

Your Pick:_____

Keyboard

Our Pick: Microsoft Natural Keyboard Pro

Your Pick:_____

Mouse

Our Pick: Logitech MX 900

Your Pick:_____

Windows XP CD

Our Pick: Windows XP Professional

Your Pick:_____

Step 1: Prepare Your Case

Before you can begin installing components, you'll need to prep your case. Open it up—on an ATX case, you'll open the left side (if you're facing the front of the case), but on a BTX case, you'll open the right side. Make sure you remove any screws or other hardware holding the door shut. You shouldn't have to pry the door open.

Once the case is opened, look for a small bag or box filled with extra hardware for your case. The box will include motherboard mounting posts, screws of all shapes and sizes, PCI slot covers, and more. Remove the extra hardware from your case and grab your motherboard. Carefully lower it into your case and line up the mounting holes on the motherboard with the mounting holes on the motherboard tray below. Note which holes you'll be able to use. We generally recommend you use at least eight mounting points for any regular size ATX board.

Remove the mobo from the case and install the mobo mounts in the holes that correspond to your motherboard's mounting holes. If your case doesn't include a built-in power supply, you should install that now, too. Each case is a little different, but most power supplies slide into the case near the top of the case and mount using four screws.

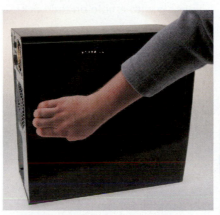

Before you can install any components, you need to prep your case. Unscrew any screws holding the door on and then remove the side panel.

Next, you need to line up the motherboard in the case, so that you'll know which motherboard risers you'll need to place and which you can leave out.

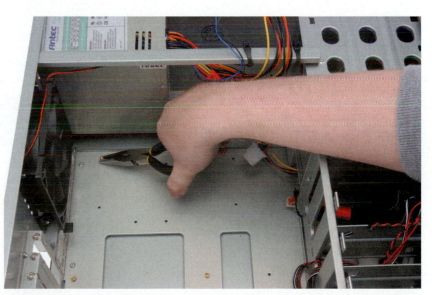

Now that you know which holes in the case line up with your motherboard, you can begin placing the risers. Screw them in by hand at first and then use a pair of pliers to tighten them to one-quarter turn beyond hand-tightening.

Step 2: Prepare the ATX Backplate Connector

Next, we need to get the ATX backplate cover ready so we can install it in the case. Take a look at the backplate your motherboard manufacturer provided. It's the shiny silver thing in the motherboard box with your IDE cables and driver disks. Look at the ATX connector block on the back of your mobo and compare it to your backplate. Make sure that every connector on the motherboard actually lines up with a hole on the backplate.

If your backplate is missing any holes, you might need to punch them out. Take a screwdriver—be careful, the metal edges can be very sharp—and gently poke metal plugs out of any holes that need it.

You shouldn't have to physically cut the holes out of your backplate.

Some people run their systems without a backplate installed. We generally discourage this. If you don't use the backplate, it can affect airflow in your system and create a nasty dust trap. If you have a backplate, you should use it.

Remove the backplate from your motherboard's box and line it up against the actual motherboard. This one lines up, for the most part...

...but you'll notice that the two FireWire ports aren't punched out of the ATX backplate. If this happens, take your screwdriver and punch out any metal covers that block any ports.

Step 3: Install Your Motherboard

Now you need to pop the backplate into your case. The lip should be on the inside of the case, with the PS2 ports near the top end of your case. Push it in from the inside, as shown here.

Now you can slide the mobo into the case. Lower it in at a 45° angle, making sure that the holes on the ATX backplate are lined up with the appropriate connectors on the motherboard. Pay close attention to any FireWire, Ethernet, USB,

and PS2 ports. There are small pieces of metal attached to the backplate that sometimes slide into the ports if you don't pay attention. In fact, they should go above the ports, as they help keep the ATX backplate from moving.

Once the motherboard is in the case, line up the holes on the mobo with the holes on the supports. Make absolutely certain that that none of the mobo supports are

hidden under the board. You need to adjust their position before you screw the mobo down or they'll short out your board and prevent it from working right. Once you've lined up all the holes, you can begin screwing them in. It's important that you don't overtighten the screws. Doing so could damage your mobo. Turn it no more than one-quarter turn beyond the point you first feel resistance.

Once the motherboard is in the case and everything's lined up right, screw down the motherboard, but not too tightly!

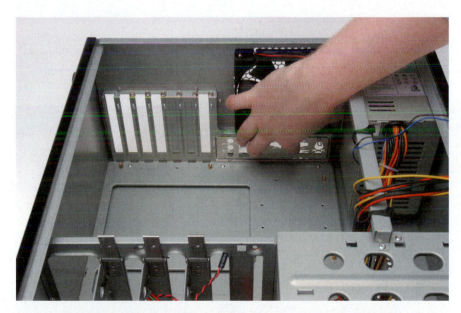

Your motherboard mounts are installed—now it's time to install the mobo. Before you do that, you need to install the ATX backplate. It's impossible to get it in after the motherboard is in place.

Step 4: Install System Memory

Installing RAM is frightening to PC neophytes because of the amount of force it requires. Never fear though—the DIMM modules require quite a bit of pushing to lock into the RAM slots.

First, line up the slot on your DIMM with the key on the RAM slot. Then line up the edges of the DIMM with the slots on either end of the slot and slide the DIMM into the slot. Next, apply pressure to both ends of the DIMM evenly. You will probably have to press down pretty hard to get the retaining clips on the slot to click into place.

If your motherboard supports dual-channel memory and you have a pair of matching DIMMs to use in it, you should consult your motherboard's manual to make sure that you put RAM in the proper slots. If you don't, they won't run in dual-channel mode.

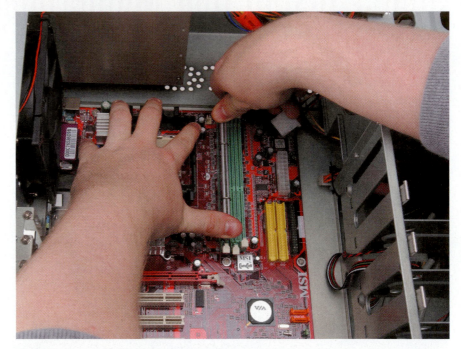

When you install your RAM, it's important that you get the slot lined up properly. Check your DIMM to make sure that it matches the key on the slot and then slide it down into the slot.

The memory chips are the only component on your system that really require force to install. Push down on the DIMMs firmly until you hear the retaining clips click into place.

Step 5: Install Your CPU

Now it's time to install your CPU. First you need to lift the locking clip on the side of the CPU socket until it's perpendicular to the motherboard. Don't worry if the socket makes an odd sound when you do this.

Next, remove it from its protective case—you should leave the CPU cooler in the packaging for the time being though—being extremely careful not to touch the pins on the bottom of the CPU. Flip the CPU over and line up the keyed pins on the bottom of the CPU with the keyed pins on the socket. Most CPUs and sockets also have a small triangle on one corner. You can use those triangles to line the CPU and socket up if you have problems telling which is which.

Before you can install your CPU, you need to lift the retaining lever. Raise it until it's perpendicular to the motherboard.

Now line up the CPU with the socket. It should only go in one way. Note that the corner with the triangle on the CPU lines up with the corner with the triangle on the socket.

Step 5 Continued

Lower the CPU into the socket. If it doesn't slide right in, DO NOT FORCE IT. The socket is called a Zero Insertion Force socket for a reason. Gently move the CPU until the pins on all four sides line up with the holes in the socket. When it does, the CPU will just fall into place. If it doesn't drop into place, lift the CPU and make sure that you have the keyed corners of the CPU and socket lined up right.

Once the CPU is nestled snugly in the socket, you need to lock it into place. Simply lower the locking lever back down until it snaps back into the socket.

Carefully lower the CPU into the socket. This should require absolutely no force at all. When you have it lined up properly, it will just drop into place.

Once the CPU's silicon substrate is flush with the socket, you should lock it into place by moving the locking lever back down.

Step 6: Apply Thermal Paste to the CPU (if necessary)

You definitely need some sort of heat-conductive substance to fill the gaps between the CPU and heatsink and ensure optimal heat transfer from the CPU to the cooler. Although we recommend using the thermal pad that comes on many CPU coolers these days—if yours has one, it will be a small gray or silver square on the bottom side of the cooler—you'll eventually need to use an aftermarket thermal paste on your system.

First, apply a small dab of thermal paste to the center of the CPU. Then use a flat, flexible edge (business cards or old credit cards work great) to spread a thin layer of paste across the CPU core. You want the thinnest possible layer that still covers the entire CPU, but if it's not perfect, don't sweat it. Do try to avoid creating clumps, though.

If you ever need to remove thermal paste or an old thermal pad, use a paper towel soaked in 90% or greater isopropyl alcohol. That takes most thermal grease right off.

If your CPU cooler doesn't come with a thermal pad, you might need to use thermal paste between your CPU and cooler. Remember, you can always add more, but it's tough to scrape it away.

Before you can mount the CPU cooler, you need to spread the thermal paste evenly over the CPU.

Step 7: Mount Your Heatsink on the CPU

Mounting the CPU cooler can be tricky, especially with older Athlon XP CPUs, which had exposed cores. Make sure that the cooler is lined up in the right direction before you set it down on your CPU. If you have to remove it after it's made contact with the thermal paste, you'll have to reapply the paste.

When you're lowering the CPU cooler on the CPU, make sure that the mounts for the cooler are lined up with the attachment point on the CPU socket. Once it's lined up, lower the cooler onto the CPU. Then slide the hooks on the CPU cooler over the pins on the socket. Once both sides are connected, flip the locking lever to its locked position.

Every CPU cooler works a little differently, and there are big differences between Intel and AMD socket designs. Make sure you read the directions provided with your CPU cooler before you try to mount it to your CPU.

Once the cooler is physically mounted to your CPU socket, you need to connect the power lead or leads. Many coolers use a small 3-pin monitored fan mount, but some use standard, unmonitored 4-pin Molex connectors (both are shown here). The 3-pin connections are preferable, as your motherboard will be able to monitor and control your CPU fan speed as the CPU temperature varies.

Once the thermal grease has been applied, you can lower your heatsink down onto the CPU. Make sure that the sides of the heatsink with the mounting clasps line up with the mounting points on the CPU's socket.

After you've gotten the mounting clasps on both sides of the CPU socket attached to the heatsink, you can move the lever to its locked position.

Step 7 Continued

This particular CPU cooler draws power from a standard four-pin Molex connector, but can still report its rotational speed back to your motherboard's BIOS using the monitored fan connectors.

Finally, we connect the CPU fan to one of the power supply's 4-pin Molex connectors.

Step 8: Install Your PCI Cards

Installing PCI cards is simple. All you need to do is remove one PCI slot cover on the case for each board you want to install. Then line up the card and gently push it into the slot, applying even force to both ends of the board.

If the card doesn't want to go in, check that you're actually pushing it into a PCI slot, and make sure that it's not getting held up by a wayward piece of metal on the case.

Once the card is all the way into the slot—you can tell because the gold contacts at the bottom of the card will not show—you should lock it into place by screwing it into the case.

You'll need to remove a slot cover for each AGP, PCI, or PCI Express board you want to install.

Line up your first card over the slot. Make sure that the card is level and then push the board into place, applying even pressure at both ends.

Once the card is firmly in the slot, screw it into the case. Make sure that the entire card is in the slot. Sometimes the portion near the front of the case can pop out!

Step 9: Install Your Videocard

Installing your AGP card is very much like installing a PCI card—you line up the card in the slot and then gently push it into place. There are a few additional concerns with a high-end 3D accelerator than with other, lesser cards, though.

Most modern videocards require more power than the AGP slot can deliver. They need to sip (or in some instances, guzzle) power directly from the power supply to function. Make sure you connect them to as many power leads as they need.

You'll also want to keep a close eye on cooling for your videocard. Because they run at such high temperatures, many cards—even the single slot Radeon cards—work best when the PCI slot directly below them is empty. After all, without the proper airflow, your card could melt down!

Installing an AGP card is much like installing a PCI card. Line it up with the slot, then apply even pressure to push it into place.

Once the card is in the slot, you should screw it into place. This helps prevent damage to the card and the rest of your machine.

Most modern videocards require more power than the motherboard's AGP slot can provide. Luckily, you can plug a 4-pin Molex connector into the board to provide the extra juice.

The AGP retention mechanism helps keep heavy AGP cards in their slots. Once the card is fully seated, you should be able to flip this up into place.

Step 10: Connect Your Switches and Lights

These little pins connect to the lights and buttons on the front of your case. You'll need to consult your motherboard's documentation to know which pin on the mobo is which, but the first one you should connect is the power.

After the power is connected, go in whatever order is easiest. Because the speaker connector was next on this mobo, we did it next.

The LED lights on the case front can be tricky. Because LEDs require a certain polarity, you need to make sure that the positive lead on the wire is connected to the positive pin on the mobo or your lights won't light. Usually the colored light (green in this case) is the positive.

The last two we will connect are the reset switch and the hard disk LED. It doesn't matter which way you plug in the reset switch, but the hard drive LED must be connected positive to positive.

Connecting the case's power switch, reset switch, and lights is another one of those steps for which we're going to have to recommend you consult your motherboard manual, but we can give you the gist, and in plain English that you won't find in any mobo manual.

These tiny little two-pin connectors carry the signals from your case's switches to your mobo, and from the mobo to the case's lights and speakers. That's right, without these little wires, not only will you not know when your hard drive is active, you won't even be able to power on the PC. Plugging in the power switch, reset switch, and speaker is as easy as lining them up with the right pins and gently sliding the connector down until it's flush with the mobo. There's no polarity involved, so you just need to make the wires close the connection.

The hard drive and power light, on the other hand, have to be mounted in the right direction or they won't work. Your motherboard's manual and your motherboard itself should tell you which of the pins designated for your power LED and hard drive activity LED are positive. As a general rule, the wire that is neither black nor white is the positive wire. For the hard drive activity LED pictured here, the positive is the red wire. For the power LED, the positive is the green wire. If you can't tell which is which, don't sweat it. You won't break anything by plugging the LEDs in backward; they just won't light up. So, if you turn on your PC for the first time and neither LED lights up, just reverse their polarity. Don't worry, you won't overcharge the flux capacitor and cause a reverse cascade overflow.

Step 11: Connecting Your Case's Front-Mounted USB, FireWire, and Audio

If your case has front-mounted FireWire or USB ports, or even a front-mounted headphone or microphone jack, you'll need to connect the ports to your motherboard's internal headers. First, find and identify the cables. As shown here, from top to bottom the cables are FireWire, USB, and then the audio connector. Although the FireWire and USB connectors look the same, they are not compatible. Plugging a FireWire cable into a USB port or vice versa can damage your mobo. If you look closely, these connectors should be properly labeled.

Once you've determined which cable is which, you need to figure out where the internal headers are on the motherboard. They should look like the yellow connectors in the second image, but if you can't find them, check your motherboard's manual for the exact location. To plug the headers into the cable, line up the connector with the header and then gently push it into the socket.

If your mobo doesn't have onboard FireWire, you can use the FireWire header labeled SB1394 on an Audigy 2 ZS card without any problems at all.

Before you do anything else, you need to identify your case's front USB, FireWire, and audio cables. Your case may or may not have them, but you need to connect them to your mobo to enable the front-mounted USB, FireWire, and audio ports. The onboard USB and FireWire share a physically identical connector, so one should be labeled FireWire or 1394. The top connector shown here is the audio header connector.

Next you need to find your onboard USB headers and plug the USB wire from the case into them. Do NOT plug the FireWire cable into the USB header—that will only end in tears. If you aren't certain which header is which, consult your mobo manual.

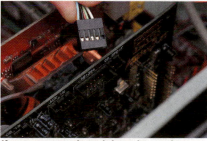

If your system doesn't have internal FireWire headers, you'll need to connect the front mounted FireWire to an internal header on another card. Here we connect the front-mounted ports to the Audigy's onboard FireWire header.

Step 12: Preparing Your Hard Drives

We used only Serial ATA drives in our system, but if you're using old parallel IDE drives, you'll need to set your drives to the proper Master/Slave setting before you mount the drive in the case. Skip ahead to step 17 if you need to configure your parallel IDE hard drives—we'll be waiting back here with the Serial ATA users.

Not everyone's case will have a drive cage or caddy for your hard drive. Whether you have a drive cage or not, this step is the same. Line up your drive with the holes, making sure that it's oriented the right way—it will be difficult to connect cables if your drive points the wrong way!

In some cases, you'll screw the drive directly into the chassis. Either way, it's a pretty simple task. Remember, to make sure that your screw is lined up with the hole properly, unscrew it for a turn before you begin screwing it. That will make sure that the threads all line up, and prevent you from stripping the holes in your hardware.

This is another step that will vary on a case-by-case basis—you might need to mount your hard drives in a drive cage or rack before you install them in your PC. Make sure your drive is pointing in the right direction!

When you screw the drive into the case or drive cage, make sure you use the right thread of screws, and be careful not to overtighten. Note that not all cases make you mount the drives by their bottom screws. With most, you screw the drives directly into the side-mounting holes.

When you're screwing any component into your PC, you should screw in opposite corners first. That makes it easier to keep the holes lined up and get the component evenly screwed down.

Step 13: Installing Your Hard Drives

In our Sonata case, installing the drive is as easy as lining it up with its slot and gently lowering it into place. Make sure you leave room for air to flow between drives!

Connect your Serial ATA cables to your drives. Without a data cable, even the fastest hard drive is nothing more than an expensive heater.

Once your cables are plugged in, gently run them through the case. Be extremely careful! It's easy to break the Serial ATA connector off of the drive, which renders the drive useless.

Installing the hard drives in our Sonata is as easy as lining the drive caddy up with its bay and gently sliding it into place. Keep in mind when you're placing your hard drives that a modern 10,000rpm drive can get up to 140° F if it isn't properly cooled. Running a drive at a high temperature won't really affect performance, but it will greatly decrease the lifespan of the drive. Keeping your drives cool shouldn't require any extra hardware—all you really need to do is leave a space between them.

Once the drives are mounted to your system, you need to run the data cables to your motherboard. We usually try to use the case chassis to help route the cables. You can slide them through gaps in the case and then secure them with zip or twist ties.

A warning for Serial ATA users: Be extremely careful when you apply any vertical force to the Serial ATA connector on the back of your hard drives. We've already heard a few reports from users who broke connectors off the drive, which rendered the entire drive useless. It might be a good idea to remove the Serial ATA cables from the drives while you route the cables and then replace them once everything is in place.

Step 14: Bring Power to Your Drives

One of the tricks we've learned in the *Maximum PC* labs is that it really pays to plan out how you're going to use the limited number of power cables in every system. In addition to the two hard drives, there's also an 8cm fan that needs power right next to these drives.

Our goal was to only run one cable down from the power supply to the front of the case, and power all three of these devices off that cable. Luckily, that's easy to do. Because the fan includes a pass-through, we simply connect one of the leads to the fan's input and then plug the pass-through into the first drive. That leaves the second Molex connector on the power

cable available for drive number two.

It's OK to use splitters and a pass-through to put a couple of drives on one power cable, but we wouldn't go further than that. If you overload one of the lines from the power supply, it can cause system-crashing sags under heavy loads.

Now it's time to power up your drives. In this image, we're also powering up a fan using the pass-through power connector that most case fans ship with. Note that we brought the power cable up between the two drives, where it is virtually invisible.

Now that the power lead from the power supply is connected to the fan, we can use the fan's power output to power our hard drive.

Rinse and repeat. We used the second Molex connector on the lead from the power supply to supply juice to the second drive.

Step 15: Let the Data Flow

The connector for Serial ATA drives is exactly the same on the motherboard as on the drive. Just make sure you have it lined up the right way, and give it a gentle push.

Connecting the Serial ATA connectors is seemingly simple, but which ones should you use? Many motherboards today ship with four or even six Serial ATA ports. Some are connected directly to the motherboards chipset, some are connected to external Serial ATA chips, and some are connected to RAID controllers. Picking the right one can be tricky.

First, you need to figure out which port is which by—you guessed it—checking your motherboard's manual. If you want to put your drives in a RAID array, you obviously need to connect both drives to the same RAID controller; otherwise, they won't be able to talk to each other. If you're using RAID and your system has more than one RAID controller, we generally recommend that you use the native chipset implementation for the RAID array you want to install Windows on.

If you're installing Windows on a single drive rather than a RAID array, the solution is much simpler. Always attach your Windows drive to the chipset's Parallel or Serial ATA ports. Otherwise, you'll have to go through the hassle of pressing F6 to install hard drive controller drivers when you install Windows.

Step 16: Procure Your Drive Rails

Before you can mount your optical drive, you need to find the drive rails. Different cases hide them in different locations in the system. Sometimes they'll be attached to the bottom of the case, sometimes to the drive cage, and sometimes—as is the case here—behind the empty drive bezels.

There has been a lot of debate on the Internet over the small vibrations that drive rails allow decreasing optical drive lifespans. As none of the major optical drive manufacturers warn against using drive rails, and as no *Maximum PC* editor has had a drive fail in a case with rails, we believe that drive rails are probably safe. That's a good thing, too! Having to open both sides of your case just to install an optical drive would suck!

Not all cases use drive rails for the optical drives, but the Sonata does. They're cleverly hidden behind the spare drive bezels. To get them out, you'll need to remove the front bezel.

Once the bezel's off, it's easy to pop the rails out. However, not all cases store spare drive rails behind the bezels. Check your manual if you can't find them.

Step 17: Prep Your Optical Drives

Now that you have the drive rails, you need to screw them onto the optical drive. Unlike the hard drive, it's important that you use the proper holes on the drive rails, or else your drive's front bezel won't line up with the front bezel of the case. And believe us, nothing looks goofier than a system whose DVD burner sticks an extra inch out of the front of the case. It's actually a good idea to hand-tighten the screws on your rails and then slide the drive into the system to see whether it's going to line up properly. If it does, you can slide it back out and tighten up the screws.

Every parallel IDE optical drive should have a label like this one showing the jumper settings for master, slave, and cable select.

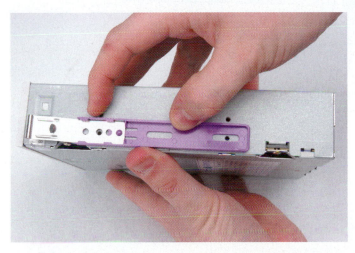

Figuring out which holes to use for the drive rails may take a little trial and error. For most cases, though, the first hole shown here is the proper one to make your drive bezels even with the front of the case.

Step 17 Continued

Deciding which drive will be master and which will be slave can be confusing. Remember that when two devices are connected to the IDE bus, only one of them can transfer data at a time, so if the master drive is sending data, the slave drive is idle. If you're going to do any disk-to-disk copying at all, you should definitely run your optical drives on different IDE channels. Even though we're not going to be doing any disk-to-disk work with this machine, we're still going to put each drive on its own chain. We set each drive to use the master setting and then connected each to its own IDE cable.

If you're just using optical drives on the IDE chain, you can always use cable select. Cable select determines your drives' master and slave status based on each drive's position on the IDE cable. The drive at the end of the cable will be the master, and the drive in the middle of the cable will be the slave. If you want to use cable select for hard drives, make certain that the drive you intend to boot off of is at the end of the cable. Some operating systems have trouble booting off of any drives that are not on the primary master. Remember, if you use cable select for one drive on the chain, you need to have cable select set on the other one as well—otherwise the BIOS won't see either drive.

We have a full guide that describes several common drive configurations in Chapter 7, "Optical Drives."

This is the jumper you move to change the master/slave setting. It's very tiny, so you might want to use a pair of tweezers or needlenose pliers.

Step 18: Install Your Optical Drives

This is really quite a simple step. With your drives already configured and mounted on rails, all that's really left is to slide them into the case. Optical drives don't generate too much heat, so don't worry about leaving a breathing gap between them.

If you don't have a case with drive rails, at this point you'll need to remove the other side of your case and line the drive up in whichever slot you want to use. Set the two screws in the back of the drive so that your optical drive won't fall and then slide it back and forth in the slot until the front bezel of the drive lines up with the front bezel of your case. Once you have the drive situated properly, go ahead and tighten all four screws.

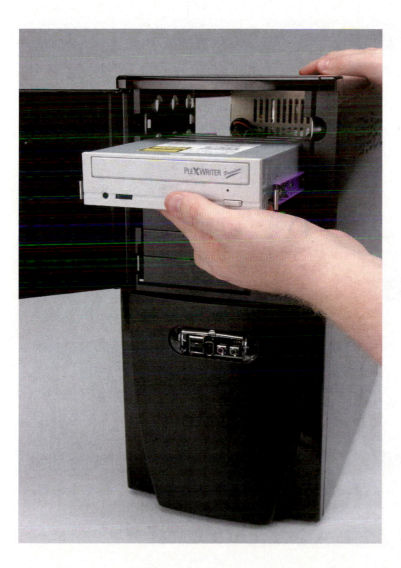

Once the jumpers are set and the drive rails are screwed in, you can slide your drives into the case.

Step 19: Connect Your Optical Drives

Once your drives are physically mounted in the system, you need to connect them to your motherboard. Get your IDE cable and connect the lowest drive to the IDE cable first—otherwise the cable will get in your way! For 80-pin IDE cables, the blue end should always be plugged into the motherboard.

If you've never connected an IDE cable before, you need to make absolutely certain that you get the pins lined up properly before you start pushing. Most cables and sockets are keyed so that they only fit one way, but not all are. If your cable isn't keyed, a good rule of thumb is that the red wire on the ribbon cable should always be on the same side of the drive as the power connector.

After the data cable is connected, you need to connect a power lead from the power supply to each optical drive. It's OK to use the same power lead for two optical drives, but we wouldn't use any power splitters to connect more components to that particular lead.

Go ahead and connect your IDE cables to the optical drives. Make sure you have the cable lined up with the connector before you start pushing, or you could bend pins or break the connector.

Once both drive's data cables are connected, you can connect the power lines. It doesn't really matter what order you do this in, but it's easier if you do the data cables and then the power lines in this case.

A normal power line provides more than enough power for two optical drives. We wouldn't recommend using a splitter to do more than that, though.

Step 20: Hitch a Ride on the IDE Bus

Connecting the optical drives to the motherboard is another potentially perilous task. After all, modern motherboards can have four or even six parallel IDE ports. Which ones should you use for your optical drives? As a general rule, your best choice is the native IDE ports that are built into the motherboard. Most of the time, a chipset's integrated IDE controller is supported by Windows without any external drivers, which simplifies the installation process. Most RAID controllers—the extra IDE connectors are almost always attached to a RAID controller—don't really know what to do with optical drives. To get the RAID controller to work, you'll need to enter the RAID controller's BIOS and switch the RAID controller from RAID mode to normal IDE mode.

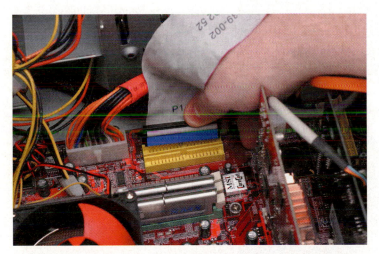

Now you need to plug the other end of each IDE cable into the IDE ports on the motherboard. It doesn't really matter which one you use for optical drives, but if you're plugging your Windows boot drive into a Parallel ATA port, you need to make sure it's the one labeled Primary.

Next we'll plug in our second optical drive. The motherboard's IDE ports should be easier to see, but you still need to make sure that you line the connector up properly with the pins.

Step 21: Connect Your Power Supply to the Mobo

This big mother is your ATX power connector. The ATX connector can only fit one way—line up the springy clip on one side with the latch on the motherboard's connector.

Push the ATX connector down until it clicks into place. It might require a little bit of force, but you shouldn't push hard enough to flex the mobo.

This is called the ATX 12V power connector. It provides more juice to the mobo than the original spec called for. Like the ATX connector, it only fits one way.

Just like the main ATX power connector, the 12V connector should click into place.

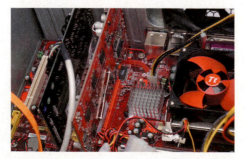

Before your system will boot, you need to connect the power supply to the mobo. First, you'll want to plug the ATX power connector into the motherboard. The ATX power connector is usually attached to the largest bundle of cables coming out of the power supply. Its 20-pin connector is usually translucent white. Once you've found it, you need to plug it into the motherboard's socket, which is usually near the RAM. Line the connector up with the socket, and press down. It should click into place when it's fully inserted.

Next you need to find the ATX 12V power connector. It's a smaller, square four-pin connector that also comes out of the power supply. Once you've found it, look on the mobo for the matching socket—it's usually near the CPU. Line the clip up with the latch on the socket and gently push it into place. Like the ATX power connector, it should click into place.

Step 22: Connect Any Remaining Fans to Power

Now you need to look around your case and plug in any remaining fans. After you've run the system for a week or two and established that the system is stable, you can begin disabling them one at a time to minimize noise, but for the time being, you should turn them all on.

When you're working with case fans on an ATX system, the golden rule is that you should suck cool air in at the bottom front portion of the case and blow it out the rear of the case near the top. Keep this in mind as you design your cooling scheme.

If you're having trouble determining whether a fan is set to suck or blow, it's easy to tell! Just pop the fan out of its mount and look on all four sides until you see the pair of arrows. One shows the rotational direction of the fan blades, but the other shows the direction air flows through the fan.

Look for disconnected fans near the front of the case, above the CPU, and even above the optical drives. Also, some power supplies include leads that let you connect your power supply fan to a motherboard header so that your mobo can monitor and adjust the speed of the power supply fan.

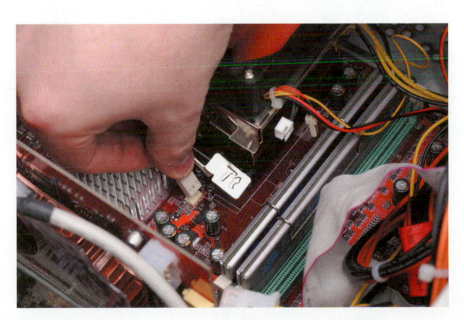

Look around your case for any fans that you haven't connected to a power supply yet and give them power!

Step 23: Tidy Up Your Mess

Before you close up the case, take a minute or two to tidy up your cables. Where it's possible, you can use the case to contain them. Slide the ATX power connector's cable under the optical drive cage where it will be out of the way and then secure it with a zip tie. Zip tie your Serial ATA cables together and then attach them to the case's frame with another zip tie.

Getting the wiring nice and tight is a little different with each motherboard and case combination, so you'll have to kind of wing it on this step. Take a close look at your power cables and IDE cables. You should be able to do some twisting and folding to keep them mostly out of sight.

A good wiring job isn't really necessary in the greater scheme of things—unless your case has a window—but it does show a level of craftsmanship and pride in your work that will separate your computer from the pretenders.

In the *Maximum PC* labs, we try to tidy up our wiring jobs without using too many zip ties or permanent fixing points. Those just make it difficult to remove and replace components later. Instead, try to use the stiffness of the wires and the natural nooks and crannies that your case provides.

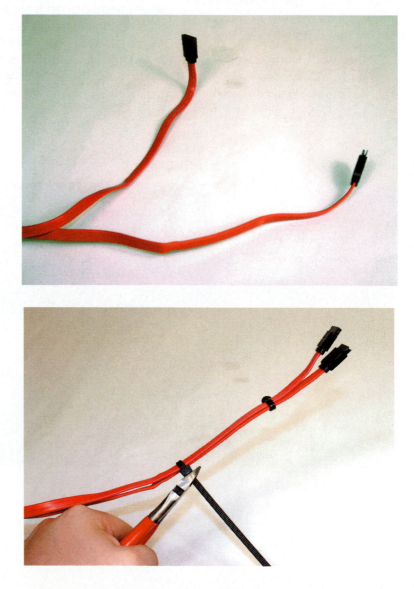

It's easy to get Serial ATA cables under control. First, use zip ties to hold them together...

...then use zip ties to attach them to the case's frame.

Step 24: Boot the PC and Enter the BIOS

```
Frequency 1MHz Stepping       133
CPU Ratio Select              Auto
CPU Vcore Select              Default
Quick Power On Self Test      Enabled

First Boot Device             CDROM
Second Boot Device            Floppy
Third Boot Device             HDD-1
Boot Other Device             Enabled
RAID/ATA & SCSI Boot Order    RAID/ATA,SCSI

C.I.H. 4-WAY Protection       Disabled
Onboard Promise IDE RAID      Enabled
Onboard 6Ch H/W Audio         Disabled
```

Before you can install Windows XP off of the CD-ROM drive, you need to make sure your computer is set to boot off of the CD-ROM.

```
System Performance        Normal        Item Help
Auto Detect DIMM/PCI Clk  Enabled
Spread Spectrum           Disabled      Menu Level  ▶
CPU Frequency Select      133 MHz
Frequency 1MHz St                       ows you to selec
CPU Ratio Select      CPU Ratio Select  r CPU Ratio
CPU Vcore Select
Quick Power On Se   Auto   ..... [■]
                    6.0 X  ..... [ ]
First Boot Device   6.5 X  ..... [ ]
Second Boot Devic   7.0 X  ..... [ ]
Third Boot Device   7.5 X  ..... [ ]
Boot Other Device   8.0 X  ..... [ ]
RAID/ATA & SCSI B   8.5 X  ..... [ ]
                    9.0 X  ..... [ ]
C.I.H. 4-WAY Prot
Onboard Promise I   ↑↓:Move ENTER:Accept ESC:Abort
Onboard 6Ch H/W A
VIA OnChip LAN            Enabled
↑↓←→:Move  Enter:Select  +/-/PU/PD:Value  F10:Save  ESC:Exit  F1:General H
   F5: Previous Values    F6: Fail-Safe Defaults   F7: Optimized Defaults
```

Make sure your CPU is running at its peak speed. Because most modern CPU cores will only run at one setting, you should set the multiplier to automatically detect the proper setting.

Now it's time to set up your PC's BIOS. The term *BIOS* stands for *basic input/output system*. This is the software that contains all the rudimentary instructions on how your operating system should communicate with your hardware.

First, turn on your newly constructed PC and punch the key that lets you enter the BIOS. It's normally the F1, F2, or DEL key. If you get a full-screen logo but no key prompt to "enter setup," hit the ESC key. This will spawn your hidden boot sequence. Now you can hit F1, F2, or DEL to enter the BIOS setup screen. Once you're inside the setup menus, you can adjust a number of parameters that will affect OS-hardware communication, but we're just going to focus on getting the machine up and running. Never fear though, we've got a whole chapter of *Maximum PC*-approved BIOS tweaks in Chapter 16, "Tweaking Your BIOS Settings."

Because you'll soon be loading Windows XP from scratch, directly from its CD, the first thing you'll want to do in the BIOS is set the First Boot Device to the CD-ROM drive. This tells the computer to boot from the CD drive before trying to boot from the hard drive, which is still blank. While you're in the BIOS, you'll also want to disable the onboard audio to make way for the Sound Blaster Audigy card.

Remember that you can't manually set the CPU multiplier (or ratio) for any modern AMD or Intel retail processors, so leave the BIOS multiplier setting at Auto (see Image 2). You should make sure that your CPU is running the right bus speed though, especially if it's reporting a speed that's slower or faster than expected. Bus speeds vary widely even within the same family of CPU, so check the documentation that came with your CPU and motherboard to find the proper speed.

If at any place in the BIOS you encounter options for "Maximum" or "Normal," go with the normal setting for now. You want to make sure everything is working fine before you try to optimize for maximum performance.

Step 25: Configure RAID

If you want to install Windows on a RAID array—remember, that's two drives that work together as one bigger drive—you need to create the array before you install Windows. To find out all about configuring RAID, turn to Chapter 15, "Add RAID to Your Computer."

Once your RAID array is installed, be aware that you'll need to do something a little special when you install Windows. When the CD-ROM[nd]based installer first starts, just after the screen turns blue for the first time, you'll see a message at the bottom of the screen that says "Press F6 to install third-party drivers." You will need to install drivers for your RAID card so that Windows will see your hard drive.

When you're installing Windows from a RAID card, you need to be quick with the F6 button or you'll never see the screen that lets you install third-party mass storage drivers.

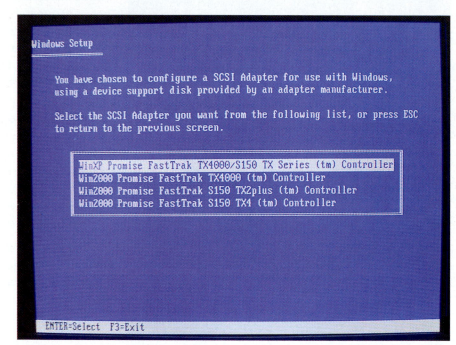

Step 26: Install Windows

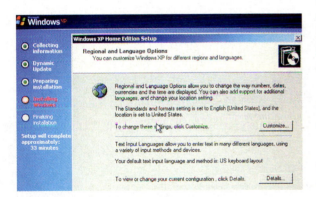

During the text-mode portion of Windows XP setup, you'll need to decide how you want to format your drive. For most users, it's best to create a smaller partition for the OS and applications, with a big secondary partition for data.

Unless you want to use a Slovakian keyboard on your new computer, you can speed by the Regional Settings screen.

To install Windows, all you need to do is pop the CD-ROM into the drive and then press the "any" key when you see a screen prompting you to "Press any key to boot from CD."

After your system has booted off the CD, the installer will start the non-GUI portion of setup (*GUI* stands for *graphical user interface*). If you want to install Windows on a SCSI drive or RAID array for which XP doesn't include built-in drivers, you'll need to press F6 as soon as you see the blue screen. Otherwise, you can wait for the Welcome screen.

Follow the prompts until you get to the partitioning screen. Assuming you're using a new hard drive, you'll need to tell Windows how you want to configure your disk. If you're using your old drive, be extra careful at this step—this part of the installer is the Win XP equivalent of FDISK and can easily wipe your drive. For maximum performance with XP, we recommend creating one big partition that spans the entire drive. If you decide you need two partitions later, it's easy to repartition the drive using a utility such as Partition Magic. We recommend that you use the NTFS format for your new drive. And always do a thorough format on a brand-new hard drive!

Once you've started the format, it's usually safe to leave the machine for 20 or 30 minutes. The formatting process is even more mind-bogglingly dull than watching paint dry.

When you return, your PC should be into the GUI stage of the install. The first screen you'll see is the language options screen. Unless you have a nonstandard keyboard layout or don't live in the U.S., you can safely continue to the next step.

The last major step you have to wade through is the setup of your network. Typical settings work for most cable modems and DSL connections, although you'll need to use manual settings if you have a statically assigned IP address or use some sort of wonky PPPoE connection. After the network is configured, Windows should reboot one last time.

Following the final reboot, you'll be prompted to activate Windows. We recommend that you hold off until you have all the drivers set up for your hardware and everything is working properly. You should have at least 30 days before your unactivated copy of Windows stops working, so take your time.

Step 27: Install XP Updates and Drivers

Windows is installed, but you're not quite done yet. Before you can begin using your computer, you need to install the latest updates, drivers, and patches to make your system safe for daily use.

Before you connect to the Internet, make sure you enable the built-in firewall. You can disable it after we've patched the OS, but it's important to keep it on before you install the critical updates, while your system is hyper-vulnerable. To enable the firewall, go to the Control Panel, click Network and Internet Connections, and then click Network Connections. Right-click on your connection and click Properties. Go to the Advanced tab and click Protect My Computer and Network by Limiting or Preventing Access to the Computer From the Internet. Now you can connect to the Net a little more safely!

Next you need to install Service Pack 2. Open Internet Explorer and go to www.windowsupdate.com. Click the Scan for Updates button and go directly to the Critical Updates and Service Packs section. Install the most recent Service Pack, and reboot your computer when prompted.

Before you connect to the Internet, enable the built-in XP firewall. It isn't much, but it will protect you from self-propagating worms like Blaster until you get your system patched.

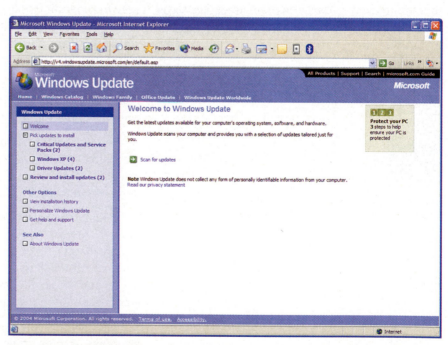

Once the Firewall is enabled, go to www.windowsupdate.com and download and install the latest Service Pack.

Step 27 Continued

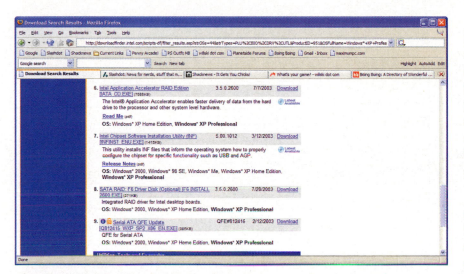

After the Service Pack is installed, you need to visit your motherboard manufacturer's website and download and install the latest version of its chipset drivers.

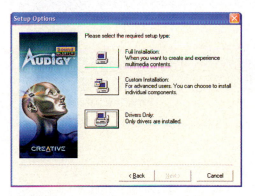

Finally, you should update to the latest version of DirectX and then install your videocard drivers, soundcard drivers, and drivers for any other hardware—rebooting as necessary. Finish by visiting windowsupdate.com again and installing all the critical updates.

Once the Service Pack is installed, you should install your motherboard's chipset drivers. You should be able to download them from your motherboard manufacturer's website. They're sometimes called 4-in-1 drivers or the chipset software, depending on the manufacturer. Make sure you reboot when you're done.

Go back to windowsupdate.com and install the latest version of DirectX. It might have been included in Service Pack 2, so if you don't see it in the Windows XP section, don't sweat it.

We're almost done. Go to your videocard chipset manufacturer's website—Radeon owners should go to www.ati.com and GeForce owners should go to www.nvidia.com—and download the latest version of your videocard's drivers. Once you install them, you'll probably have to reboot again.

Install drivers for your soundcard, network card, and any other hardware you might have. It's always best to download new driver updates from the manufacturer's website, but if you can't find any more recent drivers, you can always use the ones from the CD that came with the card.

After all your drivers are installed, you should go back to windowsupdate.com once again and install all the updates in the Critical Updates section.

Step 28: Install Your Applications and Games

Before you can truly use your system, you need to install all the apps you regularly use. We usually install Office, iTunes, and Mozilla Firefox before anything else, and then we move on to the more important stuff—games!

When you're installing applications on a new machine, think about how you can use a default file structure to keep everything nice and organized. For example, several of the *Maximum PC* editors store all their games in the c:/Games folder. That way, when an editor moves to a new machine, moving his games is frequently as easy as just copying the entire Games directory to the same place on the new hard drive. Because he installs and uninstalls game demos frequently, he installs all the demos to the same location, c:\games\demos. Every few months, he blows the contents of that demos folder away, which prevents moldy old game demos from clogging up his hard drive.

Come up with a storage scheme that suits you and then implement it from the git-go. It's always easier to do that than to try and wrap a new file storage scheme around the cluttered mess on a full 200GB hard drive.

Don't forget to turn to Chapter 18, "Create Custom Recovery Disks," to learn how to preserve your machine in its pristine form, so that you can restore it at any time, without having to reinstall Windows!

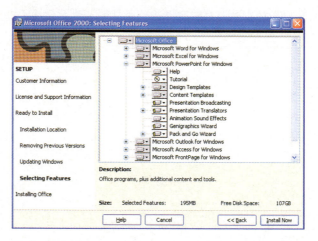

You're in the home stretch now! Install your favorite applications and games. You're done!

Don't forget cool applications like the Mozilla Firefox web browser.

You're Done! Enjoy Your Handiwork!

Enjoy! You've built your
own PC!

Chapter Fifteen

Add RAID to Your Computer

Supercharge your hard drive performance by striping together two drives

To create a RAID array, you need at least two drives of the same type and a RAID controller. Most of today's performance-oriented motherboards have a RAID controller built in, but you can also buy an add-in PCI RAID controller like this one for around $40.

The evolution of CPUs, videocards, and memory seems to occur at an almost blinding pace. The memory pipelines on yesterday's videocards pumped two or three gigabytes of data per second, whereas today's fastest cards are moving 10 times that amount. But there's one part of your PC that improves at a much slower pace: the hard drive. The fastest desktop hard drives roar along at 10,000rpm, but can barely hit a sustained transfer rate of 60 megabytes per second (abbreviated in *Maximum PC*-speak to 60MB/s). It's enough to make any geek spiral into deep depression.

Cheer up! You don't necessarily have to wait for the engineers in R&D to come up with a breakthrough if you want to improve your hard drive performance in the here and now. The solution to your transfer-rate woes is *RAID*, which stands for *redundant array of inexpensive disks* (yes, really). There are many different flavors of RAID, but they all work on the same basic principle—multiple hard drives strung together perform the duties normally handled by a single drive. The most commonly used types of RAID are RAID 0, RAID 1, and RAID 0+1. In RAID 0 (often called *striping*), chunks of data are alternately split between two hard drives, significantly boosting transfer rates.

Meanwhile, in RAID 1 (a.k.a. *mirroring*), an identical copy of each piece of data is written to two separate disks, effectively backing up all your files in real time. Finally, RAID 0+1 combines the functionality of RAID 0 and RAID 1, but requires four disks.

In this chapter, we'll focus on setting up a RAID 0 array because *Maximum PC*-caliber enthusiasts tend to be more concerned with performance than the possibility of disk failure. Implementing RAID 0+1 would be ideal, but purchasing four hard drives for a single system is simply too expensive a proposition for most folk. Be forewarned: There are drawbacks to RAID 0—your PC will boot slower, and the failure of either of the two hard drives in the array will destroy *all* your data, so you're essentially doubling your chances of data loss. That said, the faster transfer rates and access times provided by a RAID 0 array will definitely boost your rig's overall performance. The benefits will be most tangible in disk-intensive apps, such as image and video editing, and during large file transfers. Interested? Then let's back up your important data and get to building a RAID 0 array!

And, please, for the love of God, make sure you read this *entire* how-to before beginning the actual process.

Ingredients

- PCI RAID controller card ($20), or a motherboard with built-in RAID
- Two identical hard drives (same model and same firmware revision)
- Floppy disk with the drivers for your RAID card
- A copy of Windows 2000 or Windows XP (about $100)

What Is RAID?

Heard of RAID, but still think of it as the stuff you spray on ants? Never fear. You wouldn't be the first hardware maven to be at a loss for words when asked how RAID works or why it's the choice of serious performance freaks. Simply put, a single hard drive is limited in terms of what it can accomplish. It has a set speed and capacity, and a level of security that's only as good as the drive is reliable. If you want more storage capacity or faster disk performance, you can shell out the bones for a bigger, faster hard drive, but this strategy demands that you open your wallet every time you reach a size or performance plateau.

In a RAID array, two or more hard drives work together as a single volume to provide performance options that simply aren't possible with a single drive. Depending on the type of RAID array you implement, you'll see increased performance, better data security, or both.

RAID stands for redundant array of inexpensive disks—an accurate description of what RAID is and does (although the "Inexpensive Disks" portion of the phrase has been something of a misnomer until relatively recently). Redundancy is the cornerstone of a RAID setup—it simply means that the array includes drives specifically designed to back up the system's primary drive every time data is written to that main drive. Redundancy can be implemented in a variety of ways (some of which are outlined in the following sections), but its primary purpose is always the same: to minimize the downtime incurred by a drive failure. Every legitimate RAID array will offer some form of protection against data loss.

The word *array* implies a setup in which several components have the same properties, and RAID is no exception. However, it's important to note that a RAID array can only operate at the level of the smallest or slowest drive included in the setup. For example, a 40GB drive working with a 20GB drive maxes out at 40GB (20GB per drive). The moral of the story? Happy power users only build RAID arrays with identical drives.

A RAID array's work is governed by a controller that handles the task of sending and receiving data requests to all the drives. The controller can be hardware- or software-based—if you use Windows NT Server or 2000 Server, your OS can even act as a software controller! However, we recommend an add-in PCI controller card for top performance, because a software controller steals CPU cycles for every operation. Hardware controllers include onboard processors that handle all the functions your array demands, leaving your CPU and other system resources free to handle other tasks. Most good controller cards also come bundled with a monitoring utility, which provides details on the array's status.

Step 1: Backing Up Your Data

Figure Out What to Back Up

If you're building your PC from scratch, and haven't used the hard drives that you're going to RAID yet, then obviously you won't need to back up any data, so you can safely skip to step 2. Of course, if you need to move your data from your old machine to your new computer, this still applies!

Anyone who has added RAID to an existing Windows install knows that the trickiest part of setting up a RAID array has nothing to do with RAID itself; it's backing up your data in preparation for reformatting. If you forget to back up something crucial, you'll be kicking yourself for weeks to come. So don't rush the process. Make a list and check it twice. Important elements to back up include your email, browser bookmarks, documents (MP3s, text files, whatever), and saved games. Remember, you can't just make a drive image and restore it to your RAID array—Windows doesn't take kindly to you changing the IDE controller without reinstalling the OS.

Back Up Your Email in Outlook or Outlook Express

To back up your email in Outlook, click File and choose

Import and Export. Select Export To a File, click Next, choose Personal Folder File (.pst), and then click Next and select your contacts, email, and what-

ever else you want to back up. In Outlook Express, click File, Export, and choose either Address Book or Messages (you'll probably want to export both). Finally, make sure you write down your account settings. To find these, click the Tools menu and choose E-mail Accounts (Outlook) or Accounts (OE). OE will take you directly to the list of accounts, but in Outlook, you'll need to select View Or Change Existing E-mail Accounts and click Next. Importing everything you've backed up is as simple as clicking File, Import and Export (Outlook), or Import (OE).

Back Up Your Email in Eudora

Unlike Outlook, Eudora doesn't include an export feature, so you'll have to perform a manual backup. Head over to the program's folder (usually C:\Program Files\Qualcomm\Eudora) and back up all your .mbx and .toc files; the default files are In.mbx, In.toc,

Out.mbx, Out.toc, Trash.mbx, and Trash.toc. You'll also want to back up your address book. To do this, copy the NNdbase.txt file and Nickname folder from your Eudora folder. Lastly, save your account settings by copying the Eudora.ini file. After you've reinstalled Windows and Eudora on your RAID array, simply copy everything you've backed up into the program's folder and you should be set.

Back Up Your Bookmarks and Documents

To back up your Internet Explorer Favorites in Windows 2000 or XP, open the C:\Documents and Settings folder. Double-click the folder named after your login and copy the entire Favorites folder to a safe location (for example, an external hard drive, USB key, whatever). If, on the other hand, you're running the Mozilla Firebird browser, search for the bookmarks.html file and save it. Backing up your documents is easy as pie if you save all your files in the My Documents folder—simply copy the entire folder to your backup device and you're set. But if you're a rebel—or if you use programs such as TurboTax that stupidly don't save their files in the My Documents folder—you'll need to carefully scour your computer to find all your documents.

Store Everything in a Safe Place

Once you've amassed all the files you want to back up, be sure to store them somewhere safe. Copying all your files to another hard drive is the fastest and easiest way to go, assuming you have an extra drive for this purpose. If this isn't an option, burning everything to removable media (such as CD-Rs or DVDs) is the best alternative. Just remember to make absolutely certain you've backed up everything you need. Don't come whining to us if you forget to save your tax returns or lose your bookie's email address!

Before you pull the pin on your existing hard drive, you should test the backups you've already made, make sure you grabbed the little items that you'll really miss when you reinstall—IM buddy lists, emails with serial numbers and registration keys, and your username and password for your ISP. Only after you've backed up and tested the backups for all those files should you move on to the next step.

Back Up Your Save-Game Files

Finding all your save-game files can be a bit problematic, because they're not usually located in any one centralized folder. Most games throw their save files in a subfolder within the game's program folder. The subfolder will usually be named something obvious, like "Saves," so just poke around a bit. To be safe, back up the entire contents of these folders rather than individual files because some games use multiple files for each save. Also note that some RPGs save character and save-game file in different folders. Finally, some games (*C&C: Generals*, for example) store their save files in the My Documents folder, so if you're not backing up your entire My Documents folder, make sure you at least sift through it for save-game files.

Step 2: RAID Configuration

Configure Your Hardware

Once you're done with the backup, it's time to install the hardware. If you're using an add-in RAID controller, go ahead and install it in a vacant PCI slot. Parallel ATA users need to jumper both of the hard drives to "master" (consult your drive's documentation for the specifics), and connect each one to a separate IDE channel on the RAID controller. As long as your IDE or Serial ATA cables are long enough to reach from your RAID card to your drive, you can place the actual hard drives anywhere in your system you like.

Make sure you don't accidentally plug the drives into your mobo's standard IDE ports. (Usually onboard RAID ports will be colored differently than standard IDE ports.) We strongly recommend using two identical hard drives with the same firmware version to maximize performance and minimize the risk of any problems. Visit your hard drive manufacturer's website to find firmware updates. Be advised that if you don't use identical drives, at best your RAID array will be limited by the smallest and slowest drive. At worst, it won't work at all.

Configure Your System to Accept the RAID Array

If you're using your motherboard's onboard RAID support, make sure it's enabled in the system BIOS. You might also need to change the boot order in your BIOS so the system will boot from the RAID controller. Most modern motherboards will automatically change the boot order when they detect an add-in PCI RAID controller card.

While you're in the BIOS, we recommend enabling SMART (Self-Monitoring Analysis and Reporting Technology), which is an early-warning system that continually monitors your hard drives to predict possible mechanical failures. If you're using a PCI RAID controller card, you'll want to enable SMART in the RAID card's BIOS rather than in the motherboard's (see the next step). Preemptive notification of disk problems is critical when you're running a striped RAID array. For your system to receive warnings of impending hard drive failures, you'll need to run a SMART-capable RAID management utility. Most RAID controllers come with the requisite software.

Configure the RAID Array

To finish setting up your RAID array, you'll need to enter your RAID controller's BIOS. After your motherboard completes its power-on self-test (POST), a message should appear indicating that the RAID controller is looking for installed hard drives. At this point, you can enter the RAID BIOS by pressing the appropriate key combination, and it will pop up as your computer boots—after the normal boot process, but before Windows loads. Follow the onscreen instructions to establish a RAID 0 array and set it to "active."

There are a number of settings you can customize during this process, but the stripe size (or block size) setting is of particular interest. Not to be confused with stripe width, stripe size determines the size of the chunks of data that are written to each disk in a RAID 0 array (see "RAID Basics" later in this chapter to learn more about RAID levels). If you work primarily with large files (such as in video editing), a higher stripe size will yield better performance. Conversely, folks who tend to work with smaller files will reap the greatest dividends from a small stripe size. For the best overall balance, we suggest a stripe size of 64KB.

Step 3: Install Windows

For this step, you'll need a bootable Windows XP CD and a floppy disk with the drivers for your RAID controller. Most add-in RAID cards and RAID-enabled motherboards come bundled with a driver disk, but if you don't have one, you can download the appropriate drivers online. (Please do so *before* you start this how-to!) Visit your mobo or RAID-card manufacturer's website to download a utility to create a driver disk. The two biggest makers of RAID controllers are Promise (www.promise.com) and HighPoint (www.highpoint-tech.com). When you've finished preparing a driver disk, start up your computer with the Windows CD in your optical drive (make sure your BIOS is set to boot off the CD-ROM). Once the Windows setup program starts, keep an eye on the bottom of the screen. When you see a message that says "Press F6 if you need to install a third-party SCSI or RAID driver," press F6. After Setup finishes loading, it will read the RAID drivers from your floppy disk. If multiple RAID drivers are detected, Windows might prompt you to choose the correct one. From here on out, the Windows setup process should proceed exactly as it would on a normal IDE drive. After Windows is set up, you can rein-

stall your applications, and restore the data you backed up earlier.

Step 4: Maintenance

Once you're all set up, maintaining a RAID 0 array is not much different from maintaining a single IDE hard drive. When two drives are striped in a RAID 0 array, Windows will treat them as a single large drive that's size is the sum of the two drives' capacities. As with any system, you should defragment your RAID array on a regular basis to ensure stability and boost performance. You should also run Scandisk from time to time to make sure your file system is intact. Keep in mind that problems detected by Scandisk usually aren't hardware-related, so don't be terribly alarmed if bad clusters are found. However, if Scandisk consistently finds problems with your disks, it could indicate an underlying hardware glitch. Regardless, because of the increased risk of data loss that accompanies RAID 0, we recommend that you periodically back up your most coveted data. Finally, update your RAID drivers and RAID BIOS regularly—both should be available on the website of the company that made your mobo or add-in RAID card.

Step 5: Troubleshoot

In general, once Windows is installed, a RAID 0 array should work just like a single hard drive. But you might occasionally encounter problems with some programs. These problems most often stem from incompatibilities between the programs and the RAID controller, rather than any issue with RAID technology as a whole. For example, the game *Neverwinter Nights* has been known to suffer extremely poor performance on systems that use certain HighPoint RAID controllers. However, such problems are the exception rather than the rule. RAID is popular enough that most software companies take it into account when testing their products, so you shouldn't have very many issues, if any. If you do encounter a problem—say, a specific program is performing unpredictably or not running at all—first try updating your RAID BIOS and/or drivers to the latest versions. If that doesn't help, visit the website of the company that made the miscreant program. There might be a patch or some kind of relevant information available that can help you resolve your issues.

RAID Basics

Although redundancy is the cornerstone of a RAID array, increased performance and security benefits are also paramount. There are many ways to configure a RAID array, but all RAID setups employ at least one of the following features.

Striping

In a striped RAID configuration, data is *interleaved*, or woven, across all the drives in the array. The chunks of data being written to the drives, were they visible, would appear as stripes running across all the drives in the array.

Because all the drives in a striped array write and read data simultaneously, the array yields faster overall throughput. Here's another way to look at it: Imagine that you want to write the digits 1 through 10 on a piece of paper as quickly as possible. With one hand, you could write one number at a time. But if you were able to use both hands simultaneously, with one hand writing even numbers and the other writing odd numbers, you'd finish in half the time.

A striped array's performance is dictated by two factors: stripe width and stripe size. The width of the stripe is equivalent to the number of drives in the array. To understand how this affects performance, consider the following example: If a 256K chunk of data is written onto two drives in 64K chunks, each drive would be required to perform two writes—one

drive would write the first and third 64K chunks, and the second drive would write the second and fourth 64K pieces. As soon as the first drive finishes writing a chunk, it begins writing another, and the other drive does the same. The result is that each drive's work is halved, and transfer rates are nearly double those of a single drive. With each increase in an array's stripe width (that is, with each additional physical drive), performance is increased as more drives share the workload.

Mirroring

In a *mirrored* array, data is simultaneously written to two drives. The result is that if one drive fails, the second should continue working without missing a beat and with no data loss. If a system's RAID controller allows it, that replacement can happen almost instantaneously. If not, the rotten drive must be physically removed and replaced with a functional drive, to which the controller copies all the data stored on the working drive.

Mirroring typically makes for slower write speeds than if you were writing data to a single drive. And why wouldn't it? The data has to be written to two drives instead of just one. However, mirrored drives usually yield better read speeds than those of a single drive (although not as good as the read speeds of striped drives). Because the two mirrored drives carry identical data, the controller can retrieve data from one drive while simultaneously sending commands for additional data to the other drive.

Parity

Like mirroring, *parity* is a redundancy measure. In parity mode, the array's controller adds an extra bit of data to the binary information that's being written to the hard drive. When calculated by the controller, the extra sequence results in an even or an odd number. By analyzing this value, the controller can determine whether the information's integrity has been compromised and, if so, repair it instantly by replacing it with non-compromised data from another drive in the array.

Currently, the most popular method of implementing parity in a RAID array is to use a mathematical operation called *exclusive OR*, or *XOR* for short. XOR is a Boolean logic operator that analyzes a string of values—in this case, binary computer data represented by ones and zeros—and returns to the RAID controller a value of either true or false (odd numbers are true, even numbers are false). XOR is especially useful because it can reconstruct binary data that's been corrupted; if XOR has at least some details of an operation, it can fill in the data that's "missing."

Here's a representation of how XOR does its thing: Consider the operation 2 + 3 = 5. If those numbers represent data, and the number 3 is somehow taken out of the equation (that is, it's corrupted), you're left with an equation that reads 2 + "blank" = 5. Obviously, the answer is 3. And that's how XOR works: It uses two parts of a three-part equation to determine the missing third part.

Levels of RAID

The original specification for RAID, produced in 1988 at the University of California at Berkeley—and later revised in 1992 by the RAID Advisory Board (RAB), described seven RAID "levels," each designed to deliver a variety of different performance benefits. Aptly identified as RAID levels 0 through 6, the seven original levels now act as blueprints for other RAID levels, including the most popular configuration for home users—RAID 0. Because the most commonly implemented RAID configurations are RAID 0, RAID 1, RAID 0+1, and RAID 5, we'll describe those in more detail.

RAID 0 (Striped Array)

A RAID 0 array contains at least two drives, and data is written across the drives in consecutive blocks. Drives in a RAID 0 configuration are called a *striped set*. Technically, RAID 0 isn't really RAID, because it's missing the "R" (redundancy). For this reason, RAID 0 is rarely used by large corporations or in situations where mission-critical data must be protected.

The benefits of RAID 0 are increased read and write speeds, as explained above in the description of striping. The main disadvantage is that corrupted data on a single drive can hose the whole array. RAID 0 is usually used in noncritical environments that require fast writes and reads, such as high-definition digital video capturing and editing, working with large multimedia files, or high-end gaming machines and workstations that value performance over reliability.

RAID 1 (Mirroring)

A RAID 1 array contains at least two drives and all data is written to both drives. Because both drives contain exactly the same data, your chance of data loss is exponentially lower than with a single drive. In RAID 1, the controller oversees the mirroring operation. If the main drive takes a tumble, the controller reroutes work to the functional drive until the dead drive can be replaced. RAID 1 offers straight-up redundancy, nothing more.

RAID Cheat Sheet

RAID has a lot of details to keep in your ole noggin. If you have trouble keeping them straight, here's the basics summarized in a handy table

RAID LEVEL	A.K.A.	MINIMUM NUMBER OF DRIVES	ADVANTAGES	DISADVANTAGES	NATURAL APPLICATION
0	Striped Array	2	Significant improvement in read/write speeds over those of a single drive	No redundancy; doubles chance of data loss	Environments with lots of random access; desktop computing
1	Mirrored Array	2	100% redundancy; faster possible reads than those of a single drive	Slower writes than those of a single drive; double the cost per GB; performance dependent on controller card	Web servers; infrequently accessed data storage
5	Striping with distributed parity	3	Striped performance with the security of parity	Parity calculations can slow write times; expensive if done in SCSI; slower than 0+1	Enterprise servers; not usually used for desktop machines

RAID 1's benefits include the safety net of full redundancy and improved read times, as explained above in the description of mirroring. Its disadvantages include slower write times compared to those of a single drive (also explained above). RAID 1 is suitable for small corporate networks, small web servers, and people who don't need massive amounts of storage space but require 100% redundancy.

RAID 0+1 or 1+0 (Striping and Mirroring)

This configuration requiresbuffet of benefits, including the high performance of striped disks and the security of parity calculations. At least three drives are required, and both data and parity information are interleaved across all the drives in the array—hence the name "distributed parity."

It's easy to understand why RAID 5 is usually incorporated into corporate servers and mission-critical computing environments. Its advantages include speedy disk reads and writes and a serious security setup. Because parity information is distributed across the array, if one drive bites the dust, the missing data can be reconstructed on the fly using the parity information that's written on the other drives. RAID 5's major disadvantage is cost. For the most part, only high-end SCSI RAID controllers are equipped to handle this setup, which means less-expensive IDE hard drives are out. RAID 5 is traditionally deployed in "enterprise" computing environments that require terabytes of storage space and minimal downtime.

Chapter Sixteen

Tweaking Your BIOS Settings

Better performance, reliability, and boot speed—this chapter shows you how to get the most from your PC's BIOS

The brand of BIOS your PC has depends entirely on which chip is used in your system's motherboard. Different manufacturers make different settings available to end users. Large PC manufacturers such as Dell and Micron lock end users out of the really dangerous stuff, so don't expect to do a lot of tweaking with one of their PCs.

The BIOS controls your PC's hardware at the very lowest levels. It determines the speed of your CPU, memory, and even some components. Because of this, tweaking your BIOS can net you huge gains in performance and reliability. Changing one minor setting can net you a 10% performance boost, while another could cost you as much as 40%. How do you know which settings will give your system a lift or bring it to its knees? Motherboard manuals usually leave something to be desired when it comes to explaining the workings of the BIOS. Not to fear—you're reading the most comprehensive BIOS optimization guide we've ever produced. We'll show you how to tweak your BIOS three different ways:

- To maximize performance
- To minimize boot times
- To make your PC more reliable

We'd be remiss if we didn't warn you that setting your BIOS incorrectly could keep your PC from booting. Before you make any changes to your BIOS, make a note of all of the original settings. And make sure that you follow the instructions explicitly, as any deviation may do damage. If you're not comfortable with the possibility of breaking your system, you shouldn't be tweaking your BIOS.

Before you begin, reread this text and the figure caption on the chapter's opening page. Done? Let's get started then!

Editor's Note

Avid readers of *Maximum PC* might recognize this chapter as one that appeared in our newsstand special, *The Ultimate PC How-to Guide 2004*. Mark Edward Soper, a longtime computer trainer and writer, wrote this chapter. We feel that the original article is the definitive treatise on BIOS tweaks for PCs, so we would be remiss if we didn't include it in this book. We took Mark's original text and updated it with the most current information so you can tweak *your* Dream PC. Enjoy.

Tweak Your BIOS for Maximum Performance

Tweak 1: Correct Your Memory Card and CPU Speeds

Overclocking can give your system a big performance boost, but before you can try upping your system's clock speeds, you should make sure the processor's frequency and clock-multiplier are set correctly. Your CPU's speed is determined by taking your system's frontside bus speed (FSB) and multiplying it by the clock multiplier. Both of these values are set in your system's BIOS. Overclockers are generally limited to adjusting the frequency, because most modern processors will operate at just one clock multiplier.

Many BIOSes correctly detect the processor frequency and clock multiplier for you. However, a lot of systems switch to a default fail-safe setting of 100MHz if the system locks up or powers-down during initial startup. The processor or FSB frequency is multiplied by a factor of two (most AMD CPUs) or a factor of four (most Intel CPUs) to obtain the processor's rated frontside-bus speed. Thus, a 100MHz setting in the BIOS is equivalent to a 200MHz FSB on an AMD system, or a 400MHz setting on an Intel system.

If your processor is designed to use a faster FSB speed (as most newer CPUs are), this fail-safe setting results in a significant performance drop. You should find this setting in the Frequency/Voltage Control menu or the Advanced menu. To determine the correct frequency to use, check the data sheet for your processor model at the vendor's website.

Tweak 2: User-Defined Memory Timing

Step 1: Adjusting CAS Latency

Manually tweaking your memory settings can yield big performance gains. The memory timing menu is usually located in the Advanced Chipset screen, or a submenu of this screen. Before you can adjust memory timing, you must change the Configure SDRAM Timing setting from the default of SPD to User. The default SPD setting uses the settings built into a chip on the memory modules to determine the proper memory timings. If you need to determine what the standard timing values are for the memory modules you use, and the BIOS doesn't show the actual values, check the memory vendor's website for the modules' data sheet.

There are two major ways to rate the speed of memory: frequency (measured in MHz) and latency (how quickly the module can send data after receiving a request). SDR memory usually features CAS (column-address-strobe) Latency values of 2 and 3 (lower is faster); DDR SDRAM is available with CAS Latency values of 2.5 and 2. Some systems display the CAS Latency value during startup.

To improve performance, try using a lower latency value. For example, if your memory has a CAS Latency value of 2.5, use 2 instead. If the system won't run properly, go back to the default CAS latency and try other adjustments.

Step 2: Adjusting Memory Timing and Access Factors

Depending on the BIOS your system uses, you can also adjust other memory timing factors, such as row precharge time, Row Address Strobe (RAS) pulse width, and RAS-to-CAS delay. Row precharge time (also referred to as tRP) refers to the amount of time needed in clock cycles to activate the memory bank. RAS pulse width (tRAS) refers to the amount of time in clock cycles to leave the row of memory open for data transfers. RAS-to-CAS delay (tRCD) refers to the amount of time needed to switch to a different row of memory to access data not found in the current row. For maximum speed, these should be set as fast as possible (smaller values are faster).

The following options have variable effects on performance:

Enable SDRAM 1T to synchronize RAM with the CPU's FSB if both run at the same speed. SDRAM Burst Length can sometimes improve performance when set to 8QW (que words). Fast Command controls how quickly the CPU interacts with memory (Normal, Fast, Ultra). Many systems default to Fast, but Ultra can be used in some cases to improve performance. Fast R-2-R Turnaround, when enabled, improves the speed of recovery from a burst operation.

Tweak 3: Adjust AGP Settings

The AGP menu might be located on its own or be incorporated into the Advanced Chipset menu. The first setting to check is the AGP mode. It should be set for the maximum speed supported by your motherboard and AGP card (usually 4× or 8× with today's hardware).

As you might expect, other AGP settings fall into the trial-and-error category. AGP FastWrite bypasses main memory when performing writes to AGP memory, which can boost write performance by as much as 10% when enabled. However, some games have problems with this setting. AGP Master 1 W/S Read and Write settings can be enabled to use one wait state (a memory cycle that performs no operation) instead of the default of two wait states for memory transfers to and from the AGP card. However, if your system uses a default of zero wait states, enabling these options can slow down your system instead of speeding it up. AGP Read Synchronization can cause stability problems if enabled, so it should be disabled. AGP Aperture Size controls the size of the GART (graphics address relocation table) and the amount of memory address space used for AGP memory addresses. A value of 64MB to 128MB is recommended.

Tweak 4: Improve PCI Bus Performance

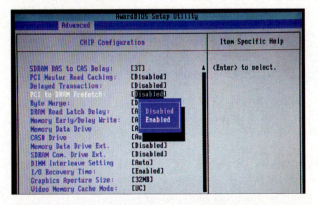

Enable the PCI Delay Transaction option (also referred to as PCI 2.1 Compliance or Delay Transaction) to improve performance if you have ISA cards. Enable the PCI To DRAM Prefetch option to improve the performance of IEEE 1394 and PCI-based soundcards. Enabling PCI Master Read Caching uses the processor's L2 cache

to cache reads from the PCI bus. Disabling this option can sometimes help performance by keeping the processor's L2 cache available for other processes. However, enabling this option in some Athlon-based systems helps lower the temperature of the processor. These options are usually located in the Advanced Chipset Features menu.

The PCI Latency Timer option might be located in the PnP/PCI Configuration menu. It configures how long each PCI device gets to control the PCI bus before allowing another device to take over. The maximum range of settings is 0 to 255, but some BIOSes provide only certain values in this range. Reducing the value from the default of 32 can improve the response time of each PCI device (0 provides the fastest response time and 255 the slowest) to fix problems with some cards. However, PCI bandwidth suffers as a result. Increase this value to increase bandwidth across the PCI bus if your PCI devices work at an acceptable rate.

Tweak 5: Power Up Peripherals

If you still use parallel ports for printers and other devices, you should configure the parallel port to run in EPP or ECP mode. (EPP is recommended for single printers, and ECP mode is recommended for daisy-chaining printers and other devices.) These settings provide the fastest input-output support available, and are typically located in the Integrated Peripherals menu. Make sure you use an IEEE 1284-compliant parallel cable to get the full benefit of this setting.

If you have switched to USB, keep in mind that using a hub to connect several USB 1.1 peripherals on a single USB 1.1 port (still the dominant type of USB port on most systems) can cause device slowdowns. Slowdowns are particularly likely if you connect low-speed USB 1.1 devices such as keyboards and mouse devices to the same port as faster devices, such as printers or disk drives. If you have more than two USB ports, make sure you enable all of them. Then use separate ports for full-speed and low-speed devices. The USB setting is also typically found in the Integrated Peripherals menu.

Tweaking the BIOS for Maximum Reliability

Tweak 1: Protect Your PC from Viruses

Although boot sector viruses are no longer the most common type of virus threat, every time you reuse a floppy disk, you put your system at risk of a virus infection. This feature is a step beyond write-protecting the boot sector, because it can distinguish between legitimate changes to the boot sector caused by operating system upgrades and boot managers and virus infections. You can find this option on the Standard CMOS Features, Advanced CMOS Features, or Boot menus of typical systems.

Tweak 2: Watch for Hard Drive Failure

Enabling this feature supports the Self-Monitoring and Reporting Technology (S.M.A.R.T.) feature of recent ATA/IDE hard disks. S.M.A.R.T.-enabled drives can warn you of serious impending problems before the drive goes kaput, giving you time to back up your data and test the drive with vendor-supplied utilities. If you don't run S.M.A.R.T.-compatible software such as Norton System Works, you will only see a warning of a problem with a compatible drive at system startup. You can find this option on the Advanced CMOS/BIOS Features menu of some systems, or as an individual configuration option for each ATA/IDE drive.

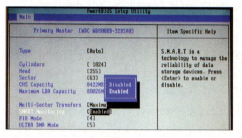

Tweak 3: Monitor Vital System Temps

This option is found on the Power Management menu of some recent systems. When you enable it, you will be warned when your CPU exceeds the temperature you specify. Typical temperature options include 70 degrees Celsius (158 degrees Fahrenheit) up to 95 degrees Celsius (203 degrees Fahrenheit) in five-degree Celsius increments. Don't substitute this for adequate processor cooling, but use it along with other stability options to warn you of problems.

Tweak 4: Watch for Faulty Fans

If a CPU or chassis fan fails, your system will crash in short order because of overheating, and you might also fry your processor as a most unwelcome bonus. Some systems monitor the CPU and chassis fans automatically if they are connected to the motherboard. However, in other cases you must enable this feature on the PC Health screen. If your motherboard or system includes software that can receive fan status messages from the BIOS, this setting provides cheap insurance against fan and system failure.

Tweak 5: Don't Fear Losing Power

If you are running a system that always needs to be on (such as an Internet Connection Sharing gateway or a server), enabling this option in the Power Management Features menu will automatically restart your system in the event of a power loss. If you'd prefer to restore the system to whatever state it was in when the lights went out, select Last State instead.

Tweak 6: Free Unused Ports

Serial and parallel ports are ISA devices that can't share IRQs with newer PCI devices, such as USB ports. Although systems with ACPI power management can assign multiple PCI devices to the same IRQ, doing so can reduce system reliability and cause conflicts between devices. If you don't use serial and parallel ports anymore, disable them in the Integrated Peripherals or I/O Device Configuration menu to help free up the settings they use for use by newer devices. Serial ports use IRQ 4 (COM 1) and IRQ 3 (COM 2) by default, and the parallel port uses IRQ 7 by default.

Tweak 7: Reserve Resources for Legacy Hardware

Some systems assume that IRQs from 3 up to 15 are fair game for PCI/PnP devices. However, if you still have non-PnP ISA devices, you'd better reserve the IRQs they use. Disabling legacy ports helps make more IRQs available, but some systems won't use IRQs below 9 for PCI/PnP devices unless you specifically adjust the PnP/PCI menu to enable these IRQs.

Tweak 8: Minimize Component Interference

The Spread Spectrum feature in some recent systems' Frequency/Voltage Control menu is designed to help systems pass CE (European) EMI interference tests. However, leaving this feature enabled, especially with large values for the voltage fluctuation, can cause loss of Internet connections and stability problems in over-clocking. You can sometimes adjust the voltage difference used as an alternative to disabling the feature completely.

Tweak 9: Use Only USB Legacy Settings If You Must

Originally, USB Legacy mode was intended to support USB keyboards when used at a system command prompt or the BIOS setup program. More recent systems can also support mouse devices and USB floppy drives. In some cases, enabling USB legacy support for devices you don't use can cause other devices to stop functioning when you try to come out of a hibernation or standby mode. The USB Legacy mode might be located on the Integrated Peripherals, Advanced, or other menus.

Tweak 10: Use the Standby State That Makes Sense to You

The Advanced Configuration and Power Interface (ACPI) standard supports several different standby modes. The most common are S1/POS and S3/STR. The S3 (Suspend to RAM) option saves more power, but doesn't work with devices that don't support the ACPI specification. If you are using older peripherals or aren't sure if the devices you have connected to the computer work in the S3 mode, enable the S1 mode. This option is typically found on the Power Management Features menu.

Tweak 11: Don't Cache the BIOS

The contents of the system BIOS are copied to L2 cache when this option is enabled (it is usually found in the Advanced BIOS Features menu). However, various problems can result when this option is enabled, including system crashes if programs try to write to the BIOS area and USB conflicts on some systems with Via chipsets. Disable this option to avoid headaches, and you'll suffer little if any real-world impact on system performance.

Tweak 12: Check Your Cache

Most systems don't support ECC memory, but if your BIOS (and your processor's L2 cache) support this option, you can get much of the benefit of ECC memory with off-the-shelf non-parity memory. It also helps improve reliability when you overclock your system. This option is typically located on the Advanced or Chipset BIOS menu. To determine whether your processor's L2 cache supports ECC, get the data sheet for your processor from your processor vendor's website.

Tweak Your BIOS for Maximum Boot Speed

Tweak 1: Switch Hard Disks from Auto to User-Defined

Step 1: Find Your Drives in the BIOS

```
AMIBIOS NEW SETUP UTILITY - VERSION 3.31a

    Standard CMOS Features                       [ Setup Help ]

   System Time              :   16:42:31       Primary IDE Master
   System Date                  Oct 03 2003 Fri   Configuration

 ▶ Primary IDE Master          Maxtor 6E040L0
 ▶ Primary IDE Slave           Not Installed
 ▶ Secondary IDE Master        LITE-ON LTR-32123
 ▶ Secondary IDE Slave         WDC AC31200F

   Floppy Drive A              1.44 MB 3½
   Floppy Drive B              Not Installed

   Boot Sector Virus Protection  Disabled
```

By default, most modern systems are configured to detect the specifics of your hard drive every time you boot your PC. Switching the setting for installed drives to User-Defined bypasses the drive-detection process and speeds boot times. The first BIOS setup screen on many systems is the Standard CMOS Feature screen. It'll display a list of drives currently installed in your PC. If you don't see a list of your drives, look for a setting called IDE Drive Auto-Detect on the main BIOS screen. It works the same way.

Before proceeding, keep in mind that there's one good reason for keeping the Auto-Detect option enabled: If you use a hardware boot selection device such as the Romtec Trios (www.romtec.com), the Auto-detect feature lets you select which drive(s) to use at startup.

Step 2: Record Drive Settings

```
AMIBIOS NEW SETUP UTILITY - VERSION 3.31a

   Primary IDE Master:Maxtor 6E040L0             [ Setup Help ]

   Type                       Auto          1-50: Predefined types
   Cylinders                  19680         USER: Set Parameters
   Heads                      16                  by User
   Write Precompensation                    AUTO: Set parameters
   Sectors                    255                 automatically
       Maximum Capacity       41111 Mb      CD-ROM: Use for ATAPI
   LBA Mode                   On                  CD-ROM drives
   Block Mode                 On            Or
   Fast Programmed I/O Modes  4             Double click [AUTO] to
   32 Bit Transfer Mode       On            set all HDD parameters
                                            automatically
```

On most modern systems, the Automatic setting displays the drive's configuration. This configuration is read by the system BIOS from the hard disk's firmware using a feature called the Identify Drive command. This feature enables your BIOS to accurately install a hard disk, even if you don't know the correct settings for the drive.

Write down the info corresponding to the Cylinders, Heads, Write Precompensation, and Sectors (per track). Also write down settings for the LBA Mode, Block Mode, Fast-Programmed I/O (PIO), and Ultra DMA Mode settings. Alternatively, you can check the drive vendor's website for this information.

Record this information accurately because you'll manually duplicate these settings in the next step. If you make an error recording the information, you will set the system incorrectly and your computer won't boot.

Step 3: Configure the Drive As User-Defined

```
AMIBIOS NEW SETUP UTILITY - VERSION 3.31a

    Primary IDE Master                            [ Setup Help ]

   Type                       User          Select <Auto> for a
   Cylinders                  19680         hard disk > 512 MB
   Heads                      16            under DOS and Windows,
   Write Precompensation      8             Select <Disabled> under
   Sectors                    255           Nerware and UNIX.
       Maximum Capacity       41111 Mb
   LBA Mode                   On
   Block Mode                 On
   Fast Programmed I/O Modes  4
   32 Bit Transfer Mode       On
```

After you record the drive's settings, move the cursor to the Type field (currently set as Auto) and change it to User or User-Defined. The values for Cylinders, Heads, Sectors For Track, and so on are now blank.

Enter the values you recorded in Step 2. Use the arrow keys to move from field to field. It's essential that the drive is configured manually the same way it was detected by the system. If you screw up one or more of the settings, the computer won't boot from the drive or be able to recognize its contents.

Repeat Steps 2 and 3 for each ATA/IDE drive installed (select CD or CD/DVD for CD-ROM or other optical drives). If you don't need to make any additional changes, save your changes and exit the system BIOS setup. Your computer will restart.

Tweak 2: Streamline the Boot Sequence

Step 1: Determine the Correct Boot Sequence

Even when you configure your drives as User-Defined, the typical system that boots off a hard drive still spends a lot of time looking for boot devices that you're probably not using, such as CD-ROM and floppy drives, Serial ATA, and others.

In most systems, the boot menu is part of the Advanced BIOS Features or Advanced BIOS Setup menu, or a submenu of that menu. Note that the floppy drive is listed first, followed by the CD-ROM drive, and then the hard disk. On systems configured this way, the floppy and CD-ROM are checked for boot files before the hard disk, wasting valuable time at each reboot.

Step 2: Make the Primary ATA/IDE Drive the First (or Only) Boot Device

Select the first boot device and change it to the first ATA/IDE drive (this might be referred to as IDE-0).

Because this drive will always be used to boot the system, you can disable the other boot devices. If you need to boot from a CD or a floppy disk in the future (such as for an operating system upgrade or repair), you can restart the BIOS setup program and reconfigure the boot sequence menu accordingly.

Tweak 3: Disable Memory Check and Floppy Drive Seek

Many systems waste time at startup by performing a memory check and a floppy drive seek. The memory check seldom finds memory problems (even if they exist). If you don't boot from the floppy drive, there's no reason to check the drive at boot time for a boot disk. To disable the memory check, open the Advanced BIOS Features or Boot menu and enable the Quick Boot or Quick Power On Self Test options. Disable the Floppy Drive Seek option in the Advanced BIOS Features or Boot menu.

Tweak 4: Disable Serial ATA (SATA) Host Adapter

If the SATA host adapter built into many modern systems is enabled but no drives are present, the BIOS wastes time trying to detect drives before giving up and continuing the boot process. The SATA Host Adapter setting is usually located in the Integrated Peripherals menu, or a submenu of this menu. In this BIOS, it is located in the OnBoard PCI Controller menu within the Integrated Peripherals menu. Disable it to more speedily boot!

Tweak 5: Disable Onboard ATA BIOS

If your system has three or four ATA host adapter connectors instead of the normal pair, it's designed to support additional ATA drives in either normal mode or as an ATA RAID array. We love ATA RAID arrays here at *Maximum PC*, but if you don't have any drives connected to the hard drive controllers, leaving them enabled just wastes precious time at boot. The ATA BIOS option should be located in the Boot menu or in the Onboard Peripherals menu.

Tweak 6: Enable PCI IDE BusMaster

Bus mastering ATA/IDE host adapters provide a huge speed boost when enabled, but if they're disabled, your drives will be stuck using slower PIO access methods. Look for this option on the PnP/PCI menu or Integrated Peripherals menu. Don't forget to install the appropriate bus mastering drivers for your motherboard chipset in Windows to finish the job.

Chapter Seventeen

Optimizing Your OS

Maximum PC presents a slew of expert tips that will help you transform your Windows XP into a faster, stronger, leaner operating system

Ingredients		%Daily Value
Speed	Page 209	14%
Security	Page 211	11%
Gaming	Page 212	13%
Interface	Page 213	20%
Day-to-day usage	Page 216	19%
Audio	Page 218	11%
Applications	Page 221	12%
Total Tips:		30+
Coolness factor:		Extreme
BS factor:		Nil
Minutes saved:		100,000,000

XP EXTREME

Warning: *Maximum PC's* Windows tips induce more powerful, speedier responses than other magazines' tips. *Maximum PC's* Windows tips may induce spontaneous bursts of excitement and unprecedented levels of productivity.

Speed Up Windows

Windows XP is pretty self-sufficient, but you can administer a few tweaks to even the best behaved XP box to squeeze more performance from it

Get the Latest Drivers

There's a reason why we mention this every time we dole out Windows tips: It should *always* be your starting point. Getting the latest drivers for your hardware can give you a big performance boost, while making your PC more stable at the same time. You don't need to update drivers for all the hardware in your machine, just the crucial components. We recommend you update your videocard, motherboard chipset, and soundcard drivers regularly, but drivers for your mouse, keyboard, and other USB devices need to be updated only when you experience problems.

Disable Windows' Bells and Whistles

The Performance Options dialog provides several options for the performance-conscious. You can either disable all the fancy-schmancy interface options that Windows XP added, or pick and choose the features you'll sacrifice.

Windows XP is the best-looking OS from Microsoft to date, but those good looks aren't free. The fancy new UI, drop shadows, and other bells and whistles can really affect your PC's performance. Luckily, these features are easy to disable.

- First, go to System Properties by pressing the Windows key and Pause/Break simultaneously. Go to the Advanced tab and click the Settings button in the Performance section.

- On the Visual Effects tab of the Settings dialog (see image), change the setting to Adjust for Best Performance. You can also pick and choose your settings by using the Custom option if you prefer. When you're done, click OK and close System Properties.

- Now cruise over to Display Properties by right-clicking an open area of your Desktop and clicking Properties. Go to the Appearance tab and then click Effects. For best performance, make sure all the options here are unchecked.

- Drawing a bunch of icons on your Desktop can really affect performance, especially if you have a lot of real estate with a multi-monitor display. If you'd rather take a solid kick to the groin than clean up the unneeded icons, you can sweep them under the rug simply and easily. Just right-click an open area of your Desktop, go to Arrange Icons, and uncheck Show Desktop Icons. Voilà, your problem is solved!

Torpedo System Tray Apps—Keep Evil Apps from Eating Your Resources

Every frickin' application we install lately seems to dump some sort of craptacular applet into our System Tray. We're so sick of it that we now summarily give these tiny apps the death penalty. Don't worry—it's easy and fun for the whole family!

To kill the apps, you need to root them out at their source. You could visit the Registry, the Startup folder, and the other secret places that software apps hide their auto-starting hellspawn, but it's easier to use the msconfig tool. To start it, go to Start, Run, and then type **msconfig.exe**. When the app opens, go to the Startup tab. The vast majority of your evil systray apps can be disabled from here.

The difficulty lies in figuring out which apps you need and which you don't. Stretch the command heading far enough to the right so you can see the entire path to the app. Most of the time, you'll be able to tell the name or manufacturer of the app by looking at the place where it's saved on your hard drive. If the path to the application doesn't give you a hint, open My Computer and browse down to the program. Right-click it and select Properties. Click the version tab and browse through the options there. Look for a company name or product name to tip you off. We recommend leaving alone any apps that use rundll32 to run—if you mess with those, you can disrupt vital Windows processes. If you can't find the app, a frequently updated list of common startup apps can be found at http://www.pacs-portal.co.uk/startup_index.htm.

To disable the startup apps, all you need to do is uncheck the box next to each app's name and reboot your PC. It's that simple.

Turn Off Unnecessary Services

By default, Windows XP Professional loads more than 20 services that do everything from facilitating easy wireless networking to monitoring your PC's health. Many of the services can be safely disabled by home users, which frees up memory and the occasional CPU cycle. To disable a service, go to Control Panel, Administrative Tools, then the Services hotkey. Right-click the service you want to disable and select Properties. Then change the Startup Type to Disabled or Manual. Disabling the wrong service could cause

Msconfig lets you selectively disable startup apps. It's tricky to tell what item goes with what app, though, because of the cryptic names. It might be obvious that NeroCheck has something to do with Nero CD burning software, but what's nwiz? The easiest way to find out is to search for the item's name in Google. Nine times out of 10, someone on the net has already tracked it down.

A service is nothing more than a fancy application that Windows runs at boot and then monitors to make sure it continues running. Disabling unneeded services can help you conserve precious system resources.

odd things to happen, so keep track of what you're modifying, and if you experience any unexplained PC phenomena, re-enable the services you've turned off. Here's our list of tried-and-true services that are safe to disable:

- **ClipBook:** This service lets you share stuff on your clipboard with other people across the network. Kill it.

- **Application Management:** Not on a network? Don't ever plan on remotely installing an app? That's what this service does, so feel free to kill it.

- **Distributed Link Tracking Client:** Another network-based service, this automatically updates your shortcuts to files on remote volumes if they're moved. If you don't use a file server, kill this one.

- **Error Reporting:** Automatic error reporting can get pretty annoying, especially if you're dealing with a misbehaving app. You can kill this service to permanently disable the error report.

- **TCP/IP NetBIOS Helper:** You only need this service running if you use NetBIOS over TCP/IP. If you don't, feel free to kill it.

Secure Your PC
Criminal Internet capers are on the rise. Protect yourself from evildoers!

Install a Firewall

This isn't so much a tip as a general guideline. Everyone whose PC is directly connected to the Net, whether it's via a dial-up or broadband connection, should install firewall software. A firewall moderates your connection to the network. Whenever an app tries to send out data or someone on the Internet tries to connect to your computer, the firewall will ask you if that behavior is allowed. You can then allow or disallow the connection.

Firewall software is freely available for personal use, and it protects your PC from most worms and viruses that spread without user intervention. We recommend ZoneAlarm (www.zonealarm.com) for ease of configuration and use, even for relative newbies.

Will Overclocking My PC Make My Windows Apps Run Faster?

Maybe. It depends on the type of overclocking you're talking about. Videocard overclocking gives you absolutely no benefit in 2D Windows apps. In fact, many videocards automatically underclock themselves when they're running in 2D mode.

CPU overclocking, on the other hand, can make a pretty significant impact on some Windows applications. Content creation apps like Photoshop can really benefit from a faster CPU, but MS Office staples Word and Excel show little to no performance boost when you upgrade from 2GHz to 3GHz, or even higher. More common tasks, such as web browsing or checking email, benefit even less than Office apps.

The only real reason to overclock is for faster gaming performance. In many games, cranking up the CPU or videocard clocks gives you a commensurate frame rate boost. If you can squeeze out 10% more from your videocard core, you could easily net a 10% frame rate boost in your favorite game.

Install Antivirus Software

Antivirus software is absolutely vital today, especially if you download email using Outlook and Outlook Express. Having the proper antivirus software installed will stop those pesky viruses that email everyone in your address book a message containing an infectious attachment. If you don't already have an antivirus program, you should definitely purchase one as soon as possible. We're not kidding. We have recommended Norton Anti-Virus 2003 in the past, but we haven't had a chance to evaluate the 2004 version yet. If you don't want to wait, download AVG 7.0 Free Edition from www.grisoft.com.

Disable Unsecure Services

We've already touched upon a few of the unnecessary services anyone can disable, but there are also some services that are actual security holes. If you're not sure how to disable services, turn back to the "Speed Up Windows" section and check the tip titled "Turn Off Unnecessary Services."

- **Messenger:** In the last year, spammer scum have realized that they can use Windows' built-in messaging service to send spam to millions of XP users. Disabling the service kills all the incoming spam, and no one uses the Messenger service for actual system administration messages anymore.

- **Remote Registry:** The only purpose of this service is to give other users access to your Registry. If no one but you should have access to your Registry, disable it.

- **Telnet:** If allowing other people to log on to your computer and do whatever they want seems like a good idea, then by all means go ahead and leave the Telnet service enabled. If you'd rather your PC not be taken over by Croatian haX0rs, you should disable it.

Don't Stop at Windows—Protect Your Wireless LAN

Once your Windows install is properly secure, turn your eyes to your wireless LAN. Most of the wizard-type access-point installations leave your wireless network wide open for any passing scammer to use. Make absolutely certain that your Wi-Fi LAN uses something other than the manufacturer's default SSID, and always encrypt data moving across your LAN with either WEP encryption or the newer, better WPA encryption. To find out how to change your SSID and enable WEP, you should consult the documentation that came with your access point.

Improve Gaming

Read on to find the perfect balance of frame rate and visual quality in today's demanding 3D games

Get an Easy, Fast Speed Bump, Without Overclocking!

This is a trick we picked up from sneaky system vendors who use it to gain a decent performance boost in exchange for image quality degradation.

1. Open your Display Properties by right-clicking the Desktop and selecting Properties.

2. Go to the Settings tab and click Advanced.

3. Go to the Image Quality tab on nVidia cards, or the 3D tab for ATI cards. Browse to the custom setting and change the texture quality to the minimum setting. Do the same for the mip-map levels slider.

Your image quality will decline drastically, but your frame rates will get much better!

Use Profiles to Make Switching from Multiplayer Settings to Single-player Settings Simple and Fast

Both ATI and nVidia have a feature in their latest control panel applications that lets you save all vendor-specific videocard settings in a profile. We recommend you set up one profile with high image-quality settings for single-player games, and a low-quality profile for online games in which you want to max out your frame rates.

Overclock Your Videocard for a Frame Rate Boost

Getting a few more frames a second can mean the difference between life and death in a heated online deathmatch. Most video-cards have plenty of headroom, which gives you a perfect opportunity to crank up the clock speeds and get a little more performance from a struggling system. Remember that overclocking voids your warranty, and just because we've never heard of anyone frying their videocard by overclocking doesn't mean that it's not entirely possible.

Our favorite videocard app is PowerStrip. Download PowerStrip at www.powerstrip.com and install it on your PC. Once it's running, right-click the System Tray icon, select Performance, and click Configure. You should see two vertical sliders: one for the engine (a.k.a. *core*) clock, and one for the memory clock. To overclock your card, all you need to do is move the sliders up.

We recommend that you take baby steps when you overclock videocards. Start with 5MHz increments for a single clock. Adjust the core clock first and then test your card by playing an intensive game. When you're playing, watch the screen for any artifacts, static, or deformed polygons. Once you are sure the card is sta-ble at the new clock rate, bump the core clock up another 5MHz. You'll know you've reached the board's limit when you see visual artifacts while testing. When that happens, exit the game and lower the core clock back down 5MHz.

Once you've tested your core clocks, it's time to get started on the memory. Don't expect to push your video-card's memory as far as you can the core clock. Also, you need to remember that the memory clock reported here is the actual clock speed of your card's double data-rate memory, not the effective clock speed that is written on your product's box. Increase the memory clock in small increments using the slider in PowerStrip and then test the changes in a stressful game.

Customize Your Interface

These simple steps allow you to turn Windows XP into your own personal OS

Force Alphabetic Sorting of the Program Menu

Clicking Sort By Name in the All Programs menu makes it a lot easier to find your applications, but Windows XP needs constant reminders to sort applica-tions this way. This tweak will permanently sort all your programs alphabetically.

- Open the Registry and go to HKEY_Current User\Software\Microsoft\Windows\Current-Version\Explorer\Menu Order.

- On the Edit menu, select Permissions.

- In the Permissions for Menu Order dialog box, click Advanced.

- In the Advanced Security Settings for Menu Order dialog box, clear the Inherit From Parent check box.

- In the security dialog box that appears, click Copy.

- Click OK to return to the Permissions for Menu Order dialog box, and then clear the Full Control Access entry for your own account and for any security groups that you're a member of, leaving the Read Access Control entry in place.

What Do Antialiasing and Anisotropic Filtering Do? Do They Need to Be On?

Antialiasing and anisotropic filtering minimize the visual impact of rendering errors in games. Antialiasing smoothes the jagged lines that form on the edges of polygons. Modern videocards antialias polygons by rendering a scene in higher detail than is requested, and then blending it down to a lower detail level. The more samples that are rendered, the smoother the edges look, but increasing the number of samples greatly increases the amount of memory bandwidth required.

You can override your games' antialiasing and anisotropic filtering settings, but it's not always a good idea.

Anisotropic filtering helps remove the artifacts created when you stretch a flat, square two-dimensional texture over a three-dimensional model. Anisotropic filtering samples several different texture qualities to ensure that textures that stretch from the foreground into the background draw properly. Without anisotropic filtering, affected textures will lose definition and appear muddy. Like antialiasing, anisotropic filtering is dependent on memory bandwidth.

Whether you should turn on antialiasing and anisotropic filtering depends on the type of videocard you have, your PC's speed, and the type of game you're playing. For single-player games such as *Knights of the Old Republic* or *Deus Ex: Invisible War*, we generally crank up the image quality all the way. As long as the frame rate stays above 30fps, we're happy in single-player games. This means that a person with a fast CPU and videocard can run single-player games with antialiasing at 4× and anisotropic filtering at 8× and experience a great-looking game. If your PC won't run your games at this high a setting, try 2× AA and 4× aniso.

On the other hand, in multiplayer games, frame rate equals life. If you're in a deathmatch and your opponent's PC renders the game at 60fps, but your PC is chugging along at just 30fps, he gets twice as many chances as you to aim and shoot. Frame rate is especially important in games like *Planetside*, where 300-person battles aren't uncommon. For multiplayer games, we generally turn down the detail (and the fancy features like antialiasing and anisotropic filtering) all the way, but run at the highest resolution we can while maintaining 60fps.

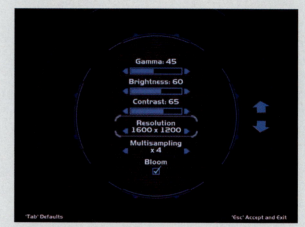

Many newer games let end users set antialiasing and anisotropic filtering in-game instead of forcing settings in the driver's control panel.

Most of the games we test today are limited by the available memory bandwidth of the videocard more than anything else. As we see more games that utilize programmable shader technology, we expect that memory bandwidth will become less an issue, and that shader capabilities will become the limiting factor. From early benchmarks, it looks like *Half-Life 2* will be limited by shader performance more than memory bandwidth. If this ends up being the case, you should be able to enable bandwidth intensive features like AA and aniso without any impact on your frame rate at all.

Group Your Taskbar More Effectively

Windows XP automatically groups applications together when the taskbar fills up, but you can make it group items whenever you'd like.

- Open the Start Menu, select Run, and type **Regedit**.

- Go to HKEY_Current_User\Software\ Microsoft\Windows\CurrentVersion\Explorer\ Advanced.

- Click Edit, select New, and then select DWORD value.

- Name this new value **TaskbarGroupSize**.

- Once named, right-click it and select Modify.

- Type in the number of windows that appear before Windows starts grouping them. We like the number 5, but use a smaller number if you want an uncluttered taskbar or a higher number if you like to see each open window.

If you want to avoid taskbar clutter, pick a low number for this setting to keep multiple windows of the same app grouped together.

Make Your Start Menu Easier to Navigate

Is Start menu clutter chapping your hide? Put a little breathing room between all those apps with this handy hack.

- Right-click your desktop and make a new shortcut.

- Select any target for this shortcut (it really doesn't matter which).

- To give the shortcut a name, erase any text in the Name field and hold down the Alt key while punching **0160** on the number pad, which will give the shortcut an empty field for a name. Click OK.

- Right-click the new shortcut and remove the target. Next, click Change Icon and select a blank icon. Now simply drag it onto the start button, and then drag it to the desired location.

We love pinning apps to the Start menu, but when the list gets too long, it's time to add one of these separators to make navigation easier.

Get Rid of Your eBooks Once and for All

Let us guess—you deleted My eBooks, My Videos, and My Music only to open up the same folder a few minutes later and find they had in fact, not been deleted after all. Get rid of them for good!

- Go to Start and then select Run.

- Type **Regsvr32 /u mydocs.dll** and hit Enter.

- Go into My Documents and delete any of those "My" folders you want—they're not coming back!

Use this little hack, which allows you to use different desktop wallpaper for each of your displays. As always, be sure to use a high-res image to reduce dithering.

• Right-click your desktop and then select Properties.

• Under the Desktop section, select Customize Desktop and then select the Web tab.

• To use an image file located on your hard drive, select New and browse to the file's location. Once you've selected the file you want, click OK and it will appear on your desktop.

• Now simply drag the image over to the second desktop, and from the image's pull-down menu in the upper left-hand corner, select Cover Desktop.

• Right-click and select Arrange By and Lock Web Items on Desktop. Now you can select a standard desktop for your primary display, and use the web object to cover the standard desktop image on your second desktop with the image of your choice.

Woohoo! I got a big one! Although a JPEG isn't a "web object," it still works as desktop wallpaper.

Optimize Your Day-to-Day Usage of Windows XP

Improve OS clutter and enhance your overall Windows experience with this collection of handy, obscure, and extremely powerful tricks, hacks, and tweaks

Monitor Your CPU Usage at All Times

Ever wonder what your CPU is up to? Keep an eye on it by sticking the CPU monitor from the Task Manager in your System Tray.

• Go to C:\Windows\System 32 and find Taskmgr.exe. Right-click it and select Send To Desktop. Go to that new shortcut and right-click it and then select Properties.

• Under the Run command, select Minimized and click OK.

• Rename the shortcut "CPU Meter" or something similar, and cut it from your desktop using Ctrl+X.

• Right-click the Start menu, select Explore All Users, and then click on the Programs folder and then the Startup folder. Paste the CPU Meter into the Startup folder.

• You should see it pop up in your System Tray. If not, open the Task Manager and under Options make sure Minimize On Use and Hide When Minimized are selected.

"I'm giving her all she's got, captain!" Keep tabs on your CPU by sticking this handy little CPU monitor in your System Tray.

Automate Hard Drive Cleaning

Want your hard drive to be fresh and ready to roll whenever you sit down to compute? So do we. This little tweak automates the hard drive "cleaning" process and keeps your drive bright-eyed and bushy-sectored.

- Right-click your desktop and create a new text file. In this file, type the following:

```
C:\windows\system32\cleanmgr.exe /dc /sage-
set: 1
C:
cd\
cd c:\windows\prefetch
del *.* /q
```

- Save the file, but change the extension to **.bat**. Name it whatever you like.

- Now run the file you just renamed. This opens the Disk Cleaner program. Select the items you'd like it to clean for you when it runs unattended, and then click OK.

- Right-click the file you created and select Edit. Change the first line to read

```
C:\windows\system32\cleanmgr.exe /dc
/sagerun: 1
```

- Save the file. Now you can execute it to automatically clean up your disks, or set it to run automatically via Control Panel\Scheduled Tasks\Add New Task.

This quick, simple batch file will keep your drive clean without your intervention.

Shut Down Your PC Faster

If you're sick of clicking Start, Shut Down, and then OK, listen up.

- Right-click your desktop and create a new shortcut.

- In the location line, type **shutdown –s –t 0**.

- Name it and click OK. You might want to give it a different icon, such as the red shutdown icon.

- Drag this icon onto your Quick Launch taskbar or leave it on the desktop. Either way, clicking it once will now completely shut down your PC.

To make a similar restart shortcut, the location line needs to read **shutdown –r –t 0**. (That's a zero at the end, not an "oh.")

Boom. One click and your PC turns itself off. Handy, huh?

Endless Supply of New Folders

This is an easy way to create new folders. Rather than using the File menu or right-clicking and selecting New, Folder, you can just use the Quick Launch toolbar instead.

- Surf over to C:\Documents and Settings\ Username\Application Data\Microsoft\ Internet Explorer\Quick Launch.

- Open the Quick Launch folder and create a new folder within this folder. Leave its name as New Folder.

- You'll see that a New Folder has appeared in your Quick Launch toolbar. To create a new folder anywhere on your PC, simply hold down the Ctrl key and drag the new folder to its location.

Drag this little folder out of your Quick Launch toolbar to create a New Folder anywhere, anytime you choose.

Choose Your Search Companion

We really hate the XP search companion, so here's a way to toggle back and forth between the OG style and the new doggy style.

- Go into the Registry and click to HKEY_CURRENT_USER\Software\Microsoft\Windows\ CurrentVersion\Explore\CabinetState.

- Open the CabinetState key, right-click inside the right-side pane and select New, String Value.

- Name this new value **Use Search Asst** and then press Enter.

- Right-click this new value, type **No** in the value data field, and then close the dialog box. Now right-click the CabinetState key and select Export. Name the file you are exporting **Disable Search Companion** and make sure the Selected Branch Option button is selected. Close the Registry editor.

- Open the Disable Search Companion Registry entry in Notepad and find the line

```
Use Search Asst = no
```

Change that value to **yes**, all in lowercase. Save this entry as **Enable Search Asst**.

Now whenever you click on each of these respective Registry keys, they take effect immediately—no reboot required.

Don't tell PETA, but we banished the puppy from our search window forever! Luckily, we can coax him into returning with just a few clicks of the mouse.

Customize Windows' Preset Folder Display

Whenever you open a file on your PC, Microsoft lovingly presents you with preset folder options on the left side of the dialog box. Thanks, Redmond, but we don't open items from our History or Favorites very often. Here's how to put what you want in that list.

- Go into the Registry and cruise to HKEY_CUR-RENT_USERS\Software\Microsoft\Windows\CurrentVersion\Policies\comdlg32.

- Create a new key called **Placesbar**. Inside this key, create a string named **Place0** and point it to the folder you want to appear on the Open dialog box, such as C:\CurrentWork, for example.

- Create another string called **Places1** and point it to another location on your drive.

An easier way to tackle this tweak is to download TweakUI (see accompanying sidebar), which will allow you to similarly customize your menus. Just open Common Dialogs, Places Bar, and then select or type the locations of your preferred folders.

Optimize Windows Audio

Tune and perfect Windows XP's audio settings

Set Your Soundcard for the Type of Output You're Using

If you're like us, you use speakers in the day and switch to headphones when your spouse, children, or roommates go to bed. However, switching to headphones from speakers isn't just a simple matter of jacking in. Modern advanced audio hardware uses complex algorithms to render audio. These algorithms are so precise that playing with headphones when the soundcard is still set to render for desktop speakers will make everything sound a little off and/or distorted.

To optimize your audio for your output device, steer to your soundcard's speaker configuration applet and look for a setting that lets you change it to 7.1, 6.1, 5.1, 2.1, or headphones. In some cases, you might have to reboot. If your card doesn't have an applet control for speaker configuration, use the one built into Windows XP. Go to Control Panel\Sounds\Audio Devices, and under Speaker Settings, select Advanced. Then pick your poison. In cards like the Sound Blaster Audigy 2 ZS or onboard audio devices such as Analog Devices' SoundMax, setting the application applet will override

Three Utilities That Make XP Tweaking Easy

Foraging around in the Windows Registry is sort of like defusing a bomb—one wrong move and it's lights out for your OS and your PC. It's also time-consuming to edit keys individually, which is why several utilities exist that allow easy and relatively safe access to myriad Registry hacks.

TweakUI: The most popular of these utilities is easily Microsoft's very own TweakUI. It's a part of Microsoft's XP PowerToys, a set of free enhancements for XP that are designed—but not officially supported—by Microsoft. This app is divided into nine major groupings, and offers tweaks for everything from Internet Explorer to Windows menus, dialog boxes, mouse movements, and so forth. Although Microsoft doesn't allow this utility to be distributed via our cover-mount disk, we've placed a link to PowerToys in the disc's Extra section—or just go to www.microsoft.com/powertoys.

X-Setup: Another useful tweaking app is X-Setup from Xteq Systems (www.xteq.com). This powerful utility goes above and beyond the settings available in TweakUI by delivering a dizzying array of tweaks most people don't even know are possible. It includes mundane tweaks such as disabling your keyboard's Windows keys, to advanced tactics such as clearing out the XP Prefetch folder, to setting timeout lengths for locked programs. Xteq calls its program the "ultimate tool for black belt system tuning," and it's not whistling Dixie.

TweakXP: (www.tweakxp.com) is the largest and most useful repository of Windows XP tweaks we've found anywhere. In fact, some of the tips found in this chapter were discovered on this website! The site is literally a clearing house for every possible Windows XP tweak available. Bookmark it now!

the Windows XP setting. Keep in mind that some soundcard drivers might need you to set both the Windows XP control panel and the soundcard applet for the setting to work properly.

Not setting the applet for the correct output device will cause audio artifacts or incorrect audio rendering.

You might have to go into the Windows XP Control Panel to set your sound subsystem to match the output device.

Enable Stereo Expansion Modes

If you have a set of 7.1 or 5.1 surround speakers hooked up to your PC and you play mostly MP3 or CD audio, you may have noticed that audio only comes out through the front pair of stereo speakers. That's because, unlike video games or DVD movies, the

source audio on most MP3s and CD audio is stereo only. Fortunately, most advanced audio hardware today features expansion modes that can filter the audio. In these filtered modes, music and vocals can be shunted to the front speakers, while instruments are sent to the rear. Other modes duplicate the front stereo to the rear for a fuller sound. To enable this, poke around in your audio applet and look for an expansion check box. In the popular Creative Labs series of Live!, Audigy, and Audigy 2 cards, it's called CMSS or CMSS2. Enabling audio expansion or just turning on Stereo Surround should give those other slacker satellites some work.

DirectSound Good, Wave Out Bad

Applications such as the popular WinAmp and many soft DVD players default to the wave out for audio. Unfortunately, using wave out does all the mixing in software, thus stealing precious CPU cycles. That might not matter if you're pushing a 3.2GHz P4 or Athlon 64 FX hog, but if you paid extra for an Audigy 2 ZS or nForce2 motherboard with advanced audio, what's the point of rendering it on the CPU? To set your PC to use DirectSound over wave out, go into the configuration or setup section of your application (in WinAmp, hit Ctrl+P and select Plug-ins, Output). Set it to DirectSound for hardware acceleration goodness. In InterVideo WinDVD 5, it's under Audio/Advance Audio. Then simply set it to DirectSound.

Setting the Creative Labs' control panel to Stereo Surround or CMSS lets the sound card up-mix stereo source material to your surround-sound speakers.

If hardware acceleration is turned down even a notch, most sound systems will turn off all acceleration.

Setting your audio applications to use DirectSound over wave out will let the hardware acceleration of your soundcard or motherboard do the heavy lifting.

I lowered the hardware acceleration for my soundcard by a little bit, and now my PC is crawling. What gives?

Sound vendors tell us one big complaint from consumers is the lack of performance that results from turning hardware acceleration off. Duh. What we didn't know, however, is that lowering hardware acceleration even a notch usually disables all hardware audio acceleration. To make sure yours is set correctly, go into Control Panel and click Sounds, Audio Devices Properties. Under Speaker Settings, click Advanced and then click the Performance tab. Make sure Hardware Acceleration is all the way to the right. Yes, the other right.

Accelerate Your Apps!

We say that when it comes to our applications, optimization is next to godliness. Here are our favorite tips for speeding up Microsoft Outlook, Microsoft Word, and Windows Media Player!

Quick Emailing in Outlook

Sometimes you just want to dash off a quick email without having to launch a big-ass app like Microsoft Outlook. Well, now you don't have to.

- Right-click the desktop and select New, Shortcut from the pop-up menu.

- A wizard launches. Type **mailto:** in the location box (don't forget the colon at the end).

- Name your shortcut something illuminating, like **New Email**.

From now on, whenever you want to dash off an email when Outlook isn't open, just double-click on this shortcut, state your business, and click Send. This trick will actually work for other email clients as well, as long as the application is the default email client.

Customize Your MS Word File Cabinet

This one is so convenient and fun, we occasionally wonder if it's illegal. You can establish a list of your own frequently used documents directly in Microsoft Word's menu bar. Add templated letters with boiler-plate text ("Dear John..."). Create a separate menu for all the documents you're plagiarizing for your term paper. Go crazy—here's how.

- Fire up Word.

- Go to Tools, Customize.

- In the Categories pane (left side), scroll down to Built-In Menus, and click on it to highlight the selection.

You can write and send a quick email using Outlook without having to launch the whole application.

Put your most frequently used documents right where you need them—on Word's menu bar.

- In the Commands pane (right side), scroll down to Work. Click on it, drag it to the menu bar, and release the mouse button.

- Don't close the Customize window yet! Click on your new Work folder to highlight it if it isn't already highlighted, and in the Customize window, click Modify Selection. A drop-down list will appear, allowing you to change the name of the folder to whatever you want. You can also add the ampersand (**&**) before a character to add a hotkey so you can access the menu with the Alt key. (For example, **St&uff** will let you access the menu by pressing Alt+U.)

- Now you can click Close in the Customize window.

- To add documents, just open them, click the new menu item, and select Add to Work Menu. Life is good. To remove them—this is a little weird—press Ctrl+Alt+- (hyphen). Your I-beam cursor will turn into a thick horizontal bar. Using this cursor, select your menu item, position the cursor over the document you want to delete, and press the trigger. Sayonara!

Microsoft puts you behind the controls of Windows Media Player 9 with TweakMP.

Tweak Windows Media Player 9

You've had your fun with TweakUI, the unsupported set of customization tools released by Microsoft for its operating systems. Now you can experience the rush all over again with TweakMP, a bundle of utilities designed to configure Windows Media Player to your taste. Go to www.wmplugins.com, select Plug-Ins & Skins from the menu bar at the top, select Toys and Utils from the drop-down menu, and then scroll down the list to TweakMP PowerToy for Windows XP. One of the first things to do is shorten the time it takes the mouse pointer and menu to disappear when you go full-screen (as shown in the screenshot).

While you're at it, you can download the Windows Media Bonus Pack at the same location. Among other things, you'll get a badass plug-in that allows you to export playlists to Microsoft Excel for perusal or printing. You can, for example, simply cut the playlist from Excel and paste it into an illustration program for creating a CD or DVD sleeve. Get the picture?

Fast URL Entry in Internet Explorer 6

When you're entering a URL in Internet Explorer that begins with **www** and ends in **.com**, all you have to do is enter the domain name itself, like **maximumpc**, and press Ctrl+Enter. The **www** and **.com** will be filled in for you, as if by magic.

Chapter Eighteen

Create Custom Recovery Disks

When you buy a new PC from Dell or Gateway, you get a set of disks that returns your system to its pristine condition. There's no reason not to do the same for your own machine!

Your Dream Machine is assembled, it's time to install your basic software on the box and then preserve its condition for all time!

Windows XP utilities such as Disk Cleanup and System Restore can be helpful in keeping your system in good health, but the truth is that there's no substitute for a top-to-bottom OS reinstall to make your PC feel like new. It's called a *clean start*, and on the following pages we'll show you how to perform one with the highest level of personal customization possible. Our time-tested (and improved) *Maximum PC* process involves backing up all your valuable files, wiping your system clean, reinstalling your OS along with all your personal settings and favorite apps, and then creating a mirror image of this perfect system profile on CD-ROMs. It'll include all your OS preferences, all your networking settings, and all the software you use on a daily basis—ready to load at any time, and ready to rescue you from disaster.

Here's what you'll need to get started:

- Recordable CDs or DVDs
- Windows XP Installation CD
- Norton Ghost 2003
- A CD or DVD burner

After you're done, you'll be able to get that "fresh-out-of-the-shower" feeling anytime you want just by popping your recovery CDs and loading in your image. System feeling groggy? Virus attack? No problem. All you need is a clean start.

Nine Easy Steps to Build Your Recovery Disks

Lest you get antsy about the sheer scope of this project, check out how easy the process really is. Here's a brief outline of what you'll be doing

1. **Test Your BIOS**. Most PCs shouldn't have a problem booting directly off a CD, but some really old motherboards might have issues with this, so it's best to check.

2. **Collect the essentials**. Before you recklessly reformat your drive, you're going to make sure you have all the tools required for the project.

3. **Format your drive**. This is the point of no return. Anything not backed up is about to be offered as a sacrifice to the god of hard drives.

4. **Install Windows XP**. This process is much easier than it was in previous Windows incarnations, but it's still the longest step here, so pay attention.

5. **Visit Windows Update**. Microsoft's online resources will help you plug security holes and stomp out bugs.

6. **Install drivers**. Many people forget this step and end up wondering why their frame rates are in the toilet.

7. **Tweak Windows XP**. Here's the part where you get to wring every last bit of performance from the OS.

8. **Install your apps**. Your PC isn't going to be much use without some software to run.

9. **Create restore discs**. Finally, we're going to take a snapshot of your pristine, perfectly configured system.

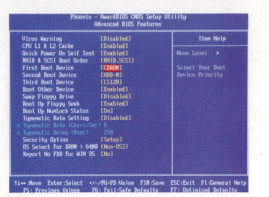

To get your machine booting from CD, you might need to go into your system's BIOS and change the first boot device setting to CDROM.

Step 1: Confirming That You Can Boot from CD

To restore your system without requiring a fragile floppy startup disk, your PC must be able to boot from a CD-ROM. Fortunately, almost all PCs that meet the minimum system requirements for Win XP can boot from the optical drive. Even so, you're still going to have to configure your BIOS so that your PC checks the CD-ROM for a bootable disc before turning to the hard drive. Here's how to do it.

Restart your computer. As soon as the screen that indicates your BIOS is loading comes up, you'll have a few seconds to press the correct key to enter the BIOS. The name of the key should appear on the screen (for example, "Press F1 to enter the BIOS"), but if it doesn't, check your motherboard documentation. If you don't have a manual, try the Delete key. If that doesn't work, try pressing each of the function keys (F1, F2, and so on) and the Escape key until you hit the right one.

After you enter your BIOS, check to see whether your BIOS is from Award or AMI by reading the title at the top. If you have an Award BIOS, enter the Advanced BIOS Features tab and scroll down to First Boot Device. It should be preset to Floppy. Because we aren't going to use the Floppy drive for boot purposes, press Enter, select CDROM from the list, and press Enter again. Now press Escape until you're back at the BIOS entry screen. Select "Save & Exit Setup" from the menu and press Enter.

If your BIOS is from AMI, select the Advanced BIOS Features tab, scroll to 1st Boot Device, and use the plus and minus keys until you've selected CDROM. Now press Escape, select "Save & Exit Setup," and press Enter.

After you've done all this, your system should be able to boot from a CD.

Before I Go On . . .

I've confirmed that my PC can boot from my CD-ROM, and I've made the CD-ROM my first boot device. I'm ready to move on.

Step 2: Collect Your Project Tools

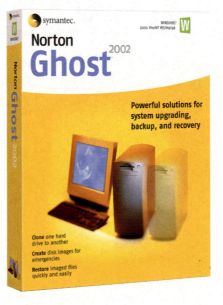

You can use Norton Ghost to make an image of your hard drive, which is a perfect copy of your drive.

It never hurts to double-check your tool box, because once you get moving, you won't want to be caught empty-handed. So, make sure you have the following:

- Norton Ghost 2003, the program we'll use to create the restore disc set.

- Your original Windows XP installation CD (either Home or Professional).

- At least three CD-Rs, CD-RWs, or a couple of recordable DVDs. (It helps to have more on hand in case there are burning errors or you need more room.)

- An optical disc that contains all the drivers you need for your hardware. We suggest that you pull the latest drivers from vendor websites. Usually the driver you've got on your CD is old and moldy, or even Windows XP–incompatible in some cases.

Try not to forget any components, because any driver that you don't update now will have to be updated every time you reinstall. Make sure you've got the most current driver releases for your videocard, motherboard chipset, soundcard, network card, USB 2.0 card, printer, and any specialized A/V cards you might have. We keep all our drivers on rewritable optical discs. That way, they all stay in one place and can be updated as necessary.

We'll warn you ahead of time that Windows might warn you that your drivers are not digitally signed. That is to be expected, especially with cutting-edge hardware. Unsigned drivers aren't necessarily a bad thing as long as the company has a good reputation for making stable drivers. We have no qualms installing unsigned drivers from companies like ATI, nVidia, and Creative Labs.

You'll also need the original installation packages of all of the applications and utilities you'll want on your clean system mirror—Office, Photoshop, ACDSee, what have you.

After you have all these parts collected, you can move on to the next step.

Before I Go On . . .

I've got Norton Ghost 2003, my Windows XP CD, plenty of CD-Rs or DVD-Rs, the latest drivers for all my hardware, and I know which apps and utilities I want to install. Now what?

Kick-Ass Construction Tip

If you're planning on installing Windows on a RAID array or a Serial ATA drive, you'll need to have a floppy disk with the drivers for your disk controller on it handy for the next step. If you're installing on a RAID array, you'll need to go ahead and configure the RAID array per our instructions in Chapter 15, "Add RAID to Your Computer." Go ahead and take care of that now, we'll still be here waiting for you.

Step 3: Format Your Drive

This is it: the point of no return. If you're trying to create rescue disks for a system that you've used before, you need to back up your mail, bookmarks, and any other files you'd like to keep. In this step you're going to permanently erase files from your hard drive. If you've diligently backed up all your data, there's nothing to worry about.

```
Windows XP Professional Setup

The following list shows the existing partitions and
unpartitioned space on this computer.

Use the UP and DOWN ARROW keys to select an item in the list.

    • To set up Windows XP on the selected item, press ENTER.

    • To create a partition in the unpartitioned space, press C.

    • To delete the selected partition, press D.

76341 MB Disk 0 at Id 0 on bus 0 on atapi [MBR]

       Unpartitioned space                    76340 MB

ENTER=Install  C=Create Partition  F3=Quit
```

Whether you're making recovery images of a new machine, or giving an older box a clean start, you'll need to format your hard drive. Beware though—formatting will destroy all the data on your drive!

Here's a final safety tip before we begin: If you used a removable drive to back up all your data and it's still connected to your PC, disconnect it now. When the XP install process begins and the formatting screen pops up, it will display the removable drive as the first partition. Many unhappy people have inadvertently formatted their removable drive—with all their backed-up data—instead of their hard drive. Whoops!

Drop the Windows XP CD into your optical drive and reboot. Because you've already set it up to be the primary boot device, you should get a message that says Press Enter to Set Up Windows XP. Do this. Once you're in Windows Setup, wait until a "Welcome to Setup" screen appears. Follow the instructions and press "Enter to Set Up Windows XP."

When the EULA (end-user license agreement) appears, press F8 to continue. If Windows is already installed on your hard drive, you'll need to press Escape to bypass the previous install and install a fresh copy. Next you should see a list of the partitions you have on your PC. Before you do anything, you need to develop a plan for the final configuration of your partitions. Partitioning is basically dividing the disk space of a physical drive among several "virtual" drives called *partitions*. These virtual drives show up as separate drives (C, D, E) within Windows. Although many people like to divide their drives into multiple pieces, we recommend that you create a single partition for every physical drive you have.

Remember that there is no helpful redundancy in creating partitions, because if a physical drive fails, all the partitions associated with the drive will die as well. It is also advantageous to create a single partition for your OS install because of the way Windows XP accesses its data. When a partition spans the entire disk, Windows XP automatically puts the large files on the outside edge of the drive, where high seek times are mitigated by high throughput speeds. The smaller, more frequently accessed files use the inside edge of the disk platters, to take advantage of low access times. When you partition the drive into two pieces, you lose most of the advantages of this ordering scheme.

At the partition setup screen, find the partitions that are associated with your primary drive (Disk 0). Make sure this is the drive you want to format. If you have a physical hard drive that is 120GB, for example, and another 60GB physical drive that you backed up your old data on, look at the format screen and check the disk size—be absolutely certain that you are drawing a bead on the right drive. Once you're certain, delete them by pressing D, then Enter, and then L.

Ask the Windows XP Doctor

Q: I'm installing Windows on my hard drive, but it only shows up as a 135GB drive no matter what I do! Did I get ripped off when I bought my hard drive?

A: Nope, you just have a version of Windows that doesn't support drives larger than 135GB. Don't worry though—once you install the latest XP Service Pack from www.windowsupdate.com, you'll be able to format the rest of the drive without any problems.

Once this is done, you will have created a pool of all the free space on your hard drive and it will be ready for partitioning. Select the unpartitioned space, press Enter, and choose Format the Partition Using the NTFS File System. For this task, we want to avoid the Quick option because it simply rewrites the TOC to make the drive think it's empty instead of actually erasing anything. A full format goes through each hard drive sector and rewrites it, so if you have a bad sector on your drive, it will be exposed now rather than later.

Now let the drive format. This will take a long time. (The larger your drive, the longer it takes).

Before I Go On . . .

I've formatted my drive and deftly avoided disaster. Windows XP is now ready to install itself. No sweat.

Step 4: Install Windows XP

After your hard drive is formatted, your PC will reboot automatically and the Windows XP install routine will swing into action. You'll be prompted along the way for basic information, and asked to enter your Product Key, which will be located somewhere in your Windows packaging.

After Windows XP asks for your desired network setup option for broadband and modem connections, the rest of the installation will progress automatically.

After your drive is formatted, you can expect to look at the basic Windows XP install screen for about 40 minutes.

When it has finished and rebooted, you'll be prompted to change your display resolution. Follow the onscreen instructions and allow Windows to boot into the familiar desktop. You'll also receive a message asking if you want to register and activate Windows. (Note that activation is required, but registration is not.) If Windows was able to recognize your network card and you use a broadband connection, you can probably activate now. Otherwise, you'll have to wait until after you have installed the network card or modem drivers (see the next step).

Before I Go On...

Okey-doke, a fresh copy of Windows is now completely installed. What do I do next?

Step 5: Run Windows Update

Our first stop after installing Windows XP is Windows Update, Microsoft's one-stop online shop for security fixes, OS updates, and certified drivers.

If you're using a network card and you connect through a standard DHCP broadband connection, you can skip to the next part about running Windows

Update. But if you're using a modem, or if you need to install specialized network parameters (username and password) from your broadband ISP to connect to the Internet, we'll need to visit the Control Panel before going to Windows Update.

Once Windows is installed, you need to visit www.windowsupdate.com and download all the critical updates for your OS.

Go to the Start Menu and click Control Panel. On the left side there should be an option that says Switch to Classic View. Click this and you'll see the familiar set of Control Panel icons. Double-click Network Connections, and on the sidebar choose Create a New Connection, next choose the Connect to the Internet option, and then select Set Up My Connection Manually. From here you can choose to connect through dial-up or broadband with a username and password. Go through the desired menu selection and enter the information that you've copied down or that your ISP has supplied you. After you're done, try to achieve a connection with your ISP. If you use a static IP, make sure you select that option in the Network Connection Wizard.

Once you're able to log on and access the Internet, go to the Start Menu on the Taskbar, select All Programs, and click Windows Update. This opens an Internet Explorer browser that automatically connects you to the Windows Update site. Once the page comes up, click the Scan for Updates option and wait while your computer is gently probed.

Once your computer is checked, you'll have three different categories of updates available to you. The first section is Critical Updates, which will automatically be selected for download. You can click on that section to review what is going to be installed, but it's best to just leave it alone and let Windows Update patch whatever security holes the hacking gurus have come up with this week.

The second section contains noncritical software updates for Windows. We recommend installing everything you think you'll need, especially Service Pack 1 and all the recommended updates.

The last section is Driver Updates, and it contains a sparse list of Windows Hardware Qualification Labs (WHQL)-certified drivers for your hardware. These drivers will usually be a bit older than the latest ones you can find on your vendors' websites. You might want to go with the latest update, even if it isn't sanctioned by Microsoft.

Before I Go On . . .

I've gone to Windows Update and brought my OS up to date. Are we done yet?

Step 6: Install Drivers

You've installed all your OS updates, and now it's time to install the latest drivers for your hardware.

A s we discussed earlier, having the latest drivers is extremely important to a well-functioning machine, but you'll want to be careful with some of the stuff you put on your freshly installed OS.

Vendor driver discs tend to contain tons of extras that most people neither need nor want. Creative Labs, for example, packs a dozen or so programs with its Sound Blaster Audigy driver CD, and it installs all of them by default. When installing from vendor driver

packs, make sure you always select the minimum possible installation without all the extraneous software that's just going to muck up your pristine box. You can always add craplets later if you feel like you're missing out on something.

Most people use videocards based on either nVidia or ATI chipsets. Although your board maker might have a specialized driver pack, it's usually little more than a reference driver with a bunch of extra crap tacked on. To avoid this, just download the latest reference driver from either www.nvidia.com or www.ati.com. nVidia and ATI make this especially easy by providing unified drivers that will work on any of its video chipsets since the TNT2 and Rage 128, respectively.

Your motherboard chipset will probably be based on either an Intel or VIA chipset, although it may also be one from SiS, ALi, nVidia, or AMD. Check the vendor's web page for the latest driver updates. Having the latest chipset driver is far more important than most people think.

These days, most everyone runs a soundcard from Creative Labs, although there are some other vendors still out there, as well as a ton of integrated audio chips. For integrated audio, check your motherboard vendor's website and you should be able to find what you need. Audio card drivers are usually available as downloads from the vendor's home page.

Once you're done installing drivers, reboot your PC and go on to the next step.

Step 7: Tweak Win XP

Before you make your image, make sure that you customize Windows to your taste. We recommend you adjust your display settings to a more friendly resolution and refresh rate than the Windows default.

You should also make any changes to Windows user interface elements before you make your images.

This is the final step in your OS installation. Here's where you turn Microsoft's Windows XP into your XP by customizing its configuration and tweaking the settings for maximum performance.

If you didn't activate Windows during setup, do that first by clicking the key icon in your System Tray. Windows will generously offer to take you on a tour, install a Passport account, and so on. Click all these reminders, then cancel them right away if you're not interested. This will prevent you from being bugged about them every time you reinstall.

Change the display resolution if you haven't already. In fact, while you're in Display Properties (right-click the desktop and select Properties), take the time to set your power-management settings and Windows décor.

Set up directories for your personal data within My Documents so you'll have a fairly easy method of backing it up later. Tweak My Documents to reflect the view you prefer. (We prefer to see file details, not icons, so go to the View menu and select Details.) If you want, you can go to Tools → Folder Options, select the View tab, and apply these settings to all your folders by clicking Apply To All Folders.

Next you should muzzle two of the most space-hungry features in Windows: System Restore and Recycle Bin. To ease up System Restore's requirements, right-click on My Computer, go to Properties, and then click the System Restore tab. Move the slider until the service takes a more reasonable amount of your hard drive—let's say 1GB. To release space from the Recycle Bin's clutches, right-click on the Bin, go to Properties, and then move the slider for something more reasonable—we like 1GB for this one, too. Also make sure you examine the Automatic Updates and Advanced

tabs to set preferences for Users, Windows Update, Performance, and Startup. Don't forget to go into Internet Explorer and specify your security settings (Tools → Internet Options → Security). If you plan on using a software firewall, you can configure that now as well.

If you prefer a more comprehensive, one-stop approach, check out programs such as TweakXP that provide easy access to all the Windows XP tweaking options within one application.

Before I Go On . . .

I installed all the drivers necessary for my hardware, and I didn't forget to install updated chipset drivers for my motherboard. What's the next step?

Step 8: Install Your Applications

Any applications you install now will automatically be reinstalled when you use your recovery disks, so pick the apps you use every day—such as Office.

The final step in building your custom OS image is to install all the key applications you want loaded whenever you do a clean-start reinstall. These apps should be installed judiciously, so wherever possible, select custom installations and limit the modules and install packages to just the ones you know you'll want to use.

Avoid installing programs that are frequently updated. For example, we're perfectly happy with Office 2000 and don't have any plans to upgrade to Office XP or 2003, so we're going to add Office 2000 to our base install. But with something like an instant-messaging client, which is updated almost obsessively, we prefer to install the latest version each time we go for a clean start.

Before you move on to the next step, make sure you try running all your programs at least once to ensure that the installs were successful.

Step 9: Create Restore Discs

When you create your image, you'll need to select the drive that you want to image. Most people will want to make an image of their C: drive and store it on their D: drive.

You've gone through a long and tedious process to get here, but remember, you won't have to do it again for a long time. In this step, you're going to create the restore discs that allow you to effortlessly refresh your system whenever you want.

Insert the Norton Ghost 2003 CD into your drive and run the setup program. It's really that simple!

The first thing you should do is create bootable rescue discs. Open Ghost and go to the Ghost Utilities section. Start the Boot Wizard and select all the default options. You'll probably need two floppy disks. These disks will help you re-image your hard drive even if you can't boot into Windows.

After you create the rescue disks, label them and open Ghost. Click on Backup. First you'll need to select the drive you want to image, and the destination for that image. We recommend you burn the image directly to a recordable CD or DVD. Press Next to continue.

Keep pressing Continue until you get to the Advanced Options page. Click Advanced Options, and then go to the Compression tab. We recommend using the high-compression setting. High compression takes up less space but takes more time when creating the image. It makes no sense at all to use the no-compression option, unless you just like spending money on media.

You'll go through several more screens before you're prompted to insert a blank CD into your burner. When that's done, click Next, pick your burner from the list, and click Finish. Make sure all your programs are closed and then press the Yes button to restart the machine and begin the imaging process. Your drive will now be compressed and the image will be saved to disc. Don't forget to label the discs consecutively when you're done. Well, golly, you've done it. You've made a complete image of a pristine system. Now, whenever you want a clean start, you can use one of the following methods to restore your system to its original state. Remember that these processes will wipe out all your personal files, so make absolutely sure you repeat step 2 and back up all your data.

Putting Your Recovery Discs to Use

Suppose the worst happens—something happens to your system, and you need to use your recovery discs to restore your computer to its original settings and situation. How exactly do you do it? **Remember that when you perform any of these procedures, all of the data you have stored on your Windows partition will be erased! Make sure you've backed up your important files before you restore your drive!!!**

Restoring from Windows (Easiest and Best)

If you want to re-image your drive and can still boot into your old install, the process is an absolute snap. Just open up Ghost within Windows and cancel past the welcome screen. Insert the first of your backup discs into the CD drive and click the Restore button. Click Select Image File and point it to the .gho file on disc one. Ghost will ask you to insert disc two, then disc one again—just follow the directions. Once that's done, click Finish, and insert the discs as requested by Ghost.

Restoring from CD

If your PC just won't boot into Windows and you're loathe to use your set of floppies (if you even made them), you can boot directly off the Ghost CD. The CD will drop you onto the command line. When you see the A:\> on your screen, type: **c:\support\ghost.exe** and then press the Enter key.

After the interface comes up, click the icon for Restore Image and then point it to disc one (which you should place in your drive now). Then just follow the instructions.

In case you were wondering, it's possible to make bootable CDs for your restore discs. But because you need the Ghost program to restore the image anyway, why not just boot from its CD?

Restoring from Floppy Disk

This is the same procedure as booting from CD, except that you will not need to enter DOS. Pop in the first of two floppies you made when you installed Ghost and reboot. Ghost will ask for the second floppy, and start up its GUI automatically.

Keeping Windows Minty Fresh

Although even the most diligent housekeeper will find it impossible to keep a system absolutely free of data dust, there are still many ways to delay quarterly cleanups a year or more, depending on your usage and degree of slovenliness. Your first defense is simple common sense. Be judicious and selective about software installation packages, customizing their installs wherever possible. Avoid installing programs that have extensive spyware—and that means most file-sharing P2P applications (unless you can find one of the unauthorized, ad-free "lite" versions online).

Even if you don't use any of the traditionally suspect software, you should still use (and update frequently) Lavasoft's Ad-aware (www.lavasoft.nu) to get rid of commercial garbage dumped into your Registry and system folders.

You can also avoid strangling the pipes with cross-linked files and file fragments by shutting down Windows the right way. Use the Start Menu → Turn Off the Computer selec-

tion. Shutting down by simply flipping off the power switch can lead to data loss, file corruption, and the little droppings mentioned above. Trust us, take the extra five seconds and shut down the right way.

Virus checks and regular defragmentation of your hard disk are also essential to keeping your PC in top shape. System maintenance packages such as Norton Systemworks contain numerous tools for Registry cleaning, disk defragmenting, virus checking, and removing old files and shortcuts. Likewise, McAfee's QuickClean (available for Windows 95b through XP) is a standalone utility that blows out the garbage from all of Windows' hiding places, deletes duplicate files and orphaned shortcuts, and safely "shreds" these files on their way out. And the next time you get a message saying that the uninstall is completed but "some elements could not be removed," QuickClean steps in and removes them for you. At this point, we think that's something everyone can appreciate.

Chapter Nineteen

Troubleshooting Your Dream Machine

Your PC is sick, and we've got the cure

Meet the Doctor

For more than eight years, *Maximum PC*'s mysterious resident Doctor has been anonymously dispensing cures for ill computers in his monthly Ask the Doctor column. For every topic, the Doc doles out both perfect advice and tough love. If you have a problem you can't solve, shoot an email to him at doctor@maximumpc.com. If your question is selected, the answer will appear in a future issue of *Maximum PC*!

Ask the Doctor

E ach month, the Doctor receives scads of questions from readers, and spends hours poring over tech manuals finding cures for the things that ail our readers' PCs. Although the Doctor can't answer every reader question—nor can he make house calls—our doc can and does provide dead-on diagnoses that are guaranteed to have your sick computer running tip-top. All of this comes without subjecting your PC to drafty and unsightly hospital gowns, cold hands, or any untoward prodding from a stranger in a lab coat.

This chapter provides some of the Doctor's most vaunted advice from the past year. Here, you'll find answers to some of your most vexing PC questions, organized so that you can find it easily. We've hand-chosen the questions here because we believe these are the most applicable to the needs of just about anyone bent on bringing their dream PC to life.

Hot or Not?

Patient: Is the heatsink/fan that came with my CPU sufficient, or should I buy a better heatsink/fan?

Doctor: The heatsink that came with your CPU is certified by the manufacturer of the CPU to offer sufficient cooling for running the CPU at its standard clock speed. If you plan on overclocking, however, it is wise to purchase an aftermarket cooling solution to handle the increased temperatures that overclocking produces.

Mo' Memory

Patient: I was wondering how much of a performance boost the AMD Athlon XP CPUs get from running on a 166MHz FSB (333MHz) in conjunction with 333MHz DDR RAM? I've seen some websites that claim there's no significant performance gain. Is this because of the 64-bit CPU-to-memory data path that the Athlon XP uses?

Doctor: The Athlon XP does experience a fair boost when its FSB is increased from 266MHz to 333MHz DDR. Although clock speeds continue to climb at a crazy pace, memory bandwidth has not. The Athlon is handcuffed a bit by its narrower bus (the P4 has a 256-bit CPU-to-memory data path), but still benefits from the added bandwidth. In general, we recommend running your system's FSB at the fastest speeds they'll tolerate.

> Be sure to see Chapter 3 to learn more about selecting a CPU, including the best ways to keep it cool.

Although you might think a bundled heatsink/fan with a CPU would be bunk, they actually work quite well.

Clock Conundrum

Patient: I recently noticed that my AMD 1.1GHz processor has changed speed. It has operated at 1.1GHz for over a year and a half, but not now it's operating at 850MHz. I haven't even fooled with anything in the case, and no one else has used my system. How did this happen?

Doctor: Your system's CMOS likely was reset. We've seen systems occasionally "forget" their configurations, and that usually indicates a bad connection on the CMOS battery, static build-up, or a dying CMOS battery. (The CMOS battery is that coin-cell on your motherboard.) What you need to do is go into your BIOS and verify that the system bus is running at 133MHz. When the CMOS lost its contents, it probably defaulted to 100MHz bus. The math backs this up: $8.5 \times 100 = 850$MHz; $8.5 \times 133 = 1,100$MHz. The other possibility is that your system builder used a remarked Athlon. That is, he took an

Motherboard Monitor

850MHz Athlon, shorted the L1 bridges, and reset it to 1.1GHz. Over time, the material that's used to unlock the bridges can wear away, and the CPU can default to its stock 850MHz speed. The Doctor believes that the first scenario is more likely the cause of your problem.

Too Hot to Handle

Patient: What is an acceptable temperature for my CPU to run at, and what is the best way to monitor its temperature?

Doctor: In general, a Pentium 4 CPU should never go above 125° Fahrenheit, and an Athlon should stay below 140°. If either CPU is hovering near those levels, it would be wise to invest in a bigger, more efficient cooling mechanism for the CPU. The best way to check your CPU's temperature is to either look at your BIOS (there's usually a screen that displays the CPU temp and fan rotation speed, among other things), or use a program called Motherboard Monitor.

Double Trouble

Patient: I was told that if you have dual CPUs, you can dedicate certain processes to each CPU. I was wondering if this would work for Intel's Hyper-Threading (HT) technology. Can I set background processes to run on the virtual second CPU, and

everything else to run on the primary CPU? Would this boost performance?

Doctor: Yes. Having a dual-processor or HT-enabled machine indeed makes it possible to dedicate workloads for processes and applications via Windows XP's Task Manager to the two "virtual" CPUs. However, keep in mind that Hyper-Threading is not the same as two physical CPUs. The single CPU still has the resources of a single CPU—it's just a little more efficient at doling them out when in HT mode. If, for example, you run two applications that both require the same functions of the CPU, the performance will be no better, and might even be worse, if the applications are not optimized for Hyper-Threading. On the other hand, if you run multiple applications that use different functions of the CPU, you can see quite an efficiency boost. HT isn't the magic bullet of computing, but it does work very well at some things.

An Intel Hyper-Threading-enabled CPU appears as two physical processors to the OS, but isn't as efficient as actually having two processors.

Who's in the Driver's Seat?

Patient: I've seen you stress the importance of chipset drivers many times in Ask the Doctor, so I decided to update the drivers on my old Dell Dimension 4100. Using an Intel chipset identification utility, I discovered that I had an 815 Intel chipset and found at least five driver updates for it on the Intel website.

However, Intel tells me that my system is an OEM version of an Intel Desktop Board BIOS and advises me not to use its drivers, but to instead call my PC manufacturer for advice. That's right, you guessed it! Dell does not offer chipset update drivers. Is it safe to proceed with the Intel drivers?

Doctor: The Doctor thinks you're confusing two different things: chipset drivers and your motherboard's BIOS. We don't recommend you try to install a BIOS—the software that resides in

For everything you need to know about motherboards, turn back to Chapter 4.

a chip on your motherboard and tells your OS how to access all the nifty features of your PC—for any board other than the one that's specified. That's a sure-fire way to kill your PC. It sounds to us like you're interested in updating your Dell mobo with an Intel BIOS, which would be bad.

On the other hand, chipset drivers work on any boards that use the chipset in question. Most of the chipset vendors make one driver that will work with all their modern chipsets for convenience.

Windows Acts Wacky

Patient: I'm having trouble getting my new PC working. It's an Athlon XP 1800+, with 256MB of RAM, and a pair of 40GB Maxtor drives in a RAID 0 array. I can't get the machine to work properly. When I try to install Windows to the RAID array, Windows locks up, even though I am using the correct drivers for my RAID controller.

If I install Windows to one of the drives without RAID, Windows works OK

for a while, but eventually I get crashes when I'm playing *Battlefield: 1942*. The system won't reboot, and I get an error in NTFS.sys or kern32.sys. Please help!

Intel lets you update chipset drivers manually or automatically over the Internet. We prefer the latter.

Doctor: The Doctor had a similar problem with one of his machines recently. Assuming you're not overclocking, which can really bork 3D and PCI devices, we'd bet your problem is bad memory. A bad stick of RAM or a faulty slot on the mobo is the most common cause for this sort of problem.

To test it, open your case and remove one stick of RAM, and then fire up the PC to see how things run. If that fixes your problem, the RAM you removed is likely faulty. If it's still wonky, swap the stick you removed with the stick that's still in the system and try again. You should also try moving the memory to the other slots in your mobo.

If your RAM tests OK, your motherboard could be faulty. The only way to confirm that is to swap your mobo with another mobo and see what happens.

Can't Take the Heat

Patient: I just installed a new processor, and as soon as I start playing 3D games, my

PC just shuts off. What is happening?

Doctor: Sounds like you didn't install the CPU's heatsink properly, as random shutdowns are almost always due to overheating. Some motherboards have built-in temperature sensors that will shut the PC off once temperatures breach preset thresholds in an attempt to save your CPU from meltdown. Our advice is to remove the heatsink/fan from your CPU, make sure it is being mounted correctly, and remount it. Also, if you aren't using any type of thermal compound to increase the efficiency of your CPU's heatsink, we highly recommend applying a dab on the top of the CPU prior to mounting the heatsink.

The Case for ATX

Patient: I am looking to buy a new case, but how do I know for sure that my motherboard will fit properly?

If your system shuts off randomly, it's probably due to excessive heat. If your CPUs heatsink/fan aren't doing their job, you might need an aftermarket unit like Thermaltake's Volcano 7.

Doctor: All cases and motherboards are designed to a certain specification, which is called its *formfactor*. There are several formfactors, but as long as the one for your case matches the one for your motherboard, you will be fine. The most common formfactor for desktop machines is called ATX, and it's what you would call the typical "tower" PC, which stands a few feet tall and is quite large. The majority of both cases and motherboards conform to the ATX specification, and are all interchangeable; that is, any ATX motherboard will fit into an ATX case. In fact, an ATX case will fit several variants of the ATX specification, but it makes little sense to buy a big ATX case if you want a smaller Micro-ATX motherboard. The same applies to the newer BTX standard. If you buy a BTX mobo, make sure you buy a BTX case. The bottom line for matching cases to motherboards is to make sure the specifications match—it's that simple.

Memory Booster?

Patient: I have an Athlon XP board running PC2700 (333MHz) memory. Should I upgrade to PC3200? Is it worth it?

Doctor: The first question here should actually be, "Will my motherboard support a 400MHz bus?" Not all Athlon XP motherboards support this faster bus speed, so be sure to consult the website of your motherboard manufacturer to see what bus speeds are supported. If your mobo supports the 400MHz bus, by all means upgrade away! nForce 2 motherboard owners should pay special attention to this situation, as some nForce 2 motherboards shipped with support for a 333MHz front side bus but are able to go up to 400MHz with an updated BIOS from nVidia. Once again, be sure to check nVidia's website to see whether your board revision will support the faster bus speed. Also note that if you are currently running PC2700, you will have to upgrade your memory, as well, because PC2700 only runs at 333MHz. You'll need PC PC3200, which is also known as DDR400, to run at 400MHz.

More Power, Scotty!

Patient: How important is the power supply when upgrading?

Doctor: Extremely important. In fact, if you're considering a major upgrade (CPU and motherboard), the power supply is the best place to start. Today's CPUs require a lot of juice, and when you consider that you might have to plug your videocard into the power supply as well, along with all your other add-in cards and a passel of power-hungry hard drives, you begin to understand how a steady supply of power will go a long way toward creating a stable system. As a baseline, we always recommend a 350-watt power supply for most "power user" type systems. In general, that should be more than enough power to run a very fast system with as many peripherals plugged into it as your heart desires. You should also purchase a high-quality power supply from a known company, rather than some cheapo unit that might save you a few bucks. We highly recommend power supplies from Antec (www.antec.com) as well as PC Power and Cooling (www.pcpowerandcooling.com).

The power supply is one of the most important, yet most often overlooked, components in a PC.

The ATX formfactor is the de rigueur standard for today's performance-oriented desktop machines, as demonstrated by this gorgeous system from Falcon Northwest.

> For everything you need to know about videocards, turn back to Chapter 8.

Worst-Case Scenario

Patient: What is the worst possible outcome of a failed attempt at videocard overclocking? How likely is a "failure" when attempting this?

Doctor: The worst outcome is that your board will simply stop working, which could be a big deal or a little deal depending on its value. However, catastrophe largely can be avoided simply by overclocking in very small increments. For example, try increasing your board's memory or clock speed in 5MHz increments. After each bump up, play a 3D game for a while and watch for signs of excessive heat, such as graphical artifacts and other anomalies. Once you start seeing weirdness in your games or your PC's behavior, back the clock speed down a notch and you should be just fine. Just remember—overclocking your videocard could shorten the card's overall lifespan.

Is 256 Just for Kicks?

Patient: Do I really need a videocard with 256MB of onboard memory for today's games?

Doctor: As we write this in mid-2004, you only *need* a 256MB card for a small number of games—*Far Cry* can fill more than 128MB of video RAM, but not much else available now will. Still, with memory-hungry games like *Half-Life 2* and *Doom 3* on the horizon, you're going to need that extra memory eventually, so if you're building now, it's a good

idea to get a 256MB card to ensure its usefulness into 2005 and beyond.

Towers of Power

Patient: What are those brown cylindrical towers all over my videocard?

Doctor: Those are capacitors, and their job is to make sure the GPU always receives a steady stream of power from the power supply without any major spikes or dips. You should be extremely careful when handling your videocard because the capacitors are only attached at their base, and can snap off quite easily.

Are Onboard Graphics Really That Bad?

Patient: Are integrated graphics any good? Will they be able to run *Doom 3*?

Doctor: Integrated graphics— that is, graphics that are built into a motherboard—are designed to provide minimal 3D performance in exchange for a greatly reduced cost. Integrated chips are not designed for gaming, but rather for simple 2D desktop work. As such, anyone serious about gaming should never consider using integrated graphics. Will integrated graphics run *Doom 3*? Maybe. Will integrated run *Doom 3* at more than slideshow speeds? Not likely.

New DirectX with an Old Card

Patient: Is it OK to install DirectX 9 on my system if I only have a DirectX 8 videocard?

Doctor: Yes, it is OK, and it's also a good rule of thumb to

We're finally seeing games that really stress a 256MB buffer like that of the ATI Radeon 9800 Pro.

make sure you always have the latest version of DirectX as well. All games require a certain version to run, so if you haven't updated your DirectX installation in a while and want to play a brand new game, you could have problems. Usually, games that require an upgrade to a new version of DirectX will include it in the installation, but not always, so be sure to check.

Vexed by AGP 8x

Patient: I'm in the market for a new videocard, and the card I'm looking at is an AGP 8x, but my motherboard only supports AGP 4x. Will this hold my videocard back quite a bit?

Doctor: Do you need an AGP 8x mobo to get the max performance from the Radeon? Yes. Do you need an AGP 8x mobo to get the max

performance from today's games? Not really. You see, current games aren't able to saturate the AGP 4x bus, which can pump about 1.06GB/sec of info from the videocard to main memory. Our testing backs this up.

We tested the Radeon 9700 Pro in a board that allowed us to disable AGP 8x. As far as our benchmarks go, there was no significant difference between 8x mode and 4x mode. We do expect to see games this year—like *Doom 3* and *Half-Life 2*—that will stress the 8x AGP bus.

Need More Funky Flow

Patient: I need to know how to upgrade the fan on my videocard. I need more cooling for my videocard, and this seems like the only way because the fan is glued on and the connector cables are soldered to the card.

Doctor: You usually cannot remove the heatsink/fan that is included with your videocard, because it is usually glued to the chip with some alien substance that will not come off. (Some newer cards have easily removable heatsinks. If you have one of those cards, disregard everything we say here.) However, we've heard of people who have had success putting the card in the freezer and, once frozen, twisting the heatsink right off. We haven't personally tried it, though, and applying any kind of force to your GPU could cause permanent damage.

If your fan's wires are soldered to the board, you need to first remove the solder using either a wick or a solder sucker, and then reattach the new fan to the same leads. (Just pulling them could cause permanent damage to your board.) If this level of hardware-hacking sounds scary, you can always install a PCI fan in the slot directly below your videocard for more cooling. You also should make sure there is a case fan directly above the AGP slot blowing warm air out of the case. You can mount a fan on the case door as well, so

Today's high-end videocards all include heatsinks on top of the GPU that can be difficult, if not dangerous, to remove. Dangerous to the card, that is.

that when it's closed the fan is blowing directly onto the PCI slots. Some cases even include these fans, but most require drilling a hole to mount them.

Crash Course

Patient: I'm experiencing random crashes in games. What's my basic troubleshooting strategy?

Doctor: First, if you're overclocking anything, stop. Even slight overclocking can cause instability. If that doesn't fix your problem (or you're not doing any overclocking), go to your motherboard vendor's website and get the latest motherboard chipset drivers. Do not confuse chipset drivers with a BIOS update. Install the chipset drivers, making sure that you reboot as prompted.

Now install the latest videocard drivers appropriate to your videocard—most likely from ATI.com or nVidia.com. Updating these two drivers in this order will fix 90 percent of all crashes in games.

If you still have problems, you should open your PC and make sure that you've got good airflow around the videocard, and that its onboard fan is working properly. You should also ensure that your finicky game doesn't have known issues with your 3D accelerator by checking the game's support page (the URL is usually listed in the game manual). Finally, don't rule out other components, such as your network card or soundcard. Again, check the game's support site for known issues.

Time to Upgrade

Patient: I get errors when I try to play some new games, but my computer meets all the games' system requirements. What's wrong?

New games like *Far Cry* bring most older videocards to their knees. If you can't afford the upgrade, you'll have to turn down the eye candy.

Doctor: The system requirements listed on the side of game boxes aren't always accurate. Frequently, a game will state that it requires a 32MB 3D accelerator, but what that really means is that you need a 3D accelerator with hardware T&L or even more advanced features. Game developers and publishers frequently fudge the minimum requirement numbers so that their game will appear to be available to a larger audience. For the record, all the GeForce and Radeon cards include hardware T&L. As we move forward, games are beginning to require programmable shaders support, too, so eventually you're just going to have to upgrade to play newer games—it's unavoidable!

A Sweet Tooth for Eye Candy

Patient: I'm running my favorite game with all its effects turned to the max—and it's dog slow. What's your opinion on which visual settings should be set to the max

whenever possible, which settings should I sacrifice, and in what order should they be sacrificed?

Doctor: The easiest way to increase frame rates is to lower your resolution. For example, at 1600×1200, the minimum number of pixels that your 3D card will draw per frame is 1.92 million. And, if you enable antialiasing, texture filtering, and other features, your card will draw considerably more than that. In contrast, at 640×480 the minimum number of pixels the card draws is about 307,200. Even at 1024×768 the card draws only about 800,000 pixels. The upshot is that lowering your resolution might even allow you to run all the fancy visual effects at full blast.

If running at low resolutions is anathema to you, try disabling antialiasing and anisotropic filtering. Both of those features are performance hogs. Decreasing texture quality and turning down the number of mip-map levels can further increase performance, but they will also severely affect your image quality.

> For everything you need to know about hard drives, turn back to Chapter 6.

Pushing the Size Limit

Patient: I just bought a 200GB hard drive and Windows is only recognizing 137GB. What's wrong?

Doctor: The specification for your hard drive's ATA interface allows only 28 bits for addressing data on a disk, which means the maximum it can "see" is 137GB. Now that hard drives are twice as large, the specification has been updated to 48 bits to reflect this jump in capacity. To take advantage of this new size limit, you'll need Service Pack 1 from Microsoft for your operating system, and possibly an updated BIOS as well. With those installed, you will be able to access all of your hard drive's capacity. Also, one way to sidestep this

You can tell Windows how much hard drive space to use as a swap file, but given how cheap RAM is these days, why not just add more if you need it?

issue is to use an add-in PCI controller for your hard drives rather than connecting them to the motherboard.

Master Your Drive Chain

Patient: Does it matter if my hard drive is the Master or Slave on its channel? Should I put it on the same chain as my CD-ROM?

Doctor: If possible, it's best to install any IDE device on its own channel to give each device full control of that channel's resources. The reason it's bad to put a CD-ROM on the same channel as a hard drive is that the channel can only send and receive data from one device at a time, so if you are using your CD-ROM and the hard drive needs something, it'll have to swap back and forth between them, slowing down both drives. Try to make your primary hard drive the Master on the primary IDE channel, and your optical drive the Master on the secondary channel.

Is ATA/133 Worth It?

Patient: I have an ATA/100 hard drive. Should I upgrade to ATA/133 or Serial ATA 150?

Doctor: Not unless you are looking to buy a bigger drive anyway. If that's the case, go ahead and get the newer interface, but don't do it thinking you'll see any recognizable speed increase. In fact, most ATA/133 drives are exactly the same internally as ATA/100 drives. Remember: The number

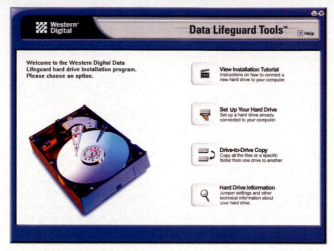

Hard drives typically include data migration utilities, but we recommend a fresh install of Windows on a new drive for peak performance.

after the "ATA" is the maximum transfer rate for the interface, not the actual speed the drive can read and write data.

Swapping Out Your Swap File

Patient: What is my hard drive's swap file? Do I need it?

Doctor: Your hard drive's swap file is a portion of the hard drive that is used when your system's memory is completely full. While you work at your PC, programs that are in use store their data in your system's memory so that you can access it rapidly. However, if you have a lot of applications open and not enough memory, programs will begin to store their data on your hard drive, which is quite slow compared to your PC's lightning-fast memory. If

you do a lot of multitasking and have scant memory, you'll need a swap file. If you have a gigabyte of RAM or more, you probably don't need a swap file.

New Drive Dilemma

Patient: I just installed a new hard drive. What is the easiest way to move all my data onto this new drive and then use my old drive for MP3 storage?

Doctor: Most retail hard drive packages include utilities for transferring your old data to the new drive. However, we always recommend a fresh install of Windows with a manual update instead. The reason for this is that if your old installation of Windows was clogged with crap, the last thing you want is all that junk on your brand-new drive. So start fresh—you won't regret it.

For everything you need to know about optical drives, turn back to Chapter 7.

Homebrew DVDs Don't Work

Patient: My DVD drive won't play a burned movie my friend loaned me. What's going on?

Doctor: Right. Your friend loaned it to you. Wink. Wink. The problem is most likely that the disc's format is incompatible with your set-top DVD player, which is rather common. When burning a DVD these days, computer users have to choose one of two competing standards—DVD+R or DVD-R. On some set-top boxes, +R works fine but –R does not. On other set-top boxes, it's precisely the opposite. The only way to find out which format is supported by your player is to check the model's specs or to just try one of each and see which works.

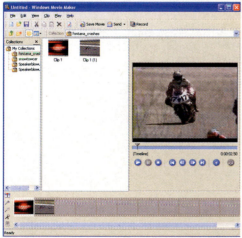

Is backing up DVDs legal or not? Not even your lawyer knows for sure.

PC Doesn't Recognize CD-RW Drive

Patient: My PC isn't recognizing my CD-RW drive on bootup.

Doctor: The only reason why any device attached to your PC would not be recognized during bootup is that it's not connected properly, or if it is connected properly, then it's not configured correctly. Once you have confirmed that the drive's 40-pin cable is firmly attached to both the drive and the motherboard, make sure the drive is correctly set to be either the Master or the Slave on its channel via the little jumpers on its rear. If another drive is connected to the same IDE chain, it should have the opposite Master/Slave setting that your optical drive has. If it's incorrectly jumpered, one or both drives on the chain can disappear from your system.

Does Backing Up DVDs Make Me a Criminal?

Patient: I've got a huge DVD collection, but just had a baby who is now almost a year old. I have heard it would be a smart idea to make backup copies of my DVDs just in case the little one gets hungry. Legally, can I do that?

Doctor: Yes, it's possible, but it might not be legal. Traditionally, it's been legal to make a backup copy of your audio or game CDs under a provision of U.S. copyright law called Fair Use. Unfortunately, this provision doesn't require manufacturers, publishers, or distributors to make backups easy, or even possible, so backups often have been thwarted by copy-protection schemes. In turn, rebel forces found ways around these schemes by using third-party applications that strip out the copy protection.

However, in 1998 Congress passed the Digital Millennium Copyright Act, which made it illegal to circumvent software copy protections for any reason. Because DVD-Video discs are encrypted, you need to decrypt them in order to copy or back up their contents, but decrypting them violates the DMCA.

When 321 Studios released DVDXCopy, which decrypts and duplicates DVDs for backup purposes, this legal blemish erupted into a full-on litigious spat that is still being hashed out in court. California courts so far have refused to issue an injunction against 321 Studios' software, so DVDXCopy remains available, if legally questionable, to consumers today.

Splitting Movies

Patient: I have a homemade movie that's about 750MB in AVI format. How can I split it into two parts so it can be burned onto a Video CD with Nero and played in my DVD player?

Like a judo chop to a piece of wood, we easily split this video clip into two pieces using Windows Movie Maker.

Doctor: The easiest way to do this is with Windows XP's built-in Windows Movie Maker. Go to Start → Programs → Accessories and launch Windows Movie Maker. Before opening your file, go to the View menu, select Options, and make sure Automatically Create Clips is unchecked. Drag your file onto the Clip pane. Click on the clip to activate the Preview window, and move the slider beneath the image to the point at which you want to edit. Once you've hit the right spot, press Control+Shift+S to split the clip into two parts. Drag the first clip to the timeline at the bottom of the screen and save the movie as a DV-AVI clip. When that's done, highlight the clip by clicking it in the timeline and delete it by pressing—yup—the Delete key. Now perform the same operation using the second half of your video.

If you don't have Windows XP, check out TMPGEnc (www.tmpgenc.net). Using this handy and effective utility can be daunting, but an explicit tutorial for the program is available at www.vcdhelp.com/ tmpgencedit.htm.

For everything you need to know about sound-cards, turn back to Chapter 9.

Audio Aggravation

Patient: Sometimes my PC's audio suddenly begins to sound horribly distorted, but only under certain circumstances. For example, the audio during the introductory screens of games sounds like it's coming out of a garbage disposal, but the audio for the game itself is fine. When I watch a movie, it sounds awful, but when I listen to music, everything is groovy.

Doctor: It sounds like you have a bad audio codec. A *codec* (short for "encoder/decoder") compresses audio and/or video so it will fit in a smaller space. Windows Media Video 9 is an example of a video codec, while MP3 is an example of an audio codec. These codecs often can be mixed and matched, so a video might use the popular Xvid codec in combination with the MP3 codec for audio, and an AC3 filter for surround sound. Ten-4? If one or more of these codecs becomes corrupted, you'll get poor sound, poor video, or no sound or video at all.

Here's how to root out the offender in Windows XP: Right-click My Computer, select Properties, click the Hardware tab, and then click Device Manager. Within Device Manager, click the plus sign next to Sound, Video, and Game Controllers, dou-ble-click Audio Codecs, and then select the Properties tab. You'll see all the codecs installed in your system. Starting from the top, double-click each codec, and you'll get a dialog box that allows you to dis-able the codec. Disable it and test your sound with a file you know triggers distortion. If that doesn't solve the problem, re-enable the codec, and target the next one in line. Keep going until you've pinpointed the culpable codec. Once you've disabled the bad codec, write down its name, then try your test file again. Your sound might work fine. However, if your media player says it can't find the right codec, enter the codec name in Google and find another source for a new or updated version of the same codec.

MP3s Are Skipping

Patient: When I'm listening to MP3s and access something on my hard drive, the sound skips. How do I stop this from happening?

Doctor: The skipping is probably due to your CPU being overloaded. An MP3 file is encoded into the MP3 codec and has to be decoded by your MP3 player, which requires calculations by your CPU. The skipping occurs because the CPU is busy decoding the MP3 when all of a sud-den it's asked to perform another task, so it puts your MP3 on hold for a tick. To solve this prob-lem, you could upgrade your CPU for more pro-cessing power, but there are less expensive ways, as well. First, try a differ-ent MP3 player. Some of the older versions of Winamp, such as the 2.0 series (available at http://www.winamp-heaven.net/), have very low CPU-utilization lev-els. You also should make sure your hard drive is defragged, because it's possible the MP3 you're playing is scattered all over your hard drive, thus exacerbating the problem. Finally, as we've mentioned before, going with an add-in soundcard will lighten the CPU's load consider-ably.

Can I "Live" Without It?

Patient: I see the Sound Blaster cards are offered with an optional drive bay for more inputs. Do I need that?

Buggy audio is usually the sign of a bad codec. Start the process of elimination here.

Doctor: If you just listen to music and play games, then no, you don't need it. The "Live Drive" add-in bay includes a slew of I/O ports used for record-ing music, including MIDI In and MIDI Out ports, Microphone In, Optical In and Out, Coaxial In, and others. However, the drive bay does include a remote control, which is a handy feature if you use your PC as a home entertainment center.

Different MP3 players have varying lev-els of CPU utilization. Winamp is an old favorite because of its low resource consumption and wealth of features.

Speakers

Ask the Doctor

> For everything you need to know about speakers, turn back to Chapter 11.

Speakers from Space

Patient: I bought the Klipsch GMX speakers and have a SoundBlaster Live. How can I get 5.1 sound out of them?

Doctor: The new Klipsch GMX-D5.1s were designed primarily for console gamers and include only Digital 5.1 support. For PC gamers, this setup sucks, because most soundcards can send only a two-channel PCM signal digitally. If you want to get 5.1 sound out of your GMX-D5.1s, you'll need an nForce motherboard or a soundcard that can output a Dolby Digital 5.1 stream. Unfortunately, the extremely popular Sound Blaster Audigy and Audigy 2 products can't do that now. If you're an Audigy-owner, your GMX-D5.1s are essentially 2.0 speakers.

Worrying About Wires

Patient: What is the best way to lengthen speaker wires that are hard-wired into the back of the satellite?

Doctor: The only way to deal with this tricky situation is to don your electrician cap and splice an extra length of wire into the main speaker wire. Grab a set of wire clippers/strippers and clip the wire at any point. Next, strip the cabling off the leading edge of the wires to expose the internal wires and connect the two sections of cable. Twist the new wires together and wrap the exposed portions of wire (the parts that used to be covered in cable sheath but are now entwined) with electrical tape and you're done.

Digital Versus Analog

Patient: I hear a lot about digital versus analog speakers. What's the diff?

Doctor: When people talk about "analog" versus "digital" speakers, they usually are referring to the speakers' connection to your PC, not the speakers themselves. Some speakers only have analog connectors, while some only have digital connectors. The best speakers have both! The difference between them is that PC games typically require analog connections, whereas DVD movies require digital connections. Most big-ticket surround sound speaker systems include only analog connectors, but Logitech's all-conquering Z-680 speakers include both types of connectors, which is why they've earned a Kick-Ass from us, as well as a Gear of the Year award—twice!

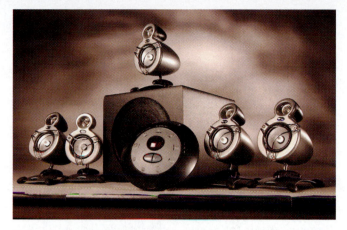

We're big fans of Klipsch speakers, but stay away from its GMX series of speakers—they're strictly for consoles.

While most surround sound speaker systems allow only analog output, Logitech's awesome Z-680 can handle both digital and analog output.

Cable Query

Patient: If I upgrade from a CRT to an LCD, do I need to upgrade my videocard as well? Will there be any issues connecting my current videocard to my new display?

Doctor: It depends on your hardware, but probably not. The standard connection for a CRT is an analog DB-15 cable, and most LCDs include this type of connector. However, some LCDs are capable of receiving a digital signal, so they use a DVI (Digital Visual Interface) connector. To use this type of connector, it must be supported on your graphics card. Luckily, most modern videocards sport both types of connectors.

Ouch...My Head!

Patient: I have a CRT monitor, and sometimes, after using the computer for a while, I get headaches. Is this normal?

Doctor: Headaches are a common side effect of an improperly set up workstation, but there are a few things you can do to mitigate the effects of this. The first thing you should do is make sure your monitor's refresh rate is set to a proper level. If it's set too low, the screen will appear to be flickering and will give you a headache in no time. Once the monitor is set to a higher refresh rate, the screen will flicker so fast that it will largely be imperceptible, which will alleviate the problem. To change your refresh settings, right-click

the desktop and select Properties, then click on the Settings tab. Next, click on the Advanced tab in the lower right-hand corner and then click on Monitor. Your refresh rate will be displayed in this screen, so simply change it to the highest setting possible.

It's also wise to make sure there is adequate light in your work area. Some people like to work in the dark because it makes the images on the screen seem more vivid. But it's common knowledge that this will hurt your eyes over time, and will definitely contribute to headaches, as well.

Finally, be sure to take breaks. As a general rule, you should take a break every half-hour. Close your eyes, roll your neck around, and don't look at a computer screen for a few minutes if possible.

Is Dual Display OK?

Patient: What do I need to run dual displays?

Doctor: Well, besides two displays, you need either a videocard with dual outputs or two physical videocards. Luckily, most mid-range to high-end videocards released in the last few years have included both an analog DB-15 connector as well as a DVI connector for an LCD. If you have one of these

The standard display connection is this DB-15 cable, which can be used for both CRT and LCD displays.

videocards and want to run two LCDs, you'll have to acquire a DVI-to-DB-15 adapter, which is available at Radio Shack.

If your videocard only has one output, you'll have to run the second display from a second physical videocard. Dual displays are supported in Windows XP, so as soon as you plug in the second display, XP will recognize it and allow you to set its resolution from Display Settings menu (right-click on the desktop and select Properties, Settings).

If you're concerned about gaming issues with dual-displays, remember that when you fire up a game it will automatically run on the gaming card and be displayed on one monitor, so the secondary display will just be for desktop work.

Almost every videocard made in the past few years is suitable for dual displays thanks to its dual outputs. The round port between the DVI and DB-15 ports is a TV Out jack.

My Start Menu Is a Big Mess

Patient: What's the best way to organize the programs in my Start menu? I'd like to group all my games and Office XP applications together, if possible.

Doctor: The easiest way to organize the Start menu in XP is to just drag-and-drop things where you'd like them to be. To drag things around inside the Start menu, click the Start button, go to All Programs, and then left-click and hold down the mouse button over the shortcut you want to move. Then you can drag the shortcut wherever you want to put it. Unfortunately, this is a tedious process.

If you want to speed things up, you can right-click the Start button, select Explore, and then right-click the Start button again and click Explore All Users. You should have two windows open now: The window that

opened when you clicked Explore All Users displays the shortcuts that appear for every user of the PC, and the other window shows only the shortcuts that are exclusive to you.

You can now drag, drop, and create new folders just like in any other Explorer window. If you're using a shared computer, be sure to only make changes to the files in your personal folder rather than to those in the All Users folder.

Spyware Be Gone!

Patient: What's the best way to rid my XP system of spyware and adware?

Doctor: Spyware, adware, malware, and scumware are apps that hide on your system and perform various nefarious actions without your knowledge. There are several different free apps available that can help rid your PC of spyware for good.

Ad-aware (www.lavasof-tusa.com) has been the front-runner for a long time, but its definitions (similar to virus definitions used by an antivirus program) are updated infrequently, it seems. These days, we really like Spybot (security.kolla.de). It works much like Ad-aware, but also includes the ability to clear the history from many popular apps. It's not a bad idea to occasionally scan your computer with both Spybot and Ad-aware.

Messenger Messages Are Driving Me Mad

Patient: I have a home LAN using Windows XP Home edition. My family and I will be playing online games or watching a movie in the living room when, all of a sudden, we get a pop-up message on our desktop. Can I fix this problem without resorting to third-party software?

Doctor: The Windows Messenger service—not to be confused with Windows Messenger, the IM client—is the latest front in the war against spam. Luckily, these messages can be stopped by activating XP's built-in firewall.

All you need to do is open up the Properties for your Internet connection, go to Start → Control Panel → Network Connections, and then right-click the icon for your Internet connection. (If you use a cable modem or DSL, it will probably be a Local Area Connection, but if you use an analog

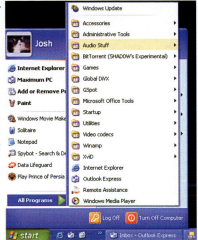

The Windows XP Start menu can get wily in no time! Tame it by creating new folders for groups of applications, such as Games and Utilities.

modem, it will be named after your ISP.) Click Properties, and then click the Advanced tab. Check the box labeled Protect My Computer and Network By Limiting or Preventing Access to This Computer From the Internet.

Double Disks?

Patient: Can I install Windows XP on two of my home computers, or do I have to purchase two installation disks?

Doctor: Unfortunately for consumers, Microsoft's licensing rules for Windows XP allow the OS to be installed on only one machine at a time. However, if you already have a copy of XP and want to upgrade another machine, you can save a few bucks by buying an extra license without the CD and manuals. You can order additional licenses for XP Home and Professional at http://shop.microsoft.com/.

Spyware is probably installed on your machine right now, tracking what you do on your PC and reporting back to its creator. Nuke it from orbit with Spybot.

Index

X - Y - Z

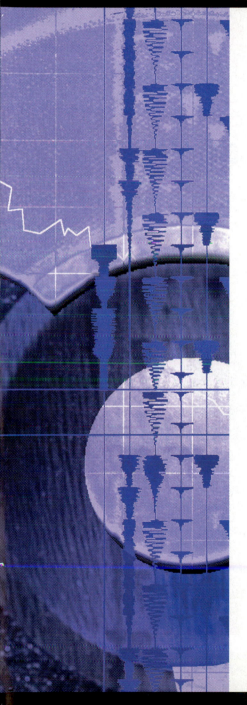

MAXIMUM... BOOKS?

300 PAGES EACH!

ALL COLOR! NO ADS!

Yes. It's true. **MAXIMUM PC** introduces the next generation in computer books!

Maximum PC Guide to Building a Dream PC

It's the biggest, meanest, *most complete* PC building guide we've ever created! Not only do we show first-time PC builders *everything* they need to know about assembling a computer from scratch, we also divulge the truth behind competing hardware technologies, and show you how to make the smartest parts choices. Includes configuration plans for six different Dream Machine archetypes. *By Will Smith, technical editor*

● **$29.99; AVAILABLE IN SEPT 04; ISBN 0-7897-3193-2**

Maximum PC 2005 Buyers Guide

Get an insider's peek at 2004's most exciting Lab experiments, plus forward looks at the gear you *must* know about in 2005. Includes the hidden story behind *Maximum PC* benchmarking, and a full compendium of our most positive—and brutal—2004 product reviews. Special Ask the Doctor and Watchdog wrap-ups make this a veritable *Maximum PC* almanac! A must-have reference book for faithful readers of the magazine. *By George Jones, editor-in-chief*

● **$29.99; AVAILABLE IN SEPT 04; ISBN 0-7897-3194-0**

Maximum PC Guide to PC Hardware Hacking

The most complete, most descriptive, most *helpful* book on case-modding ever published! Loaded with stunning illustrations and 100 percent *actionable* instructions, we show you how to construct a mind-blowing mod of your own. Painting, lighting, drilling, cutting, cooling... *every* topic is covered! Case-modder extraordinaire Paul Capello shares the tricks and insights that have made him a legend among hardware hacking experts. *By Paul Capello & Jon Phillips*

● **$29.99; AVAILABLE IN DEC 04; ISBN 0-7897-3192-4**

ALSO
Maximum PC Ultimate PC Performance Guide

All of *Maximum PC's* "newsstand only" special issues bound into a single book! Five issue's worth of content—a must-have treasure for *Maximum PC* fanatics.

● **$29.99; AVAILABLE IN SEPT 04; ISBN 0-7897-3317-X**

www.quepublishing.com

Available online and at book stores everywhere.
Check out www.maximumpc.com
for special ordering and pricing information!